Vol. XCI   No. 2

Bible Expositor and Illuminator

SPRING QUARTER   March, April, May 2019

Looking Ahead 2
Editorials 3

New Teaching

UNIT I: New in Christ

Mar.   3—A New Loyalty—I Thess. 1:1-10 4
Mar. 10—A New Affection—I Thess. 3:1-13 18
Mar. 17—A New Way of Life—I Thess. 4:1-12 32
Mar. 24—A New Understanding—I Thess. 4:13—5:10 46

UNIT II: New Growth

Mar. 31—A Growing Confidence—II Thess. 1:1-12 60
Apr.   7—A Growing Awareness—II Thess. 2:1-12 74
Apr. 14—A Growing Resolve—II Thess. 2:13—3:5 88

UNIT III: The T_____

Apr. 21—Remember the True Gospel! (_____ ____0 102
Apr. 28—The Source of Paul's Gospel—_____ 116
May   5—The Gospel of Faith Foretold—_____ 130
May 12—The Gospel: Faith in Christ—Ga_____ 144
May 19—Heirs Because of the Gospel—_____ 158
May 26—The Gospel in Action—Gal. 6:1-1_____ 172
         Topics for Next Quarter 188
         Paragraphs on Places and People 189
         Daily Bible Readings 190
         Review 191

Editor in Chief: Todd Williams

Edited and published quarterly by
THE INCORPORATED TRUSTEES OF THE
GOSPEL WORKER SOCIETY
UNION GOSPEL PRESS DIVISION

Rev. W. B. Musselman, Founder

Price: $5.00 per quarter*
$20.00 per year*

shipping and handling extra

ISBN 978-1-59843-825-3

LOOKING AHEAD

This quarter begins with seven lessons from Paul's two letters to the Thessalonians. These letters touch on a number of important issues.

Lesson 1 reminds us of the importance of godly character and actions as it points to the impact the Thessalonians' faith, hope, and love had on the lives of others. The second lesson reveals the deep affection Paul had for this church, as exhibited by his concern for them and prayers on their behalf.

Lesson 3 urges us to excel in all aspects of our Christian lives. We should not be content with less than our best when it comes to obeying God, loving others, and working.

Lesson 4 introduces the great hope of our Lord's return in I Thessalonians 4 and 5. Paul explains key details of Christ's return and how we should live in light of it.

Lesson 5 takes us to II Thessalonians 1, where Paul encouraged this persecuted church with the certainty of divine justice. Our sixth lesson covers Paul's correction of a misunderstanding regarding the end times. He urges them to cling to God's written revelation. The final lesson in the Thessalonian epistles reminds us of our responsibility to exhort, encourage, and pray for one another.

The final six lessons, primarily from the book of Galatians, focus on the doctrine of salvation and how it relates to works. Lesson 8 introduces the problem presented by false teachers. They taught salvation by works rather than the true gospel, which is clearly based in Christ's resurrection, a truth we will explore in Matthew 28.

Lesson 9 records Paul's defense of his teaching against charges leveled against him. He defended the gospel of grace he preached and his authority to preach it.

Salvation by grace alone is the consistent teaching of the Bible. The Apostle Paul set forth the scriptural argument very clearly, as lesson 10 demonstrates.

To this day there is much confusion about the Mosaic Law and how it relates to Christians. Lessons 11 and 12 tackle this subject and explain how the law served as a tool to bring us to Christ.

Our final lesson reminds us that the gospel of grace we embrace is not merely a confession but a reality that is lived out.

—*Jarl K. Waggoner.*

Witnessing Then And Now

WAYNE J. VASILENKO

Many people at times feel as though their life experiences are unique. I remember that many years ago I was on a cross-country hike with a friend. We were off the trail, using map and compass, hiking to a fire tower some three miles distant. We stopped for a break on the top of a ridge, taking in the view.

I remarked to my friend, "We could be the first people ever that have enjoyed this view."

At first my friend agreed, but then he started to laugh as he pointed to the ground at my feet. There we were in this "virgin land," thinking that we were possibly the first humans in history to be there as my friend pointed to a cigarette butt just inches from my foot! Neither one of us smoked. So much for us being the first to hike that ridge! As Christians, many of us feel as though we are trailblazing, facing unique issues or challenges, especially when witnessing to people or engaging in the discipleship of a new convert to Christianity. Interestingly, it seems at times we are fighting against more religious groups than non-Christian groups.

Why do you suppose that is so? Perhaps we can learn by exploring what it was like for the early Christians when they witnessed to the people back in their day.

When Jesus walked the earth, He mainly dealt with legalistic Judaism and the pagan gods of the Gentiles. Since that time, many different religions or denominations have sprung up claiming Christian roots; so surely it must be easier for Christians to evangelize than it was back then. After all, there are radical differences between the law of the Jewish faith, the pagan gods, and the message of grace preached by Jesus and His followers! So what, if anything, is different now as we engage in evangelism in modern times?

The Bible tells us that history has a habit of repeating itself: "The thing that hath been, it is that which shall be; and that which is done is that which shall be done: and there is no new thing under the sun. Is there any thing whereof it may be said, See, this is new? It hath been already of old time, which was before us" (Eccles. 1:9-10).

The fact remains that most things have been done or experienced before; this not only applies to everyday life but to religious teachings and practices as well. During Old Testament times, it was all about the law. It all started out with a short and simple law given to Adam and Eve. However, as even the casual student of the Bible knows, that one law became hundreds of laws over time, and they were subject to many differing interpretations. Exodus 25 through 29 gives the details of the priesthood and God's expectations pertaining to worship as it relates to the law, and it is indeed a long and detailed list.

This system of laws and worship lasted thousands of years, and in the process the priesthood became a very powerful influence over the common people. The priests were the teachers, the keepers, and the enforcers of the law, thus giving them lots of power over the people.

History teaches us that powerful people usually end up craving more power, and we can see this clearly continuing in the modern church. We can also see it in modern civil government.

What evolved in Old Testament times was a very structured system of worship overseen by a very powerful elite group. This was reinforced

(Editorials continued on page 186)

Scripture Lesson Text

I THESS. 1:1 Paul, and Silvanus, and Timotheus, unto the church of the Thessalonians which is in God the Father and in the Lord Jesus Christ: Grace be unto you, and peace, from God our Father, and the Lord Jesus Christ.

2 We give thanks to God always for you all, making mention of you in our prayers;

3 Remembering without ceasing your work of faith, and labour of love, and patience of hope in our Lord Jesus Christ, in the sight of God and our Father;

4 Knowing, brethren beloved, your election of God.

5 For our gospel came not unto you in word only, but also in power, and in the Holy Ghost, and in much assurance; as ye know what manner of men we were among you for your sake.

6 And ye became followers of us, and of the Lord, having received the word in much affliction, with joy of the Holy Ghost:

7 So that ye were ensamples to all that believe in Macedonia and Achaia.

8 For from you sounded out the word of the Lord not only in Macedonia and Achaia, but also in every place your faith to God-ward is spread abroad; so that we need not to speak any thing.

9 For they themselves shew of us what manner of entering in we had unto you, and how ye turned to God from idols to serve the living and true God;

10 And to wait for his Son from heaven, whom he raised from the dead, even Jesus, which delivered us from the wrath to come.

NOTES

A New Loyalty

Lesson Text: I Thessalonians 1:1-10

Related Scriptures: Acts 17:1-4; Romans 6:17-23;
I Corinthians 2:1-5; Ephesians 2:1-13

TIME: A.D. 51   PLACE: from Corinth

GOLDEN TEXT—"They themselves shew of us what manner of entering in we had unto you, and how ye turned to God from idols to serve the living and true God" (I Thessalonians 1:9).

Introduction

Some people are remembered for their words. Will Rogers, Mark Twain, Benjamin Franklin, and, of course, King Solomon readily come to mind as men known for their wit and wisdom. However, such people are exceptions to the general rule, undoubtedly because their writings have been preserved through the years.

The people most of us remember are those whose lives have had a profound impact on us. And we remember their character and their deeds long after their words have faded from our memories. There might be a few wise words we remember from parents and grandparents, but for the most part, we remember such things as their faithfulness, kindness, love, diligence, attitudes, and particular things they did that exhibited their honorable qualities.

When the Apostle Paul wrote his first letter to the Christians in the city of Thessalonica, he had things he wanted to teach them and remind them of. The first chapter, however, is devoted primarily to remembering the godly character and actions of the Thessalonian believers. Such reminders of their godly example would encourage them to continue faithfully following Christ and challenge others, including us, to set a Christlike example for others to follow.

LESSON OUTLINE

I. **GREETING THE THESSALONIANS**—I Thess. 1:1-2

II. **REMEMBERING THE THESSALONIANS' GODLY EXAMPLE**—I Thess. 1:3-8

III. **AFFIRMING THE THESSALONIANS**—I Thess. 1:9-10

Exposition: Verse by Verse

GREETING THE THESSALONIANS

I THESS. 1:1 Paul, and Silvanus, and Timotheus, unto the church of the Thessalonians which is in God the Father and in the Lord Jesus Christ: Grace be unto you, and

peace, from God our Father, and the Lord Jesus Christ.

2 We give thanks to God always for you all, making mention of you in our prayers.

This important letter begins with a greeting that is familiar to readers of the New Testament. Paul identifies himself as the author and the Thessalonian church as the recipient. Silvanus, another name for Silas, and Timothy are also mentioned alongside Paul's name. Silas had been with Paul when the Thessalonian church was first established (Acts 17:4), and Timothy had recently visited the Thessalonians and reported back to Paul (I Thess. 3:1-2).

Paul was writing on behalf of these two men as well as himself. But Paul was the one who actually wrote the letter, as indicated by his use of "I" throughout (2:18; 3:5; 4:9, 13; 5:1, 27).

Thessalonica was in the Roman province of Macedonia, which covered much of northern Greece. The city was situated on a gulf off the Aegean Sea. A major Roman road passed through the city. Paul had brought the gospel to the city on his second missionary journey (Acts 17). Many Gentiles came to the Lord at that time, but only a few Jews. In fact, the Jews were largely hostile toward Paul. They forced him to leave the city and even followed the apostle to Berea to disrupt his work there.

Still, the church in Thessalonica was founded during Paul's short stay there. It was, in fact, amazingly well-grounded in the faith, as Paul's letter shows. The letter of I Thessalonians followed shortly after the establishment of the church. It was written from Corinth and was one of Paul's earliest letters, probably preceded only by Galatians.

More important to Paul than his own contribution was that the Thessalonian church was "in God the Father and in the Lord Jesus Christ" (I Thess.

1:1). The word translated "church" is *ekklesia,* a familiar term in Greek and Jewish society for an assembly. It literally means a "called-out assembly." It was adopted as the distinctive name for the assembly of Christians. Here "'God the Father' distinguishes it from any pagan assembly . . . while 'and the Lord Jesus Christ' distinguishes it from Jewish assemblies" (Hiebert, *The Thessalonian Epistles,* Moody).

Paul's distinctive greeting was "Grace be unto you, and peace." His desire was for his readers to experience fully God's unmerited favor (grace) and the deep, abiding peace with God that results from receiving His grace.

Paul and his companions expressed their thanksgiving to God for all the Thessalonian believers. This they were doing constantly by praying for them. The apostle could offer no greater encouragement to them than to assure them of his personal gratitude to God for them and of his continual prayers on their behalf.

REMEMBERING THE THESSALONIANS' GODLY EXAMPLE

3 Remembering without ceasing your work of faith, and labour of love, and patience of hope in our Lord Jesus Christ, in the sight of God and our Father;

4 Knowing, brethren beloved, your election of God.

5 For our gospel came not unto you in word only, but also in power, and in the Holy Ghost, and in much assurance; as ye know what manner of men we were among you for your sake.

6 And ye became followers of us, and of the Lord, having received the word in much affliction, with joy of the Holy Ghost:

7 So that ye were ensamples to all that believe in Macedonia and Achaia.

8 For from you sounded out the word of the Lord not only in Mace-

donia and Achaia, but also in every place your faith to God-ward is spread abroad; so that we need not to speak any thing.

Examples in their character (I Thess. 1:3). Paul's thanks to God for the Thessalonians was not merely a formality. As he and the others prayed, they remembered "without ceasing" the exemplary character of the Christians in Thessalonica. Particularly, Paul mentioned their faith, love, and hope and what these Christlike virtues produced. Their faith produced work. Apart from a living faith in Christ, there would have been no work. Their faith was not yet fully-grown (3:10), but it was evident from their works.

Their love produced labor. The word here describes intense, exhausting labor. Their love for the Lord moved them to toilsome acts of compassion and self-sacrifice.

The Thessalonians' hope produced "patience" (1:3), or perseverance. Because true Christian hope is not merely a longing but a certainty based on God's promises, the Christians in Thessalonica persevered in their faith through persecution and hardship. Because their sure hope of eternal life was in the Lord Jesus Christ, they could endure anything and everything they faced. This is true of us as well.

Faith, love, and hope are not abstract ideas or beliefs; they are "the active ingredients of the Christian life, finding expression in active work, patient toil, and enduring constancy" (Hiebert). They should be active in our lives and seen, not just heard, by others. These virtues are effectively worked out in our lives as we live with the constant awareness that we stand in the presence, or "sight," of God.

Examples in their response to the gospel (I Thess. 1:4-7). Because the Thessalonians' faith was evident in their works, Paul was convinced of their "election of God." They were not only his "brethren" but also God's "beloved." Paul knew they were indeed chosen by God and belonged to Him. As further evidence of this, Paul recounted the founding of the Thessalonian church.

The gospel, the good news of Christ, had come to Thessalonica, not in "word only, but also in power" (vs. 5). The gospel is proclaimed by words, but the emphasis here is on the message, not the messengers. The gospel itself has power (cf. Rom. 1:16), and this power was evident at Thessalonica. The wording probably suggests that the Holy Spirit empowered the spoken word and gave assurance to the messengers that the gospel would accomplish God's will.

Paul then added a note about how he and his companions had selflessly conducted themselves in Thessalonica. This is expanded later in the book (I Thess. 2:1-12), probably to counter false charges made against them. "Paul, Silas, and Timothy impeccably lived out what they preached so powerfully. Their godly character validated their God-given gospel" (Mayhue, *1 & 2 Thessalonians,* Christian Focus).

Paul and Silas had preached the gospel of the resurrected Christ in Thessalonica (Acts 17:2-3), and many had "received the word" (I Thess. 1:6). They had responded in faith, and this was evidenced as they became followers of both the missionaries and the Lord Himself. The word for "followers" here literally means "imitators." Their lives were transformed so that they began to live like Paul and his companions and their Lord. This response further assured Paul that they were God's elect.

The manner in which the believers had embraced the gospel message made them examples to many others. They had received it with faith even though it meant "affliction," or oppression. And they had received the word "with joy." They were not deterred by unpleasant outward circumstances but experienced the inner joy produced by the Holy Spirit. Only those who trust in Christ can know the inner peace and joy that comes from knowing and following the Saviour and having a hope that extends beyond the pleasures or pains of this life.

The Thessalonians' joy and hope in the midst of difficulty encouraged others to remain faithful to the Lord as well. Specifically, Paul mentioned fellow Christians throughout Macedonia and Achaia, the province immediately to the south. These believers were no doubt facing persecution and pressures similar to what the Thessalonians experienced.

We can speak endlessly and correctly, but our words will have only limited impact on others unless they are accompanied by a life that reinforces our words. It is the example we set, especially in times of great difficulty, that makes the greatest impression on others. As we look to the examples of others to inspire and encourage us, let us also be examples to others.

Examples in their ministry (I Thess. 1:8). The believers in Thessalonica proved to be encouraging examples in the way they embraced the gospel and remained faithful and even joyful in the face of severe challenges. They were also examples by the way they proclaimed the word to others. Just as the gospel had come to them by way of Paul, they had taken the gospel to others.

Their ministry is described as sounding forth the word of the Lord. The expression pictures the reverberating sound of a trumpet or of thunder. "It emphasizes the resounding nature of the witness borne by the Thessalonian church" (Morris, *The Epistles of Paul to the Thessalonians,* Eerdmans).

The Thessalonian believers were taking the "word of the Lord" to others in their own province and to Achaia, which included Athens and Corinth. Even beyond Achaia, the gospel message was sounded forth wherever these vibrant believers traveled.

The experience of the Thessalonians reminds us that we do not need to wait for organized campaigns or church programs to reach our cities and counties and states with the gospel. We simply need to grasp the joy of knowing Christ through faith and faithfully share that truth in everyday life, wherever we go.

Paul said that the Thessalonians' testimony was so widespread that he did not need to tell anyone of it. The work of God among them was well known and apparently even aided Paul's ministry by revealing the power of the Lord he was preaching.

AFFIRMING THE THESSALONIANS

9 For they themselves shew of us what manner of entering in we had unto you, and how ye turned to God from idols to serve the living and true God;

10 And to wait for his Son from heaven, whom he raised from the dead, even Jesus, which delivered us from the wrath to come.

Paul's witness to the faith, love, and hope of the church in Thessalonica was not a solitary testimony. As reports came to him in Corinth, he saw that others affirmed what he said. This too was an encouragement to him, as well as to the Thessalonians themselves.

Those who confirmed Paul's words concerning the Thessalonians are not identified. They could have been believers from Macedonia or Achaia who had seen or heard of what had happened in Thessalonica, or even people of more remote areas who had encountered the new believers. However, these people consistently affirmed three things about the Thessalonians.

First, they affirmed the manner of the

missionaries' approach in Thessalonica. Paul and Silas and their fellow workers had not manipulated their hearers with eloquent and deceptive words. Rather, they had preached the simple gospel of Christ (cf. vs. 5).

Second, these people testified to the fact that the Thessalonians had "turned to God from idols to serve the living and true God" (vs. 9). The Greek word translated "turned" is frequently translated "converted" (cf. Acts 3:19). It means to "turn back" or "turn around." The word catches the essence of biblical conversion, which is turning away from sin and toward God.

All who knew the Thessalonian believers testified to their having turned away from lifeless idols to serve the living God. The implication is that the vast majority of the believers were Gentiles who had formerly worshipped idols, or false gods. Their faith in Christ was clear from their conversion. To know the true God is to reject all other so-called gods.

"Serve" in I Thessalonians 1:9 refers to serving as a slave. The believers lovingly served God as their true Master. Turning from idols and serving the true, living God gave evidence of the Thessalonians' faith and love (cf. vs. 3). The third affirmation witnessed to their hope.

Third, the witnesses testified that the Thessalonian Christians were also waiting for God's "Son from heaven" (vs. 10). This is Jesus Christ, whom God the Father raised from the dead. The resurrection is central to the gospel of Christ and was understood and fully accepted by the original readers (cf. Acts 17:3-4).

Jesus is further described as the One who delivers from God's coming wrath. God's wrath is His righteous anger against all that contradicts His holiness. As the Creator and the Holy One, He is entirely just in expressing His wrath against sin and sinners in either eternal judgment or temporal judgments.

It is possible that the temporal judgments of the end-times tribulation are envisioned in this wrath and that the Bible is saying believers will be spared from this. The context, however, seems to suggest that it is the eternal judgment of hell that is particularly in view here. Through the work of Christ, all believers have been delivered from everlasting judgment.

Only a risen Lord can return, and only a Lord who has delivered us from sin can provide a sure hope. This is the Son of God whose return we await even today, as the Thessalonians did before us. Let us be examples to all of Christlike faith and love and of the certain hope of Christ's second coming.

—Jarl K. Waggoner.

QUESTIONS

1. Why did Paul mention Silvanus and Timothy in his greeting?
2. What had the Apostle Paul experienced in Thessalonica?
3. What virtues did Paul commend in the Thessalonian Christians?
4. What convinced Paul the Thessalonians were chosen by God?
5. How did the Thessalonians' reception of the gospel encourage others?
6. How does the apostle describe the evangelistic ministry of the Thessalonians?
7. To where had news of the Thessalonians' faith spread?
8. Besides Paul, who affirmed the faith, hope, and love of the Thessalonian church?
9. How is their conversion described?
10. What sure hope did the believers embrace and anticipate?

—Jarl K. Waggoner.

Preparing to Teach the Lesson

In this first unit, we learn about the brand new life in Christ. Being born into the kingdom of our Lord Jesus through faith brings about many positive changes. Over the next few weeks, we will learn about some of these changes for the new believer.

In this first lesson we learn about a shift in loyalty from our old lives to the new.

TODAY'S AIM

Facts: to show how the new believers in Thessalonica turned from their idols and their old way of life to the living God.

Principle: to learn that when we put our faith in Christ, we become brand-new people.

Application: to turn around and know exciting new life in our Lord Jesus despite our past.

INTRODUCING THE LESSON

A Christian organization reported the healing of a Hindu woman in India who had been sick for ten years. When the missionaries came and prayed for her, she was healed and turned from her previous faith to our Lord Jesus. This is a good example of the way that the message of Jesus transforms people and turns them toward Him, away from idols.

DEVELOPING THE LESSON

1. Remembered by Paul (I Thess. 1:1-3). Unlike some of Paul's other letters, he had co-authors in the writings of this particular letter. Silvanus (Greek for Silas), a fellow preacher (cf. II Cor.1:19), and young Timothy are mentioned as such. Paul begins this letter with his usual greeting in the name of God the Father and Jesus Christ.

Paul tells us that Jesus is preeminent in all his preaching, and He is the cause for which he was doing everything. Paul had firm priorities. He knew firsthand what it was to be transformed by the gospel. Then he turns his attention to the Thessalonian believers. Every time Paul prayed, he thanked God for them. How often do we thank God for our local congregations?

Notice the detail with which Paul prays for these believers. He remembers them by name and goes on to recount specific details of their faithfulness, demonstrated by the things they did (their good works of love) because of their faith in Jesus. They showed both patience and love to each other. These were real marks of change.

Through faith in Jesus, we become new people. We are free from sin and realize that only the true and living God can do this. The past is left behind. The Thessalonian believers are a good example for us to follow. If someone looks at our own local churches, will they be able to give this kind of a report about us?

2. Chosen by God (I Thess. 1:4-7). We must not misunderstand this to mean that unless God chooses us we have no hope. He has opened the door for all of us through Jesus. We do have to make a choice to follow our Lord, and that makes all the difference. God knows all the choices we will make before we make them.

In verse 4, Paul talks about "your election of God." God loves every one of us so much and wants us to be part of His own people. He is overjoyed when one of us makes the decision to follow Jesus. Paul reminds those in the Thessalonian church that God loved them first, before they ever knew that they had to choose Him.

Paul goes on to explain that the gospel is powerful. This is seen in the way the good news is powerfully demonstrated (the word here gives us the idea of *explosive* power). It is evidence that the Holy Spirit was working in their lives. Paul and his companions were an undeniable example of transformation. They knew Paul's history; it was real!

The testimony of your response to the gospel message is your most powerful tool in evangelism. People not only need to hear the message of the gospel preached, they need to see it's transforming power.

The gospel demands a response. Paul commended the believers in Thessalonica for their close relationship with Jesus. We can choose to follow Jesus, or we can reject Him. Encourage the class to make the right choice. These believers made hard choices despite the possibility of severe suffering because of them. They did it with joy because they had discovered that the power of the gospel was real! They were willing to pay that price. Are we?

3. Serving God (I Thess. 1:8-10). When Christians follow Jesus in all their ways, the world hears about it. Word spread beyond Greece about the transformation of the believers in Thessalonica. Something special was happening there! What are people saying about your own local church? Is your faith in Jesus changing lives?

The Thessalonian church was seen as genuine because of their hospitality, shown to Paul and his companions. They also served the true and living God and had turned away from serving all idols. Their faith was undeniably real. Their lives were now very different from their previous lives. Is our faith helping others to know the true God?

What keeps you going in your Christian faith? The Thessalonian believers are an example here as well. They were waiting for Jesus, the Son of God, to return from heaven. He alone had freed them from the wrath of God against sin, and they knew it. Are you expecting Jesus with the fervent zeal that these early believers had? They show us how to wait for Jesus, their Deliverer, with passion. The whole world needs to know about this Deliverer!

ILLUSTRATING THE LESSON

The example of the Thessalonian Christians teaches us to turn from idols and worship the living God.

TURN TO JESUS

TURN AWAY FROM FALSE GODS

CONCLUDING THE LESSON

From these early Christians we learn that faith that is real must be demonstrated in a way that draws others to our Lord. The world wants to see the real thing—turning from meaningless idols to Jesus, our Deliverer.

ANTICIPATING THE NEXT LESSON

Next week, we learn how to love others as a mark of the new life in Jesus.
—*A. Koshy Muthalaly.*

PRACTICAL POINTS

1. A portion of our prayers should involve giving thanks (I Thess. 1:1-3).
2. The knowledge that we were specifically chosen by God gives us confidence in our work (vss. 4-5).
3. Just as we emulate spiritually mature Christians, we should anticipate that others will emulate us (vss. 6-7).
4. Our lives can be examples for nonbelievers (vs. 8).
5. Every Christian should discard the idols in their lives and turn to God (vs. 9).
6. Because of Christ's work on the cross, we have been delivered from God's wrath (vs. 10).

—*Charity G. Carter.*

RESEARCH AND DISCUSSION

1. Why is it important to give thanks when we pray? How would our lives change if we shifted our prayers to more thanks and fewer requests (I Thess. 1:2)?
2. If we truly believe that God chose us to accomplish His will, how should that impact our attitudes toward our work (vs. 4)?
3. In what ways would you like other believers to imitate you? How does knowing that people may imitate you influence the way you live (vs. 6)?
4. List several ways in which you knew people were followers of Christ by simply observing them.
5. Why is it necessary to completely turn away from idols when we join God's family (vs. 9)?

—*Charity G. Carter.*

ILLUSTRATED HIGH POINTS

Remembering without ceasing

Sadly, but not unexpectedly, some of the 9/11 memorials have lost their original splendor—they are deteriorating. As of May 1, 2016, the memorial in Nassau County, New York was marred by graffiti, missing several marble tiles, oozing adhesive, flying filthy flags, and strewn with litter on its dry fountain bed.

In the physical world, science tells us, all things tend toward decay.

The only true and lasting memorials are those embedded into the hearts and minds of people. Paul remembered the Thessalonians' "work of faith" without ceasing. With every word and action, we build our memorials, brick by living brick, within the hearts of those we meet.

Followers of us. . . . ye were ensamples

In the year 2000, primatologist Lisa Rapaport observed a Brazilian golden lion tamarin monkey teaching one of her offspring. When feeding her young, she emits a specific feeding call. Rapaport observed as the female stuck her arm into an old log and withdrew it—empty-handed. She then proceeded to summon her youngster with the special call, prompting the youngster to reach into the same log. He complied and swiftly pulled out a small frog—his dinner.

When cheetah cubs are about ten weeks old the mother calls them to the carcass of a fresh kill. Later the mother will let the rowdy cubs accompany her on hunts. In the end, they are fully trained to hunt and someday teach their own young.

The Thessalonians were first followers of Paul, then they were examples to Macedonia and Achaia. The students had become teachers.

—*Therese Greenberg.*

Golden Text Illuminated

"They themselves shew of us what manner of entering in we had unto you, and how ye turned to God from idols to serve the living and true God" (I Thessalonians 1:9).

The word loyal in the *American Heritage Dictionary of the English Language* is defined in two ways: "Steadfast in allegiance to one's homeland, government, or sovereign" and "Faithful to a person, ideal, custom, cause, or duty" (Houghton Mifflin Harcourt).

Believers are called to be loyal followers of the Lord Jesus Christ throughout their lives. Thankfully, they have also been given the power to be faithful even amidst times of great difficulty and temptation. A new and persevering loyalty, in fact, is what sets Christians apart, for they have been freed from the power of sin and made new in Christ (Rom. 6:17-18).

A clear example of lives changed by the gospel is found in I Thessalonians. This was a young church that the Apostle Paul began in a Jewish synagogue (Acts 17:1-2). The Bible tells us that as Paul preached in the power of the Holy Spirit (I Cor. 2:4; I Thess. 1:5), many there were converted (Acts 17:4).

Since he was unable to stay and continue to minister to his new brothers and sisters (Acts 17:10), Paul was overjoyed when news reached him concerning their reputations. It was evident that the Thessalonians had not merely been showing superficial courtesy when they received Paul and his helpers or that they regarded the gospel they preached as a mere intellectual stimulus.

The Thessalonians' lives of faith, love, and hope (I Thess. 1:3) and the way they imitated Paul, Silvanus (Silas), and Timotheus (Timothy) in spreading the gospel impacted others well beyond their immediate area (vs. 8).

Paul wrote a letter to the church to express his gratitude for them and also to encourage them in their witness. The joy with which they encountered affliction as they lived their new lives stood out (vss. 1:6-7)!

The golden text tells us that Paul, Silas, and Timothy were receiving many encouraging reports that the gospel they had shared had profoundly changed the Thessalonians' lives. Their message had not fallen on deaf ears or cold hearts but had created a new loyalty within those converted.

The Thessalonian believers had changed loyalties, leaving behind their idols (false objects of worship that had no power) to serve and live under the authority of the living and true God.

Furthermore, the Thessalonians' faith endured and impacted many. Why? Because it was rooted in God's power, not man's wisdom (I Cor. 2:5).

Romans 6:22 describes the Thessalonian believers' new loyalty well: "But now being made free from sin, and become servants to God, ye have your fruit unto holiness, and the end everlasting life."

As you look at your life, can you say that it stands as an accurate and convincing witness to your new loyalty to Christ since becoming a believer? If not, why not ask God to make the changes that only He has the power to make within you? If you have not yet been made new in Christ, do not wait another day. Repent, turn to the living God, and let your life stand out!

Once you have been given new life, your loyalty to Jesus will grow stronger with each act of obedience. Help is but a prayer away!

—*Christine M. Morrison.*

Heart of the Lesson

A person's reputation, whether good or bad, stays with him or her for a lifetime. My mother was known as a prayer warrior. After Mother's death, a woman in the community spoke of times when she had asked her to intervene on her behalf. Even though the woman herself was praying, she knew Mother would stay in communion with God until an answer came. Because of Mother's reputation, the woman waited with hopeful anticipation, knowing that God would solve her problem. Everyone has a reputation—so what is your life saying about you?

1. An introduction: Paul's greeting (I Thess. 1:1-4). This book is a letter Paul wrote to the church of Thessalonica. Paul had recently visited there during his second missionary trip with Silas and Timothy. His time was cut short, and when he was prevented from returning, he sent Timothy as his representative (3:2). Since Paul was physically unable to be there, he continually prayed for them. He felt a responsibility for the believers since he had helped them understand their need for salvation. Paul also highlighted his thankfulness for their faith, hope, and love.

Christians need to follow Paul's example by continually praying. When a person is heavily burdened, the load can be lightened by sharing the afflictions with someone else. Believers should keep such requests in their prayers.

2. The conversion: Paul's message (I Thess. 1:5-6). Paul was confident he had preached the gospel to the Thessalonians. He knew the message he expounded had come from the Holy Spirit. Because Paul lived in accord with that message, the people knew his heart and trusted his intentions. Therefore, they became followers of Christ too.

Followers of Christ need the confidence Paul showed when speaking of salvation. People can quickly discern when speakers know little about a subject or do not believe in their own cause. Believers must speak with conviction if they want the unsaved to listen.

3. The example: the Thessalonians' impact (I Thess. 1:7-8). Paul was encouraged that the people of Thessalonica had become an example to Macedonia and Achaia. Paul realized that the impression he had on the Thessalonians had caused them to influence others. The church's impact did not stop in Thessalonica but spread far and wide.

Individuals who trust in Jesus need to be examples for nonbelievers. To have an influence on the unsaved, Christians need to live a godly life that others can follow. Their influence will widen accordingly.

4. The hope: Christ's return (I Thess. 1:9-10). The Thessalonians awaited the second coming of Christ. People in the Old Testament anticipated the Messiah's arrival, and people today are still looking for His return. For some, Christ's coming again has been proclaimed for so long, they believe the time will never arrive. Jesus keeps His promises, which means He will return. The book of Revelation assures believers that He is coming back to earth, and the time is imminent. Therefore, believers must be continually watching.

What message is your life conveying? Will you prove to be loyal and true? Will others follow in your footsteps, like the Thessalonians who followed in Paul's footsteps? Someone is watching everything you say and do. What do you want people to say about you? What kind of legacy will you leave?

—Catherine Moore.

World Missions

She was only there for two years, long ago, but the image never left her memory. It was supposedly a religious celebration of good over evil, but the idol looked anything but good, the scene anything but holy.

Once back in the quietness of her room, the young missionary penned these words:

Bright red and yellow lights drape across the bamboo poles to form a festive awning over the stairs. At the top, street children gather behind a flimsy bamboo fence, staring, not at us, but at the goddess.

She has ten arms, one plunging a sword into the side of a man. A lion roars beneath her right foot. "Deceived, deceived," she seems to say and laugh, her proud eyes wide over the bowed heads of worshippers, her lips . . . slightly curved upward despite the violence in her hands.

The noise is loud and more frenzied than festive. Hands beat quickly in rhythm on the drums. Men chant, half singing, as they bow. Candles burn, incense giving off a heady, sickly sweet fragrance. Smoke rises.

"Deceived, deceived," it seems to whisper.

The smoke and the smell spread, filling the courtyard, engulfing the worshippers. Priests bow, throw flowers to the goddess mother, pray. Their heads are adorned with a sacred string, their shoes left outside in reverence, defying all that is truly holy.

"Deceived, deceived," it murmurs—gleeful, triumphant.

Satan's voice?

The children watch in fascination. The people keep coming. Offerings of coconuts and fruit near the front display devotion, and provide a feast for the ants.

The chanting continues; the fragrance is overpowering. For nearly a week the wild abandon of Hindu worship will continue. At the end, a procession of the devout, the seeking, the curious will come to their destination at the river's edge. The mother goddess will float out and sink from sight under the murky waters. The people worship; their hearts have sent her to the other world for another year, washed from the earth's filth by her journey through water.

My heart aches as I watch. The people return to their homes, to their other gods and goddesses. There will be other Puja festivals, thirteen in each year. Devotion need not cease.

Deceived, deceived.

Holy, righteous, angry, pained.

God's voice?

They are sincere, they are devout, yet hell awaits, its greedy hands reaching to grasp their souls.

If it hurt me so much to see this, how must You feel, O God? Maker of all, the only Truth, You hold out pierced hands, ready and willing to grasp the hands of those once deceived.

Since that day, twenty years have passed. There have been twenty more Durga Puja festivals, and two hundred forty other Hindu festivals where men and women offer food that could have fed their children, begging gods and goddesses for favor, for life, for health, for hope.

Will it ever change? Will they ever turn from idols to the living hope of Jesus Christ?

How can they if they do not know, if no one will go tell them?

—Kimberly Rae.

The Jewish Aspect

Thessalonica was a large and populous city of commerce and had a strategic location near the Aegean Sea. It was the capital of the province of Macedonia, was a self-governing community, and was an important city for the early spread of the gospel. Trade brought Jews to Thessalonica, and there were enough Jews to have a synagogue. Paul had trained under the renowned Rabbi Gamaliel and was permitted to speak in the synagogue. He did this for at least three consecutive Sabbaths, and some believed the gospel (Cole, "The Church That Makes An Impact [I Thessalonians 1:1-2]" www.bible.org). Paul, Silas, and Timothy, visited the city of about two hundred thousand people on Paul's second missionary journey. Silas was a Jewish believer and Timothy had a Jewish mother.

The believers there suffered violence and persecution. Paul and Silas left Thessalonica due to trouble from a mob of unbelieving Jews. But Paul wanted to return there to see how the believers were doing. He wrote his two letters to the Thessalonians while he was in Corinth, and he sent Timothy, who was like a son in the faith to Paul, back to Thessalonica with the letters to encourage the believers there.

Those who responded to the gospel message in Thessalonica were Jews, God-fearing Greeks, leading women of the city, and many who formerly had been idol-worshipping pagans. Paul began his letter to the Thessalonians with a salutation of grace and peace. "'Grace' was a common Greek salutation that meant 'greeting' or 'rejoice.' 'Peace' is the Greek equivalent of the Hebrew 'shalom' meaning 'favor,' 'well-being', and 'prosperity in the widest sense,' especially prosperity in spiritual matters" (Newton, "Perspective: A Study of 1st and 2nd Thessalonians," www.bible.org).

Paul was grateful to God for the Thessalonians' endurance through suffering and persecution. Paul wrote to the Thessalonians to encourage them in their good progress in their faith and to provide additional instruction to contribute to their spiritual growth. He had heard from traveling tradesmen that the Thessalonians were boldly sharing their new faith. Impacted by their testimony, the tradesmen were spreading what they had heard throughout all Macedonia and Achaia.

When Paul commended the Thessalonians for turning to God from idols to serve the living and true God, he was referring to numerous exhortations throughout the Hebrew Bible to turn to Israel's God and away from all others. Other exhortations are found in Leviticus 19:4, Jeremiah 10:10, Ezekiel 6:9, and Ezekiel 14:6. "The fact that God is a living Person was precious to the Jews and to Paul; this is the characteristic by which God was most often distinguished from so-called gods in the Old Testament. He is the only living God; all other gods are not alive and therefore not worthy objects of worship" (Walvoord and Zuck, eds., *The Bible Knowledge Commentary,* Cook).

The Thessalonians left slavery to idols to become slaves of God. The Greek word translated "serve" (I Thess. 1:9) referred to being a bond servant to Christ rather than a slave to sin. Throughout his letters to the early church, Paul spoke of the new believers' freedom to serve God as they had previously served sin. Paul commended the Thessalonians for no longer being slaves of sin but slaves of righteousness.

—Deborah Markowitz Solan.

Guiding the Superintendent

The word "new" suggests something that is different, better, changed, or maybe even fresh. For the next few weeks we will be thinking through what it means to be *new* in Christ.

The salvation experience is not the end of the road but rather the beginning of a life long journey. When a person comes to Christ, several new things will happen.

Our lesson this week will examine the idea that the Christian experience ushers in a new loyalty to Christ. In the first chapter of the first epistle to the Thessalonians, the Apostle Paul describes this new loyalty, to which the believers in that town had come.

DEVOTIONAL OUTLINE

1. New loyalty praised (I Thess. 1:1-3). Paul was a man of great prayer. Most of his letters grew out of his prayer life. The beginning of First Thessalonians is no exception. His thoughts about the believers in Thessalonica turns into a prayer of thanks for who they are in Christ.

Their new loyalty is expressed in three terms—faith, love, and hope. By faith, he is looking at their entire Christian experience that works out in daily life. Their faith was not theory, but very practical.

Second, Paul sees their new loyalty in terms of a love that enters into life with a desire to reach out and serve others with the love of Christ.

Third, this new loyalty is manifested in terms of a hope that produces endurance. Hope looks to the future and enables a person to live in the uncertainty of the present. Consequently, Paul is thankful for their endurance, which did not waiver.

2. New loyalty modeled (I Thess. 1:4-7). Paul reflects on how God brought the gospel to their church and the natural sequence that followed. The Word of God came in and did its natural thing. It went out to the country around them.

The text describes this new loyalty as being "followers . . . of the Lord" and as examples to all that believe. The idea here is that they modeled the gospel to those around them.

3. New loyalty reported (I Thess. 1:8-10). Paul is so pleased with the report that has come back to him about the people in Thessalonica. A turning to God is never a secret affair. People will see it and tell others.

The way their conversion is described is very significant: "how ye turned to God from idols to serve the living and true God." True conversion, then, results in a new loyalty to Christ and always starts with a turning to God and then a turning away from idols. Both elements are necessary. Conversion involves an entire re-orientation of one's life and loyalty to God and Christ.

The apostle is very thankful for this good report received about them.

CHILDREN'S CORNER

text: **Numbers 16:23-34**

title: **God's Servant Moses**

The nation of Israel is in the middle of their wilderness experience and Moses, the God appointed leader of the nation, has a problem. A group of fellow Israelites lead by Korah, Dathan, and Abiram directly challenged God's chosen leader. The rebellion came to an abrupt end when God opened up the earth and it shallowed the rebel and their entire families. Case closed. Moses was not self-appointed. He was God's leader and God had his back.

—*Martin R. Dahlquist.*

Scripture Lesson Text

I THESS. 3:1 Wherefore when we could no longer forbear, we thought it good to be left at Athens alone;

2 And sent Timotheus, our brother, and minister of God, and our fellowlabourer in the gospel of Christ, to establish you, and to comfort you concerning your faith:

3 That no man should be moved by these afflictions: for yourselves know that we are appointed thereunto.

4 For verily, when we were with you, we told you before that we should suffer tribulation; even as it came to pass, and ye know.

5 For this cause, when I could no longer forbear, I sent to know your faith, lest by some means the tempter have tempted you, and our labour be in vain.

6 But now when Timotheus came from you unto us, and brought us good tidings of your faith and charity, and that ye have good remembrance of us always, desiring greatly to see us, as we also to see you:

7 Therefore, brethren, we were comforted over you in all our affliction and distress by your faith:

8 For now we live, if ye stand fast in the Lord.

9 For what thanks can we render to God again for you, for all the joy wherewith we joy for your sakes before our God;

10 Night and day praying exceedingly that we might see your face, and might perfect that which is lacking in your faith?

11 Now God himself and our Father, and our Lord Jesus Christ, direct our way unto you.

12 And the Lord make you to increase and abound in love one toward another, and toward all men, even as we do toward you:

13 To the end he may stablish your hearts unblameable in holiness before God, even our Father, at the coming of our Lord Jesus Christ with all his saints.

NOTES

A New Affection

Lesson Text: I Thessalonians 3:1-13

Related Scriptures: Philippians 2:19-22; Acts 17:5-9;
John 15:9-13; Philippians 1:3-8

TIME: A.D. 51   PLACE: from Corinth

GOLDEN TEXT—"Timotheus came from you unto us, and brought us good tidings of your faith and charity, and that ye have good remembrance of us always, desiring greatly to see us, as we also to see you" (I Thessalonians 3:6).

Introduction

"Absence makes the heart grow fonder." So says the old adage. In other words, when we are apart from those we love, our affection for them grows stronger. Whether this is actually the case, of course, is debatable. But there is one thing we can say with certainty: if we truly love someone with a Christlike love, absence will *not* make our love grow weaker. This is because the kind of love the Bible calls us to have for others is unconditional.

We who are parents of grown children might especially understand this. When we no longer have some degree of control over our children's circumstances and decisions or even know everything they are facing in life, we often become all the more diligent to pray for them. Our love for them might take different forms when they are older and on their own, but it is just as strong. We are concerned for their welfare. We long to see them and to know they are living joyously for the Lord.

The Apostle Paul demonstrated such concerns and hopes for his spiritual children in the ancient city of Thessalonica.

LESSON OUTLINE

I. TIMOTHY'S MISSION—
I Thess. 3:1-5

II. TIMOTHY'S RETURN—
I Thess. 3:6-10

III. PAUL'S PRAYER—
I Thess. 3:11-13

Exposition: Verse by Verse

TIMOTHY'S MISSION

I THESS. 3:1 Wherefore when we could no longer forbear, we thought it good to be left at Athens alone;

2 And sent Timotheus, our broth-er, and minister of God, and our fellowlabourer in the gospel of Christ, to establish you, and to comfort you concerning your faith:

3 That no man should be moved by

these afflictions: for yourselves know that we are appointed thereunto.

4 For verily, when we were with you, we told you before that we should suffer tribulation; even as it came to pass, and ye know.

5 For this cause, when I could no longer forbear, I sent to know your faith, lest by some means the tempter have tempted you, and our labour be in vain.

His commission (I Thess. 3:1-2a). In chapter 2, Paul recounted his ministry in Thessalonica. His work there had been short in duration, and he longed to go back but had been prevented from doing so (vs. 18). His concern for them and desire to see them again were due in part to knowing they had been suffering persecution even as he had.

Following his ministry in Thessalonica, Paul traveled first to Berea and then to Athens, where Timothy and Silas joined him (Acts 17:10-16). Unable to return to Thessalonica for some reason, Paul found himself at the point of being unable to endure not knowing about the spiritual welfare of the young believers in the church there (I Thess. 3:1).

Paul and Silas decided to dispatch Timothy, a younger man, to Thessalonica. Timothy's departure would be a loss to Paul and his ministry, but it was worth it to him to continue his ministry in Thessalonica through Timothy.

The apostle described Timothy as a "brother," a "minister of God," and a fellow worker in the gospel ministry (vs. 2). Though Timothy was well known to the believers in Thessalonica, Paul reminded them again of the qualifications of this young man to carry out the mission entrusted to him. He was a true follower of Christ who had faithfully labored with Paul in proclaiming the gospel.

His purpose (I Thess. 3:2b-5). Paul set forth the purpose of Timothy's mission as being to "establish" them and to "comfort" them with regard to their faith. "Establish" means "to strengthen or make firm." "It contains the thought of making firm or solid by providing a support or buttress" (Hiebert, *The Thessalonian Epistles,* Moody). Timothy would seek to strengthen the faith of the Thessalonians (cf. Rom. 1:11).

The Greek word for "comfort" can also be translated "encourage" or "exhort." The grammatical construction indicates that establishing and encouraging are two parts of a larger whole, the idea being that encouragement or exhortation was the means of establishing the believers in their faith (Hiebert).

"Faith" can often refer to the body of Christian doctrine (cf. Jude 1:3), but here it seems to refer to both the belief and the conduct of the Thessalonian Christians. Paul was concerned that they understand the truth and live it out in their lives. We see both emphases in his letters to this church (cf. I Thess. 4:1, 13; II Thess. 2:1-2, 15; 3:13).

Paul's concern for the believers in Thessalonica was related to the persecution and suffering they were experiencing. It was crucial that they be established in their faith so that they were not "moved by these afflictions" (I Thess. 3:3).

"Moved" may simply mean "disturbed" or "disheartened." Continuing persecution can cause those who are not firmly grounded in the faith to surrender to discouragement and even compromise their faith in order to escape the suffering.

The Greek word for "moved," however, was also used of a dog wagging its tail, and from this came the idea of fawning or flattering. If this is the thought in this verse, Paul was warning that the afflictions in Thessalonica could cause the believers to listen to the "smooth talk [of those who]. . . were urging them to abandon the Christian way and accept Judaism, which would immediately free them from their plight" (Morris, *The Epistles of Paul to the*

Thessalonians, Eerdmans).

In either case, the temptation was to compromise or abandon the Christian faith in order to escape persecution. The potential for the believers to give in to such temptation necessitated Timothy's immediate ministry.

Some interpreters have taken the "we" in I Thessalonians 3:3 as making this verse a reference to Paul's afflictions rather than those of the Thessalonians. This would mean Paul was concerned about how his own suffering might negatively affect the Thessalonian Christians.

However, it seems Paul is simply making a general statement that is true of all Christians: we are all "appointed," or destined, for suffering of some kind. This is a truth Paul voices elsewhere (cf. Acts 14:22; II Tim. 3:12). Persecution and suffering may take various forms, but none of us can escape it entirely. We must be prepared for it, and we prepare by growing strong in the faith through our mutual ministry within the body of Christ, the church (cf. Eph. 4:11-16).

The fact that the Thessalonians would suffer was not unknown to them. Even while he was still with them, Paul had warned them this would come to pass. It is reassuring that no matter what we face in life, God knows about it and has always known about it, and He is present to see us through it.

While Paul knew the Thessalonian Christians would suffer persecution, now that they were, he was anxious to know about their faith (I Thess. 3:5). The use of "I" here indicates a more personal concern on Paul's part than we see in verse 1. "His concern was for their faith—that it was standing the test of time, in the midst of the temptations of Satan" (Ryrie, *First and Second Thessalonians,* Moody).

The apostle recognized that the devil can use afflictions to tempt God's people in various ways. Had the Thes-

salonians given in to Satan's temptations, the work of Paul and his companions would have been "in vain." While their ministry in the city had not initially been in vain (2:1), Paul had sent Timothy to make sure that this remained the case even as the church endured their current situation.

TIMOTHY'S RETURN

6 But now when Timotheus came from you unto us, and brought us good tidings of your faith and charity, and that ye have good remembrance of us always, desiring greatly to see us, as we also to see you:

7 Therefore, brethren, we were comforted over you in all our affliction and distress by your faith:

8 For now we live, if ye stand fast in the Lord.

9 For what thanks can we render to God again for you, for all the joy wherewith we joy for your sakes before our God;

10 Night and day praying exceedingly that we might see your face, and might perfect that which is lacking in your faith?

The report (I Thess. 3:6). Timothy had now returned from his visit, and as Paul wrote this letter, he disclosed what Timothy reported concerning the believers in Thessalonica. Paul characterized the report as "good tidings," using the very word that refers to the preaching of the gospel. The good news concerned the Thessalonians' "faith and charity," or love. He was probably referring specifically to their faith in God and their love for others (cf. Col. 1:4).

Timothy also reported that the Thessalonian Christians fondly remembered Paul and Silas and desired to see them again, just as the apostles longed to see them.

The response (I Thess. 3:7-10). As we might imagine, Paul rejoiced in Timothy's report. In fact, it might have been the impetus for Paul to write this letter to the Thessalonian church. While Timothy was sent to "comfort" (vs. 2), or encourage, the church, Paul reports that he and his friends were "comforted" (vs. 7) by Timothy's report about their faith. Their faith was not perfect, but it had endured through the "affliction and distress" they had suffered, and this greatly encouraged Paul and others.

Indeed, Paul writes, "Now we live, if ye stand fast in the Lord" (vs. 8). "If" could be translated "since" here, as Paul was convinced they were in fact standing strong in their faith in the Lord. This truth, as Timothy had reported it, brought new life to Paul. It had "refreshed, rejuvenated, and energized. It is likely that he [had] a new lease on life because a heavy burden of concern for the Thessalonians [had] been lifted" (Mayhue, *1 and 2 Thessalonians,* Christian Focus).

The report of Timothy was cause for thanksgiving. Using the form of a question, Paul in fact said that thanks was to be rendered to God (vs. 9), meaning it was due Him. It was something that was owed to God because of what He had accomplished. The joy that the Thessalonian believers brought Paul and his companions ultimately was not due to the missionaries or to the Thessalonians but to God's work in them, strengthening them to stand strong in the faith.

When we stand strong and trust the Lord through persecution and suffering, we encourage others, as the Thessalonians encouraged Paul. We bring great rejoicing among fellow Christians, set an example of faithfulness, and present a powerful testimony of God's grace to the world.

As important as it was for Paul and his fellow workers to offer God the praise due Him for His work on behalf of the Thessalonians, they were not content with that. They also offered up continual prayers regarding their brethren. Their prayers were consistent, "night and day" (vs. 10), and they were intense, or fervent, as indicated by "exceedingly." The particular word for praying here, *deomai,* means "to ask" or "beg" but implies "an asking that is motivated by a sense of personal need" (Hiebert).

Paul and his companions keenly felt the need to see the Thessalonians again, and they asked God for this opportunity. Yet their desire was not merely to experience the joy of seeing their faces again. They also wanted to see the Christians in Thessalonica in order to help "perfect" what was lacking in their faith. As much as Paul was encouraged by the Thessalonian church, he knew his work was not yet done. He wanted to see their faith perfected, or brought to completion, and this could most effectively be done in person.

There was much to rejoice about concerning this church, but there were still issues that needed to be addressed in order to make their faith complete. This is clear especially in II Thessalonians, where Paul had to confront false teaching to which some in the church had inclined (2:1-2), as well as the refusal of some to work and provide for themselves (3:8-12).

PAUL'S PRAYER

11 Now God himself and our Father, and our Lord Jesus Christ, direct our way unto you.

12 And the Lord make you to increase and abound in love one toward another, and toward all men, even as we do toward you:

13 To the end he may stablish your hearts unblameable in holiness before God, even our Father, at the coming of our Lord Jesus Christ with all his saints.

Concerning Paul and his companions (I Thess. 3:11). At this point Paul offers a prayer to God with regard to the perfecting of the Thessalonians' faith. The prayer expands on verse 10 and begins by repeating the request that God would direct the steps of Paul and his friends back to Thessalonica to see the brethren there.

The prayer is directed to "God himself and our Father" (vs. 11). The all-powerful, eternal God is also our Father. He is One we can fully trust to do what we cannot do. With regard to his own situation, Paul recognized that only God could overcome Satan's hindrance (2:18) and allow him to return to Thessalonica.

The prayer is also directed to "our Lord Jesus Christ" (3:11). Often we think of praying only to God the Father through Jesus Christ, but since Jesus and the Father are one (John 10:30) and Jesus is fully God, it is also appropriate to pray to Him (cf. John 14:14; Acts 7:59; I Cor. 1:1-2; Rev. 22:20).

Concerning the Thessalonians (I Thess. 3:12-13). Paul's prayer for the Thessalonians was that the Lord would make them "increase and abound in love." Paul's return to the city would aid the believers there, but only the Lord could increase their love to the point of abounding. "Increase" and "abound" are essentially synonyms, though the latter has greater force. The believers' love was evident (I Thess. 1:3; 3:6; II Thess. 1:3), but Paul's desire was for their love for one another and all people to grow and match the love he and his companions had exhibited (cf. I Thess. 2:7-8).

The prayer of the apostle also looked to the future. He prayed that the Lord would "stablish [their] hearts unblameable in holiness before God" (3:13). "Stablish" represents the same Greek word translated "establish" in verse 2. Timothy had been sent earlier to establish the Thessalonians in their faith, but in the end it would be God who established them in holiness, that

is, a state of being set apart to Him, a state characterized by a purity of life that withstands any charge against it.

It was Paul's prayer that "when Jesus Christ would return He would find them blameless before men and holy before God" (Walvoord and Zuck, eds., *The Bible Knowledge Commentary,* Cook). He mentioned Christ's coming "with all his saints" (vs. 13), or holy ones. This may refer to believers, angels, or both. It likely refers to the believers mentioned in 4:14 who will return with Christ at the rapture.

This prayer gives us an admirable model for praying for one another. We can always pray that the faith of our fellow believers will come to completion and that they will grow in love and live holy lives.

—Jarl K. Waggoner.

QUESTIONS

1. Why did Paul and Silas send Timothy to Thessalonica?

2. How could Timothy strengthen the Thessalonian church?

3. What temptation did persecution bring the Thessalonians?

4. What did Paul indicate is common to all Christians?

5. How did Paul describe Timothy's report?

6. Why did the report encourage Paul and his companions?

7. How did the apostles respond to the news from Timothy?

8. What did Paul and his friends pray that God would allow them to do?

9. Why did the Thessalonians' faith need to be brought to completion?

10. What two things did Paul pray for with regard to the Thessalonian Christians?

—Jarl K. Waggoner.

Preparing to Teach the Lesson

In our lesson this week we learn that new teaching also means learning new affections. Christians are called to display a new way of showing love to others. We learn about this from a church that demonstrated this quality.

TODAY'S AIM

Facts: to show how the believers in Thessalonica acted out their faith through good deeds and love for others.

Principle: to be new creations in Christ that show their faith through their love for others.

Application: to be followers of Jesus called to love others and to meet relevant needs.

INTRODUCING THE LESSON

Is it not interesting that many Christian organizations are actively involved in showing love and charity to those in need? This seems to be the hallmark of their outreach to the community. Giving freely identifies the Christian community because of their faith. We are called to give of our resources because this is how Jesus shared His life. This week, we learn how faith and love go hand in hand as we learn from the church in Thessalonica.

DEVELOPING THE LESSON

1. Paul sends Timothy (I Thess. 3:1-4). Paul was at Athens. He expressed his longing to see the Christians in Thessalonica. He was encouraged by their growth and the good report he had received, but since he could not personally go to visit them at that time, he sent Timothy in his place.

In verse 5, the phrase "no longer forbear" tells us that Paul had great love for those believers and desired strongly to see them again. Have you ever experienced a love so strong for someone that you could not stand being away from them? That is what Paul was experiencing. We must love our fellow Christians with that same intensity of love.

Timothy was a worthy ambassador of Paul to this church. Paul respectfully described him as "our brother, and minister of God, and our fellow-labourer in the gospel of Christ" (vs. 2). Timothy was young and inexperienced and being mentored by Paul. Paul had seen Timothy's commitment to the gospel and valued him highly.

The use of the phrases "our brother" and "fellowlabourer" point to the fact that Paul respected him as an equal despite his youth and inexperience. What an honor it must have been to serve our Lord Jesus and then be commended by Paul! Paul recognized that young Timothy was the best person to encourage the believers in Thessalonica since Timothy had worked alongside Paul and displayed Paul's same priorities. Timothy would help them to become grounded and comforted in their faith.

Christians at that time were persecuted for trusting in Jesus. Paul addresses this issue in the very next verse (vs. 3). Paul counseled the believers in the church at Thessalonica that putting one's faith in Jesus is a risky endeavor. It held the potential to bring them suffering and pain.

Christians are called to affliction. Paul says here that "we are appointed thereunto." Ours is a costly faith. There is a price to be paid for our faith, and we must be prepared to pay that price if we are to remain faithful. Both Paul and Timothy knew firsthand what is meant by suffering persecution for Jesus. This church had heard about those sufferings, so they trusted Timothy when he sought to encourage them. Are we ready to suffer as Paul and Timothy did?

2. Timothy gives a good report (I Thess. 3:5-8). Paul repeated his strong desire to see the Thessalonians again. He could hardly wait to know more about them. Communication was slow in those days. He wanted to know whether they were still faithful. He hoped that they had not been turned away from Christ by the evil one. Paul did not want his work among them to be ruined. Here we see the heart of Paul and his deep love for the church there.

Paul found relief in learning from Timothy that the church was still faithful. Their faith had been displayed in their actions that showed their love for others. The church's outreach comes from our faith. Is your congregation involved in helping others?

Timothy reported that these believers wanted to see Paul as much as he wanted to see them. This comforted Paul's heart. Do we desire to see spiritual growth in our fellow Christians in faith and action? Paul's own afflictions seemed smaller now that he knew that these Thessalonian believers were still faithful despite the sufferings and persecution they endured.

3. Paul prays for the believers (I Thess. 3:9-13). Paul writes with sheer joy. Joy moved Paul to gratitude. Are we able to genuinely rejoice over a neighboring church that is stronger than we are?

Paul prayed for these Christians night and day and wanted to go there in person to help them in their growth in areas "lacking in . . . faith" (vs. 10).

Each new step in our faith journey is a discovery. With good pastoral leadership, we can grow together. Paul wanted to meet with them quickly and prayed that they would increase in love. Love marks the follower of Jesus.

Love makes the heart strong, blameless, and ready to stand before the throne of God. Is this not our ultimate goal? We need to aim to finish this earthly race strong, blameless, and holy.

ILLUSTRATING THE LESSON

Christian believers love and encourage one another.

CONCLUDING THE LESSON

When Christ takes over our lives, we learn to love like Christ. Our lesson this week brought out this fervency of love between Paul and the little church in Thessalonica. We too are called to love as they did. It sets us apart from the world.

ANTICIPATING THE NEXT LESSON

In our lesson next week, we learn about a new way of life and how we can please God.

—A. Koshy Muthalaly.

PRACTICAL POINTS

1. We should make every effort to help those who are struggling in the faith (I Thess. 3:1-2).
2. Being a Christian does not exempt us from hard times (vss. 3-4).
3. We should disciple those we lead to Christ (vss. 5-6).
4. When new believers grow in faith, others are encouraged (vss. 7-8).
5. The beauty of Christian community is that we grow in faith as we learn from others (vss. 9-10).
6. We should always pray for God's direction and guidance (vs. 11).
7. As we grow closer to God, we grow stronger in faith (vss. 12-13).

—*Charity G. Carter.*

RESEARCH AND DISCUSSION

1. The Bible states that we will have difficulties on this earth. Why do some people believe that becoming a Christian means there will not be any more problems (I Thess. 3:4; cf. John 16:33)?
2. How can we encourage new believers in their faith (I Thess. 3:5)?
3. Why was Paul so encouraged to know that the people of the Thessalonian church were still going strong in their faith (vss. 7-8)?
4. Why is it important for Christians to fellowship with one another (vs. 10)?
5. How can we demonstrate a growing concern for our brothers and sisters in Christ (vs. 12)?
6. How does the Lord establish our hearts and make us blameless before God (vs. 13)?

—*Charity G. Carter.*

ILLUSTRATED HIGH POINTS

Comfort you concerning your faith

At times, we each need a little comfort concerning our faith. Consider the 15-year-old boy who posted the following inquiry, along with his workouts, to a bodybuilding forum: "Am I strong for my size and age? I was just wondering if I could get some opinions from you guys out there. My friends say I'm not that strong. . . . Just wondering if you think I'm decent for my size and age."

Someone wisely posted the following response, "Progress is more important than anything . . . at age 15, you can add just a bit every year."

Rest assured, if our faith is growing, it is enough for today.

Joy for your sakes

Forced by persecution to leave the barely three-week old believers of Thessalonica, Paul was relentlessly worried for the spiritual saplings he had left behind without adequate leadership.

Gerald "Jerry" Krueger, a retired teacher, finds his greatest joy in watching the progress of his former students. "I still look with great pride," he says, "at some of those students who excelled and made their marks in communities across the country." He reflects effusively on his past students having become "successful business owners, outstanding farmers, renowned surgeons, noted realtors, and so many, many more." When Timothy brought word of the Thessalonian's remarkable spiritual growth and strong faith, Paul was comforted from his trials and overjoyed with the progress of his former students. He truly had the heart of a teacher!

—*Therese Greenberg.*

Golden Text Illuminated

"Timotheus came from you unto us, and brought us good tidings of your faith and charity, and that ye have good remembrance of us always, desiring greatly to see us, as we also to see you" (I Thessalonians 3:6).

Evident throughout Scripture is the deep and genuine affection that existed among believers. They prayed for each other, offered encouragement in difficult times, and shared a love that neither distance nor time seemed to diminish.

The relationship that Jesus had with His disciples is one example of great affection that people share. Knowing the great sorrow and persecution that lay ahead for His followers, Jesus instructed them to continue in love and care for one another (John 15:12).

Another example of a deeply knit bond between believers is the one between Paul, Silas, Timothy, and the Thessalonian church. Having been separated from the young believers through some kind of interference by Satan (I Thess. 2:18), a longing persisted in the hearts of the three men and the church to be reunited.

Furthermore, Paul shared a concern for his friends in Thessalonica similar to the concern that Jesus had for His disciples. The apostle knew that the fledgling believers would face severe difficulties (3:4). Satan could use such situations to undermine their faith (vs. 5).

Although Paul was confident that the initial work that God had begun within the Thessalonian believers was not in any danger, his love nonetheless compelled him to visit his friends.

Therefore, Paul and Silas remained in Athens but sent Timothy to visit the Thessalonians. His visit was twofold: he was to strengthen, comfort, and encourage the church (I Thess. 3:1-3) as well as confirm the well-being of their faith (vs. 5).

The golden text reveals the results of Timothy's visit to Thessalonica. Without a doubt, Paul was delighted!

In his letter, Paul expressed Timothy's good tidings. Despite Paul's previous concerns, the church had remained steadfast in faith. Their devotion and trust in the Lord was evidenced by the love and charity that marked their lives.

It also delighted Paul's heart to hear that the Thessalonians thought fondly of him, Silas, and Timothy, just as the three disciples esteemed the church in their hearts.

The affection that was established between the believers created a deep desire to be together again.

Truly amazing is the devout affection that seems to quickly develop and prevail when fellow Christians meet. Such love could only come from God and is reflective of His relationship with the church (cf. Eph. 5:25-27).

When someone becomes a Christian, the Scriptures declare that such a person is made brand new. We read in II Corinthians 5:17: "Therefore if any man be in Christ, he is a new creature: old things are passed away; behold, all things are become new."

Following conversion, new affections begin to permeate one's life. The Lord is delighted to bring believers together to help one another and to serve together.

Thank God for His gifts of salvation, love, and friendship!

—*Christine M. Morrison.*

Heart of the Lesson

Imagine you have two plants. One plant is showered with love. It sits in the sunshine and is fed and watered regularly. Soon it is thriving. Its leaves become shiny and bright. With the other plant, you are not so diligent. It receives little care. Neglect of this plant causes it to wither. Its leaves turn brown and dull, and its head droops toward the soil. With a little attention, however, this poor, pitiful plant will become just as vibrant as the other one.

A church and its members are like those plants. Providing encouragement to a church will cause it to flourish.

1. Paul's substitute (I Thess. 3:1-5). Paul desired to visit the church in Thessalonica but was unable to make the journey. Therefore, he sent Timothy as his representative. Paul, along with Silas and Timothy, had previously visited Thessalonica, but he was now in Corinth. Since the Thessalonians knew Timothy, he would be a great encouragement to the church. Paul knew that Satan could quickly destroy the Thessalonian church. With Timothy guiding them, Paul knew that these people would be able to endure their hardships.

Members of the church need encouragement. Everyone encounters difficulties. Believers know that Satan wants to destroy anything that comes from God's hand. A smile can brighten a person's dark mood, and a kind word can refresh a disheartened church. A few encouraging words can lift a weary person's heart and give him strength to carry his heavy burden.

2. Timothy's good news (I Thess. 3:6-8). When Timothy returned, he brought good news: the Thessalonians' faith had remained strong. Their love for others was also thriving. These people knew Paul personally, so they did not believe the false rumors about him. This report renewed Paul's faith in the Thessalonian church. He was also thankful that his work had prospered.

When a church member shares good news, the whole congregation rejoices. They are encouraged to see God working in the lives of fellow believers, and it spurs them to give God praise. Good news for one believer is an encouragement to all.

3. Paul's prayer (I Thess. 3:9-13). Paul was overjoyed when he learned that the Thessalonians' faith had remained strong. He had rejoiced over them and had prayed for them often. Paul thought he could better help them grow if he could join them in person. This caused him to ask God to allow him to go to them and help them continue to grow. Paul wanted the church body to increase in their love toward one another and toward others. Finally, Paul prayed that the church might be holy and blameless before God. While Paul was encouraged by what he had heard about the Thessalonians, he also desired that they would be spurred on by his example.

Christian people need the prayers of others. Just as Paul prayed for the Thessalonians, the church body needs to be praying for one another. Believers should pray that God will direct the church as a whole as well as the individual members. Worshippers need to ask God to help them express their love for all fellow beings. A church sign I recently read sums up this lesson: "The most important blessings you can give are words that encourage, hands that help, and a heart that loves."

—*Catherine Moore.*

World Missions

Paul's experience with the Thessalonians is a wonderful example of God's global mission plan. Paul went as a missionary, willing to endure public shaming and physical harm to share the gospel. He started a church, then moved on to other places, but he never stopped praying for each body of believers. He kept in touch, asking how they were doing, encouraging them, and making sure the afflictions they endured had not caused them to waver in their faith.

In missions today, there is more opportunity than ever for the global body of Christ to remain connected, encourage one another, and keep track of how to pray and help one another.

Ashley Tallent's church in Hudson, North Carolina, has a caring relationship with a group of believers in Haiti. For years, Ashley's church has led teams to Haiti to serve by giving much-needed food, teaching seminars, and sharing the gospel. On one trip Ashley helped organize, representatives from nine different churches came together to serve. Their team included at least one child. What an apprenticeship, and what a testimony!

When Hurricane Matthew hit, devastating an already impoverished area, people in Haiti were able to send photos over social media within days. Those photos showed churches destroyed, but later ones showed believers worshipping anyway, praising God in the open air on the foundation of their church, now without walls or a roof.

Ashley was able to ask God's people to pray, and she could give specifics. Thanks to the internet, she was able to find out just what the Haitian believers in that area needed prayer for, including missing people. She and others traveled to Haiti and were humbled and amazed to hear believers, some who had lost nearly everything, expressing concern for them. "I had friends that were homeless," Ashley says, "everything wiped out—and they were worried about us."

Now Ashley plans another trip to Haiti, and she is using social media to connect with believers far beyond her own area to raise funds for bricks to rebuild the church that was destroyed. Each brick for the church costs one dollar. Eighteen thousand dollars would build a new church. She feels overwhelmed at the amount that must be raised, but in comparison with the cost to build a church in America it is not much at all.

When asked what the qualifications of being a missionary are, Ashley said, "Being willing to let the Lord tell you 'Go,' and then saying, 'Here I am.' You have to have love and compassion. People that are willing to do whatever is required of them. Workers. Servants. If I'm needed to carry water or carry cinder blocks, that's what I'll do."

The partnership of Ashley's church with the church in Haiti is the body of Christ working as Jesus intended: serving together, caring for one another, bearing one other's burdens.

Is there a body of believers on the foreign field that your church can "adopt," caring for them and praying for them regularly? God is pleased when we build each other up, support each other, and work for the kingdom together.

—Kimberly Rae.

The Jewish Aspect

The first letter of Paul to the Thessalonians is one of the most gentle and affectionate of Paul's writings. He assures the Thessalonians of his continued heartfelt concern for them. He sends Timothy to comfort and encourage them (I Thess. 3:2). The Lord, and His relationship with His people, is described by the prophet Isaiah, "As one whom his mother comforteth, so will I comfort you; and ye shall be comforted in Jerusalem" (66:13). Paul uses a similar analogy when he writes, "But we were gentle among you, even as a nurse cherisheth her children" (I Thess. 2:7).

When he refers to being taken away from them (I Thess. 2:17), the Greek word he uses means "being orphaned." "The verb translated 'left behind' (*kataleipo*) is an intense and picturesque term that is used of a child leaving his parents (Eph. 5:31) or of the death of one's spouse (Mark 12:19). In 2:17, Paul said that he felt 'orphaned' from his friends in Thessalonica, and the Greek word can also mean 'bereaved.' To leave these new believers was like an experience of bereavement. . . . Paul so loved the Thessalonian believers that he would have risked his own life to return to them. He wanted to give of himself and his resources for them, as a parent provides for his or her children" (Krell, "Built Faith Tough [I Thessalonians 3:1-13]," www.bible.org). This selfless love was also described in the Gospel of John, "Greater love hath no man than this, that a man lay down his life for his friends" (John 15:13).

Paul told the Thessalonians that he gave himself, not just his message, out of love for them, not personal gain. By working and not being a financial burden on them, he was following the tradition of Jewish rabbis, for whom receiving money was considered shameful. "Paul likely first taught the Thessalonians in an 'insula,' a workshop-like apartment where a series of shops would face the street and living quarters of owners and their families would be in the rear. This was an ideal setting to spend time with people, while he worked his trade during the day, and over meals in the evening. . . . He was forming community, a new kinship model to help them solidify the gospel in their lives" (Wiebe, "Love Each Other More," watershed online.ca).

When Paul said he could no longer hold back his concern, he used another maternal metaphor from the prophet Isaiah, "I have long time holden my peace; I have been still, and refrained myself: now will I cry like a travailing woman" (42:14).

Paul was concerned about the Thessalonians because of the persecutions they had suffered and endured. He worried that in his absence they would become disoriented and start to lose their faith. He sought assurance that they had not been led astray by the tempter (Satan). Paul hoped that his labor would not be in vain (I Thess. 3:5). Paul expressed a deep longing to see the believers at Thessalonica again, praying night and day (according to the Jewish calendar, every day starts and ends at night).

He was relieved when Timothy reported back that they still held him and the gospel affectionately in their hearts. He was grateful that they missed him as much as he missed them. And he was filled with joy that the believers were standing firm in their faith. "For now we live, if ye stand fast in the Lord" (3:8). He thanked God for the Thessalonians' endurance through suffering and that they did not waver in their commitment to Christ

—*Deborah Markowitz Solan.*

Guiding the Superintendent

Jesus said that people will best know who His disciples are by the way they love one another (John 13:35). This thought could not be better illustrated than in the way Paul and the believers in Thessalonica interacted with one another, as documented in the third chapter of the first epistle to the Thessalonians.

DEVOTIONAL OUTLINE

1. Love and present suffering (I Thess. 3:1-9). Chapter three of the first letter to the Thessalonians is perhaps one of the most personal sections in all of Paul's epistles.

The church in Thessalonica was established during Paul's whirlwind missionary tour of Greece. It seems that no sooner would Paul come to a town and establish a fledgling church than persecutors would arise and force Paul and company out of town. Churches were established in quick succession at Philippi and Thessalonica. Then Paul found himself in Athens before moving on to Corinth (Acts 16—18).

All the while Paul was deeply concerned about what persecution would do to the believers left in his wake. "When we [Paul and company] could no longer forebear" (I Thess. 3:1) Paul sent his assistant Timothy to the church back in Thessalonica to see how they were doing. Timothy was given the task of encouraging the church and strengthening them in their sufferings. Among Paul's concerns was that the tempter would lead them astray.

Paul was relieved when Timothy returned with the good news that the folks in Thessalonica had pleasant memories of Paul and his helpers. Their faith and love was still strong. Further, Paul was deeply comforted by the news that their faith was holding up under suffering. Hearing all this good news brought joy to Paul's heart.

Truly, Christian love had triumphed over all adversity.

2. Love and future growth (I Thess. 3:10-13). Love is never sedentary. Christian love is always acting and progressing.

Timothy's good report not only brought joy to the apostle's heart in his current struggles, but it also challenged him to pray night and day that the Father and Christ would bring them back to Thessalonica soon. He desired to fill in whatever gaps were left in their knowledge of God.

Paul had two prayers for them in the meantime. First, he wanted the Lord to make their love for one another grow and overflow. Even though they were already known for their love, there would always be room for more growth in love. Persecution can cause people to turn inward. More love is always the Christian answer to suffering.

The apostle's second goal was that the Lord would strengthen their hearts to become more holy before God.

CHILDREN'S CORNER

text: **I Samuel 17:43-51**
title: **God's Servant David**

It was the literal David/Goliath fight. A young shepherd boy by the name of David was amazed when he walked into the camp of the Israelite army to see them all cowering before the giant champion of the Philistine army.

Goliath had everyone scared except for David. David went after the giant and killed him. This was not because of some special ability he possessed. No, it was because of the God that David believed in. "I come to thee in the name of the Lord" (I Sam. 17:45).

—Martin R. Dahlquist.

Scripture Lesson Text

I THESS. 4:1 Furthermore then we beseech you, brethren, and exhort you by the Lord Jesus, that as ye have received of us how ye ought to walk and to please God, so ye would abound more and more.

2 For ye know what commandments we gave you by the Lord Jesus.

3 For this is the will of God, even your sanctification, that ye should abstain from fornication:

4 That every one of you should know how to possess his vessel in sanctification and honour;

5 Not in the lust of concupiscence, even as the Gentiles which know not God:

6 That no man go beyond and defraud his brother in any matter: because that the Lord is the avenger of all such, as we also have forewarned you and testified.

7 For God hath not called us unto uncleanness, but unto holiness.

8 He therefore that despiseth, despiseth not man, but God, who hath also given unto us his holy Spirit.

9 But as touching brotherly love ye need not that I write unto you: for ye yourselves are taught of God to love one another.

10 And indeed ye do it toward all the brethren which are in all Macedonia: but we beseech you, brethren, that ye increase more and more;

11 And that ye study to be quiet, and to do your own business, and to work with your own hands, as we commanded you;

12 That ye may walk honestly toward them that are without, and that ye may have lack of nothing.

NOTES

A New Way of Life

Lesson Text: I Thessalonians 4:1-12

Related Scriptures: Colossians 1:9-11; II Timothy 2:19-21;
I John 3:22-24; II Corinthians 8:1-5

TIME: A.D. 51   PLACE: from Corinth

GOLDEN TEXT—"We beseech you, brethren, and exhort you by the Lord Jesus, that as ye have received of us how ye ought to walk and to please God, so ye would abound more and more" (I Thessalonians 4:1).

Introduction

Billy Mills won the gold medal in the ten thousand–meter run at the 1964 Olympics in Tokyo, Japan. That is a simple historical fact duly listed in the Olympic record books. But the record books tell only what happened in a little over twenty-eight minutes one day in 1964. They do not reveal the incredible determination of this athlete to achieve what nobody thought was possible.

Mills had won a spot on the U.S. Olympic team, but no one imagined he would even contend for a medal. His best time in the event was almost two minutes behind that of the world record holder, against whom Mills would be competing. Determined to improve each lap by a few seconds, Mills began a training regimen that saw his time steadily improve. By the time of the Olympics, however, his best time was still a full minute slower than the favored runner. The U.S. team hoped at best that Mills would compete and have a good showing. Mills, however, was determined not just to compete but to win. With an incredible burst of speed at the end, he won the race in one of the greatest sports upsets ever.

As Christians, we are not called merely to "compete" in life—to be content to be average or compare well next to others. God wants us to exceed expectations. He calls us to a new way of life, a life of excellence.

LESSON OUTLINE

I. **EXCELLING IN HOLINESS—**
   I Thess. 4:1-8

II. **EXCELLING IN LOVE—**
    I Thess. 4:9-10

III. **EXCELLING IN WORK—**
     I Thess. 4:11-12

Exposition: Verse by Verse

EXCELLING IN HOLINESS

I THESS. 4:1 Furthermore then we beseech you, brethren, and exhort you by the Lord Jesus, that as ye have received of us how ye ought to walk and to please God, so ye would abound more and more.

2 For ye know what command-

ments we gave you by the Lord Jesus.

3 For this is the will of God, even your sanctification, that ye should abstain from fornication:

4 That every one of you should know how to possess his vessel in sanctification and honour;

5 Not in the lust of concupiscence, even as the Gentiles which know not God:

6 That no man go beyond and defraud his brother in any matter: because that the Lord is the avenger of all such, as we also have forewarned you and testified.

7 For God hath not called us unto uncleanness, but unto holiness.

8 He therefore that despiseth, despiseth not man, but God, who hath also given unto us his holy Spirit.

Exhortation to holiness (I Thess. 4:1-2). Up to this point in I Thessalonians, Paul's teaching had been primarily by way of personal example—displayed by both him and the Thessalonian Christians. With chapter 4 he begins to address some specific issues, and he does so through straightforward instruction and exhortation.

The apostle introduces his comments with an exhortation to please God. "Beseech" indicates a request made by one whose familiarity to the hearers "lends authority to the request" (Trench, *Synonyms of the New Testament,* Eerdmans). "Exhort" means "to urge" or "admonish." Paul's appeal, while personal, is based on the Thessalonians' relationship with Jesus Christ. He can exhort them to "please God" because they are followers of Christ.

Paul himself had taught the Thessalonian believers how they were to live in order to please God. This is a general reference to the whole Christian life. They had been instructed in how they should live, or walk, in a way that was honoring to the God they served. Paul's exhortation was "not new in content, but rather a reminder of fact and a motivation to reach new levels of spiritual excellency" (Mayhue, *1 & 2 Thessalonians,* Christian Focus).

Paul repeatedly commended this church for their faithfulness. However, he never encouraged them to be spiritually content but urged them to "abound more and more" (4:1; cf. 3:12; 4:10), excelling in godly living.

One author reminds us that "pleasing God is not a matter of choice for the Christian, it is a necessity which grows out of his relationship to Christ" (Ryrie, *First and Second Thessalonians,* Moody). The Christian life was never meant to be static. There is to be constant growth and excellence in obeying God and pleasing Him.

How Christians are to walk is defined by the commandments of God. Paul reminded his readers in Thessalonica that they were aware of what God expected of them because he and the other missionaries had taught them the Lord's commandments. Furthermore, these commands had been given by the authority of the Lord Jesus, the One the Thessalonians claimed as their Saviour and Master.

Example of holiness (I Thess. 4:3-6a). To please God, one must walk in holiness, obeying His commands. Holiness is really the first issue Paul took up in this chapter. This is reflected in his affirmation that God's will for the Thessalonians was their "sanctification," a word that is also translated "holiness" in our English Bibles. It literally refers to being set apart, or separated, to God. Here it is progressive sanctification that is in view, that is, the continuing growth in holiness in one's daily experience.

As followers of Christ, we are all

to be growing and abounding in holy living (cf. II Cor. 7:1; I Pet. 1:15). This is God's clearly stated desire for His children. While we might fall into sin on occasion, our lives should be characterized by progress toward Christlikeness.

While Paul could have gone in any of several directions with regard to sanctification, or holiness, he focuses on personal holiness with regard to sexual conduct. Sanctification does not consist only of abstaining from fornication, but it certainly includes such abstinence. The Greek word *porneia,* translated "fornication" in I Thessalonians 4:3, refers here to any and all sexual immorality, or intercourse, that is outside the bounds the Creator has established. It includes both adultery and fornication, which were especially prevalent in the Greek world of Paul's day.

There is no indication Timothy had reported any actual cases of immorality among the Thessalonian believers. However, Paul was well aware of the moral climate in their city and throughout the Gentile world. Sexual immorality and perversion were pervasive and integral to worship in the pagan religions.

D. Edmond Hiebert notes, "Writing from Corinth, a notoriously licentious seaport, Paul well knew the penetrating moral taint to which his converts in the seaport of Thessalonica were constantly exposed. Further, the warning was timely since many of the readers, until a few months before, had lived by the low moral standards prevailing in the pagan world around them" (*The Thessalonian Epistles,* Moody).

While the Thessalonians might not be tempted by the pagan religions of their city, the immoral practices associated with them and sanctioned by Greek society at large confronted them at every turn.

Society today is not much different. While the religious aspect of immorality is largely absent in the modern world, the glorification of so-called sexual freedom is pervasive—in the media, the arts, education, and advertising. Almost everywhere we turn, the biblical teaching on these matters is under assault, ridiculed, and rejected. The pressure to surrender to the world and compromise is unrelenting.

Paul's admonition regarding fornication is to abstain from it. The verb tense here indicates a constant, ongoing effort. The apostle does not leave it at that, though. He goes on to explain how Christians can abstain from such immoral behavior.

First, and positively, he states that each person should "know how to possess his vessel in sanctification and honour" (vs. 4). To "know" indicates that abstaining from sexual sin is "a matter that requires instruction and self-discipline" (Hiebert).

But to what does "vessel" refer? Some argue it refers to one's wife and that having and honoring a wife prevents immorality (cf. I Cor. 7:2; I Pet. 3:7). While there is truth in this, it is probably better to understand "vessel" as referring to one's body (cf. II Cor. 4:7; II Tim. 2:21). In this case, Paul is saying believers must devote their bodies to God in holiness, showing proper honor to the bodies given them by the Creator.

Negatively stated, abstaining from immorality involves avoiding lustful attitudes with regard to one's body and relationships. "Lust of concupiscence" (I Thess. 4:5) describes a powerful craving to fulfill selfish and evil desires. As we commit our bodies to honoring God and to holy uses, we will avoid immorality and the lustful passions that characterize unbelievers, or "Gentiles," as Paul refers to the pagan world of his day.

Seeking sanctification, or holiness, in sexual matters protects the believer from personal sin, but it also protects others around him from the effects of such sin. To commit immorality is to go beyond what is right and take advantage of a brother ("defraud" in verse 6). The brother here may be widely understood as any person who is harmed by sexual sin.

The lust and selfishness that is expressed through such sin has devastating and wide-ranging effects on many people. We must continually recommit our lives to holy living.

Motivation for holiness (I Thess. 4:6b-8). Holiness has application to all areas of life. Paul saw that in Thessalonica the temptation to sexual sin was especially strong, even as it is today, and he warned that it must be avoided. He now gives three reasons or motivations for avoiding immorality.

First, sexual immorality invites the judgment of God. He is the one who will ultimately avenge those who have been wronged by such sin (vs. 6). There are serious consequences to immoral actions, and we should rightly fear them, for God Himself will see that such sin is punished. For the Thessalonians, this was simply a reminder of what Paul had already taught them.

Second, immorality should be avoided because of the high calling of God. He calls us to "holiness" (vs. 7), which is the same word translated "sanctification" in verse 3. Uncleanness, or moral impurity, has no place in God's plan for us. If we take seriously God's desire and demand for us to be holy as He is holy (I Pet. 1:15-16), we will avoid sexual immorality.

A third reason for living pure lives is that immorality is rejection of God Himself. "Despiseth" in I Thessalonians 4:8 has the sense of rejection or disregard. The apostle was saying that the utter disregard for others exhibited by fornication, adultery, and other sexual sins and perversions is actually rejection of God. This does not mean people

are not harmed by such sins, for they certainly are. It simply means that in the ultimate sense, the sin expresses rejection of God. This was the perspective of David, who when he acknowledged his sin of adultery, as well as murder, declared to God, "Against thee, thee only, have I sinned" (Ps. 51:4).

Paul reminds his readers that God has given His children the Holy Spirit to empower them to live holy lives. To practice immorality is to show contempt for the One who is always present, holy, and guiding us into truth and holiness.

EXCELLING IN LOVE

9 But as touching brotherly love ye need not that I write unto you: for ye yourselves are taught of God to love one another.

10 And indeed ye do it toward all the brethren which are in all Macedonia: but we beseech you, brethren, that ye increase more and more.

The next topic Paul addresses is that of "brotherly love" (vs. 9). "Brotherly love" is a single word in Greek (*philadelphia*), combining the word for love with the word for brother. While this is not the more common word for love (*agape*), there is no real distinction between the two in this verse since the phrase "love one another" later in the verse expresses the same thought using *agape*.

Love for one another was not something the Thessalonians were lacking. In fact, Paul affirmed they were faithfully exhibiting such love toward the brethren throughout Macedonia (vs. 10). Clearly, however, this was a topic of great importance to Paul. So he urged the Thessalonian church to continue to increase, or excel, in their love (cf. 3:12).

Such mutual love seeks what is best for others and most honoring to God. It promotes holiness and protects against the temptations of the world, the flesh, and the devil. Brotherly love is vital to the spiritual health of the church.

EXCELLING IN WORK

11 And that ye study to be quiet, and to do your own business, and to work with your own hands, as we commanded you;

12 That ye may walk honestly toward them that are without, and that ye may have lack of nothing.

The third topic Paul addresses in this passage is the Christian's labor. Here the focus shifts from loving relationships within the body of Christ to how believers present themselves before the world.

"Study" means "to strive" or "to be ambitious." There are three things Paul wanted the Thessalonians to strive for. First was a "quiet" life. This is a life that "does its best to avoid unnecessary contention and to be at peace with all men in so far as it is humanly possible" (Mayhue). It is resting with contentment in Christ and all He has given us.

Second, Paul wanted his readers to take care of their own business. They were to make sure their own practices and affairs were in order. While they were to be concerned about others, such concern would be seen only as meddling if their own lives were not in proper order. Giving proper attention to our personal affairs will help us live quiet, God-honoring lives.

Finally, Paul stresses the importance of working with one's own hands. Manual labor, which was and still is often despised, is in view. The temptation to be lazy or work halfheartedly in such labor is always present (cf. II Thess. 3:10-12). Paul had taught the Thessalonians—even commanded them—to work diligently. Any honest job is honorable and honoring to God when performed with excellence and for the Lord (cf. Col. 3:23).

The result of pursuing a quiet life, working diligently, and keeping their own affairs in order was that the Thessalonians would "walk honestly" (I Thess. 4:12), that is, behave in an honorable manner, before unbelievers. The believers' efforts would commend them as people who were honest and helpful. And by providing for themselves, they would not be a burden on others or an excuse for others to reject Christ.

Our attitudes toward our work, whatever it might be, and the goals we bring to it are important testimonies to the watching world. Let us seek to excel in all our labor, for ultimately all our work is for God.

—Jarl K. Waggoner.

QUESTIONS

1. On what does Paul base his appeal to "please God" (I Thess. 4:1)?

2. To what does sanctification refer (vs. 3)?

3. What example of sanctification does Paul give?

4. Why might the Thessalonians have especially needed Paul's warning against immorality?

5. What is meant by the term "vessel" in verse 4?

6. What does Paul say characterized the Gentile world of his day?

7. In what way is immorality a rejection of God?

8. Why is the practice of brotherly love so vital to the church?

9. Why does Paul stress the importance of working with one's hands?

10. How does our labor relate to our witness?

—Jarl K. Waggoner.

Preparing to Teach the Lesson

In our lesson this week we learn how to please God as we live our daily lives. Paul taught the Thessalonian Christians how they were to walk and please God. We get a challenging picture of how they conducted their lives.

TODAY'S AIM

Facts: to show Paul's instructions to the Thessalonian church on how they were to live their lives pleasing God.

Principle: to live a new way of life in Christ that will always please Him.

Application: to do all things to please Jesus if we say that we love Him.

INTRODUCING THE LESSON

Most of us who read a lesson like this sincerely want to please God. At the same time, however, there is so much that takes our focus away from what is really important in this journey. It is easy to be distracted and follow what is not godly. We lose our focus on the eternal and slip away into that which is natural and temporary, and this often comes very easily for us. It is hard to focus solely on pleasing God in all things. But it is also important to keep this as our priority.

In our lesson this week Paul teaches us through his dealings with the church at Thessalonica that we are to seek to please God in everything. This should also dictate how we ought to live the Christian life.

DEVELOPING THE LESSON

1. Please God (I Thess. 4:1-5). We need to please God always. This thought should drive our thinking this week. Paul encouraged the believers in Thessalonica to live a holy life that pleases God. He did this in the name of our Lord. Paul knew that they were doing this already, but he sought to encourage them even more. He commended them for remembering and practicing what he had taught them. Is this not good advice for us as Christians too?

Paul taught these Christians that holiness and sexual sin could not go together. We learn that one who follows Jesus has to learn to gain control over the physical body. Only when this happens can one truly live in holiness and honor. The word "sanctification" (vs. 3) means to become holy and clean. This pleases God.

This is in striking contrast to what those who do not believe in Jesus do. These unbelievers fulfill their lusts without any regard for the laws of God or what He tells us about how we are to live. The word "concupiscence" (vs. 5) means lustful desire. God has given us His laws in His Word. We can no longer live in ignorance of what He expects of us. We cannot live as the world around us does. We must strive to please God in all our ways.

2. Live holy lives (I Thess. 4:6-8). Paul encouraged the believers in Thessalonica to live holy lives. He made this point in particular, referring to sexual sin. They were never to be involved in sexual sin, for it did not please God. It violates holiness. After all, Paul had reminded them of this before. Christians are called to live holy lives and live by the rules of God. We are called to have the fear of God that calls us to follow His laws about this.

When we live impure lives we are not disobeying human laws but God Himself who put His Holy Spirit within us. Dare we disappoint God as believers? We dare not forget that when we chose to follow Him, we were called to live holy lives. We cannot now turn back on that commitment as Christians. It is easy to live like the pagans around us. If God has called us to purity, then we dare not reject His Spirit who guides us.

If we are believers in Christ, we have been saved from God's wrath. He demands holiness. Because we could not achieve this on our own, Christ came to pay the price for our sins. Gratitude for this gift should motivate us to obey God's law. He is a good and gracious God, and He is worthy of praise and obedience.

Help the class discuss how we often reject the guidance of the Spirit, especially when it comes to sexual sin. How can we hear and follow the Spirit's gentle warnings?

3. Love fellow Christians (I Thess. 4:9-12). We see that Christian brotherly love supplants the sexual impurity that is prevalent among unbelievers. Paul told the believers in Thessalonica that he knew their commitment and so did not need any further teaching in this area. God Himself was their divine Teacher. He is love.

These believers in Thessalonica were already known for their love to the Christians in all of Macedonia. And Paul encouraged them to love their fellow Christians even more. By this they would avoid the pattern of impure sexual living. This is done through brotherly love in the congregation.

Paul then explained further. He gave them three pieces of advice. They were to live a quiet life, mind their own business, and work with their hands. We could use these bits of advice ourselves. It would clear up a lot of problems we have in our churches today. Ask the class which of these would help them the most in their situations. Paul is really saying that if we live busy and profitable lives, then we will not have time for impure sexual distractions.

Two good things will happen as a result of this. First, unbelievers will respect our manner of life and will look up to us. Second, we will become financially self-sufficient if we work hard. This makes sense! Biblical instruction transcends time and is still relevant today. We can learn from this.

ILLUSTRATING THE LESSON

Unbelievers seek impure sexual pleasure. Christians seek to please God.

CONCLUDING THE LESSON

The conclusion is very clear. If we work hard and keep our minds and hearts busy, we will not have time for the wrong way of life. Following Jesus means that we must please our Lord in all things at all times. We give ourselves to Him fully to use us as He wills. Are we prepared to please Him in all things?

ANTICIPATING THE NEXT LESSON

In our lesson next week, we learn of a new understanding that involves a new hope because we have Jesus.

—A. Koshy Muthalaly.

PRACTICAL POINTS

1. The Bible gives clear instructions for life (I Thess. 4:1-2).
2. Abstaining from sexually immoral behavior should be second nature for us (vss. 3-4).
3. We have an obligation to ensure that our behavior does not deceive or cheat others (vss. 5-6).
4. God has called us to live a holy lifestyle (vs. 7).
5. When people ignore sound Christian counsel, they are really ignoring God (vs. 8).
6. We should extend love to all our Christian brothers and sisters (vss. 9-10).
7. When we mind our own business, we walk in obedience (vss. 11-12).

—*Charity G. Carter.*

RESEARCH AND DISCUSSION

1. Why do we remind people to do what they already know they should be doing (I Thess. 4:2)?
2. How can we follow God's will regarding sanctification when popular culture has a completely different viewpoint (vss. 3-4)?
3. Why does God insist that we lead holy lives (vs. 7)?
4. Why should we refuse to take offense if people reject biblically based advice (vs. 8)?
5. How are we taught to show kindness to others (vss. 9-10)?
6. What are some practical steps we can take to mind our own business (vs. 11)?

—*Charity G. Carter.*

ILLUSTRATED HIGH POINTS

The Lord is the avenger

Our thirteen-year-old granddaughter is clever. Having learned a bit about product expiration dates, she took it upon herself to examine my pantry and toss any "suspicious" items. Being frugal, I often buy discounted items nearing their sell-by dates.

My granddaughter did not understand that, according to the USDA, there are several different label designations. "Expiration date" is a mandate to toss the offending product. Other label terms are "Sell by" and "Best if used by," which are merely indicators of peak quality. Before long, the trash bin was brimming with our packaged foods.

We may size-up our enemies and conclude (in our estimation) this unworthy person's life, freedom, or progress is expendable. But we fail to realize we are not adept at reading human hearts. It is not our pantry, it is God's.

Walk honestly

In December, 1985, the Racquetball championship had been played and one of the leading sports magazines, "National Racquetball" featured the game's true champion on the cover. He was not the winner, but the man who lost: Ruben Gonzalez.

He nearly won his very first championship when, in the final match, he made his "kill shot." The referee declared that the shot was good; yet, in that moment, Gonzalez turned and declared that the ball had "skipped," touching the floor before hitting the wall. This incident has gone down in sports history as, "The Skip."

Asked why he was willing to forfeit he said, "It was the only thing I could do to maintain my integrity." Maintaining this, he lacked nothing.

—*Therese Greenberg.*

Golden Text Illuminated

"We beseech you, brethren, and exhort you by the Lord Jesus, that as ye have received of us how ye ought to walk and to please God, so ye would abound more and more" (I Thessalonians 4:1).

Many people who profess to know Jesus Christ live lives that appear to contradict that profession. Still choosing to be ruled by the flesh, they dishonor God and often become stumbling blocks to others (Rom. 14:21). This is both sad and unnecessary (cf. II Pet. 1:3).

Although fully aware of our sinfulness (Ps. 103:14), God graciously calls us and then helps us (Heb. 13:6) to live righteously. Good fruit in the Christian's life should not be hard to see (cf. Col. 1:10).

Granted, babes in Christ (cf. I Cor. 3:1-3) do not become fathers in the faith overnight (cf. I John 2:13). Sanctification is a process. However, when someone has been made new in Christ, a new way of life should emerge.

As expressed by the golden text, living a new way of life was precisely the admonition that the Apostle Paul and his helpers Silas and Timothy put forth to the young Thessalonian church.

Scripture reveals that prior to this challenge, the three men prayed for the Thessalonians, requesting that the church's ability to live in a new way would be accomplished through the Lord's power and presence in their lives (cf. Col. 1:9-11; I Thess. 3:12-13). All believers can live fruitful lives through God's power, including you and me.

Paul and his helpers then urged their fellow believers to live lives pleasing to God. They were to be vessels of honor, holiness, and love (I Thess. 4:4, 7, 9).

Paul made this appeal to the church not in his own name or authority but in that of the Lord Jesus. This made sense; after all, it was the Lord who called and purposed them to live in this new way (cf. II Tim. 2:20-21), and He would be the one to help them.

Furthermore, the Thessalonians were not ignorant of God's ways. They had listened to and watched the lives of their teachers. They had been instructed on how to live godly lives (I Thess. 1:5-6).

Also, Paul clearly pointed out the vast contrast between those who intimately know the Lord and seek to please him and those who do not. Those whose lifestyles are polluted with such things as fornication (I Thess. 4:3), lust (vs. 5), or fraud (vs. 6) do not know God; they have effectively rejected Him (vss. 5, 8).

There are many other passages in Paul's letters affirming that genuine salvation leads to a new way of life (Gal. 5:16-18). This is indeed a vital theme and mandate throughout the entire Bible.

As the Thessalonians continued to grow in faith, they would increase more and more in the likeness of the Lord. This of course was the will of God for them (I Thess. 4:3) as it is for all believers.

We too have godly instruction available today, through the precious Word of God and in the example of committed teachers who love the Lord.

Being made new in Christ is the most wonderful gift we could receive. May we as believers respond to this gift by showing our thanks to Jesus through a new way of life in imitation of Him!

—*Christine M. Morrison.*

Heart of the Lesson

Do you ever question whether the way you conduct your life matters? I learned this lesson as a young adult. Running late for church one Sunday, I arrived just as the first hymn began. Later that afternoon, I encountered a cousin who had only recently started visiting church. The subject of my tardiness came up. He mentioned that he watched for me each Sunday and wondered whether I would arrive on time. I never dreamed that anyone was that interested in my life. Thankfully, my cousin is now saved and attends church regularly. This example illustrates Paul's message to the Thessalonians: Christians need to be aware of their conduct.

1. The model walk (I Thess. 4:1-2). Paul was sure that he had taught the Thessalonians how to properly please God. Yet he lovingly exhorted them to be cautious about how they conducted their lives. If the church was attentive to their Christian walk, their good works would greatly abound.

Believers should not only want to please God but also strive to grow in grace and knowledge. By studying God's Word and learning to walk with Him, Christians' good deeds will multiply greatly.

2. The believer's walk (I Thess. 4:3-8). Paul defined some guidelines that the Thessalonians needed to follow in order to remain holy. The first was to refrain from fornication. Another was to avoid swindling other people. Paul wanted the church members to know they could not live in sin and be in close communion with God. With sin in their lives, they would not be able to grow in wisdom.

These virtuous doctrines seem to be old-fashioned in today's modern society. Sexual impurity is so prevalent that it has now become acceptable. Every day, the news speaks of people and companies being scammed. This is not the life of a child of God. He or she must follow the guidelines outlined in the Holy Scriptures. Christians who live in sin will damage their relationship with God. Only after the believer repents will he or she again return to close harmony with God.

3. The believer's hope (I Thess. 4:9-12). The Apostle Paul spoke of how the Thessalonians should conduct their lives. He explained that they should increase their love toward all people. Although they were already showing love to others, there was room for improvement. Next, he urged them to learn to be quiet—something that everyone needs to learn! He also asked that they abstain from being busybodies.

Paul continued by saying that God wanted them to work quietly at their respective professions. Most of all, they needed to walk in a manner that would merit others' respect. In other words, the Thessalonians needed to live holy lives.

These principles are as relevant today as they were then. Everyone should adhere to them in order to earn the respect of others for the cause of Christ. Christians should desire to live sanctified, holy lives. In order to bring the unsaved to salvation, believers should live in such a manner that makes nonbelievers want to emulate them.

Trying to live like the unsaved while professing to be a Christian will dissuade nonbelievers from coming to know the Saviour. Will a sinner want to imitate your life if he cannot see Christ through you? Living a life that reflects Christ leads to heavenly rewards.

—Catherine Moore

World Missions

Colossians 1:9-11 lists these goals for new believers:

- learn wisdom and spiritual understanding
- walk worthy of the Lord
- be fruitful in every good work
- increase in the knowledge of God

Are we "old" believers walking worthy of the Lord, being fruitful in every good work?

At a Bible training school in Indonesia, students do not graduate until they have planted a church. Such a requirement is hard to imagine in our Bible schools or seminaries. Have we lowered the spiritual standard? Are we missing something important?

Is it possible to walk worthily of the Lord if we are not involved in growing His kingdom by reaching the lost? James S. Stewart says, "The concern for world evangelization is not something tacked on to a man's personal Christianity, which he may take or leave as he chooses: it is rooted indefeasibly in the character of the God who has come to us in Christ Jesus. Thus, it can never be the province of a few enthusiasts, a sideline or a specialty of those who happen to have a bent that way. It is the distinctive mark of being a Christian."

Missionary Henry Martyn said, "The spirit of Christ is the spirit of missions. The nearer we get to Him, the more intensely missionary we become."

It has been said that a vast majority of Christians have never personally won another person to faith in Christ. This is a concern of eternal proportions.

One does not need a fancy method or memorized speech to broach spiritual topics with a lost person. It can start by simply asking questions about them, including questions on what they believe. Most people enjoy being asked about themselves; it makes them feel cared for. They may then naturally respond with those same questions back, giving you an opportunity to tell your own personal story of encountering Jesus and all He has done for you.

Another hindrance to witnessing is the thought that we must confront them with eternal judgment. However, there is a simple way we can help people see their own need by utilizing the Five Layers of "Why?" This technique is used for the Ritz Carlton's customer service, but it can serve well in our conversations with the lost.

For example, if someone says that they think they will go to heaven when they die, ask, "Why?" They may say they are a good person. Ask them, "Why do you think that?"

After their list of good things, ask, "Why do you think those things will get you into heaven?"

After five "Whys" a person often discovers the fallacy in their own thinking. They may realize their root untruth, for example, that God is like a nice Santa who will let everybody in because He loves them. At that point you can express through John 3:16 that God does indeed love people, and that is why He sent His Son to deliver them from sin. From there, they may ask more questions, or you could invite them to church or give them a tract or Bible.

Talking to a lost person will likely be uncomfortable at first, but like any new thing it gets easier with practice! Let us witness for Christ, abounding more and more in our walk and pleasing our Lord.

—*Kimberly Rae.*

The Jewish Aspect

Paul commended the Thessalonians for obeying his earlier commands. However he also provided further instructions concerning Christian conduct to the new believers. He taught moral purity, love for one another, and the importance of supporting oneself through work, all of which were consistent with Jewish laws and commandments.

False prophets had convinced some of the believers that they no longer needed to support themselves. Many of them had stopped working their daily jobs and had become a financial burden on the Thessalonian church. Paul told the Thessalonians that they could demonstrate their love to one another by being self-supporting and not being a burden to others. Paul commanded them to engage in meaningful labor and daily work.

"The Greeks deplored manual labor and relegated it to slaves as much as possible. But the Jews held it in esteem; every Jewish boy was taught a trade regardless of his family's wealth" (Walvoord and Zuck, eds., *The Bible Knowledge Commentary,* Cook). "The word for work in Hebrew, *avodah,* is the same used for prayer. Avodah connotes service. . . . Work is not only a necessary part of life, it is a form of service to the world, to the rest of humanity, and to God. . . . Though work is our vocation, it has the potential to accomplish *tikkun olam,* 'repair of the world.' Every job, every work interaction has value" (Stress feld, "Avodah: Vocation, Calling, Service," www.myjewishlearning.com).

Paul did not want the Thessalonians to give up hope in Jesus' return but wanted them to recognize that Christ might not come back right away. In the interim he wanted them to live as the Lord had commanded them. When he instructed them to be quiet and to mind their own business (I Thess. 4:11), he was referring to a sense of restfulness rather than talkativeness. "It denotes a condition of inward peace and tranquillity reflecting itself in outward calmness" (Constable's Notes on 2 Thessalonians, bible.org).

Paul also instructed them to walk in a way that was pleasing to God, which meant to abstain from fornication. (I Thess. 4:4). "The Greek word *ktaomai,* translated as 'control' or 'possess' in verse 4 means 'to procure for oneself, acquire, obtain.' It carries the idea of gaining mastery over something" (*Vine's Expository Dictionary of Old and New Testament Words,* Nelson). Jewish believers knew that to be sanctified meant to be set apart for the Lord, to be made holy by God and for God. God's command to be sexually pure was in opposition to the prevalence of sexual immorality, which was common in first-century Greek culture. Thessalonica had a civic cult that celebrated the supposed return of the god Cabarus with sexually immoral behavior. Sexual immorality also characterized many groups that believed that the end of the world was at hand (Kidd, "Paul and the Thessalonians," third mill.org).

Paul reminded the Thessalonians that learning how to control their bodies in holy and honorable ways was required by God. Sexual intercourse was reserved by God for marriage (Gen. 2:24). "Marriage is referred to as *kiddushin,* which comes from the Hebrew word for 'holy.' In Judaism, holy things are things that are set apart and made special and unique. When sex is within marriage, it too is considered holy," (Staff, "Jews and Premarital Sex," www.myjewishlearning.com).

—Deborah Markowitz Solan.

Guiding the Superintendent

Contrary to what many might think, the Christian experience can be characterized by "more and more" (I Thess. 4:1, 10) and not less and less. Becoming a Christian does not mean giving up everything, it means taking on an entirely new way of living. There just is no end to what a believer will have in his relationship with Christ. The Apostle Paul calls this "more and more" experience a "walk" (I Thess. 4:1, 12; cf. Eph. 4:1, 17; 5:2, 8). In chapter 4 of I Thessalonians, Paul reminds his readers of the new way of life that Christ has brought them (4:2, 9).

DEVOTIONAL OUTLINE

1. New life of holiness (I Thess. 4:1-8). Like people living today, some people in New Testament times had too much leisure time on their hands. For many this led to a life of immorality. Paul therefore calls his readers to a life of sanctification, which is manifested in holy living.

God's will is very clear for the readers. They are to live a life of sexual purity by controlling their passions. Paul reminds them that to reject this teaching is to reject God and His Holy Spirit in their lives.

2. New life of love (I Thess. 4:9-10). A life of love is never static. There is no end to living a life of love. Paul encourages his readers to a life of more and more even though they already had a strong reputation for showing Christian love to many of the folks around them.

You should always look for opportunities to serve. Doing God's work of loving others in spite of your suffering is an incredible witness.

3. New life of quietness (I Thess. 4:11-12). A life of sexual purity and Christian love will focus itself on others.

The third characteristic of the new way of living also focuses on others.

The readers are encouraged to be very diligent to live a quiet life by minding their own business and working with their hands. The Christian life is very practical. Believers should focus on others by helping those in need.

If one is to follow these teachings about others, Paul tells his readers that a life that focuses on others will in the end win the respect of nonbelievers.

This new experience of living a life of holiness, Christian love, and quiet diligence will please God. In fact, it will be God's will.

CHILDREN'S CORNER

text: **II Chronicles 32:1-8, 21-23**
title: **God's Servant Hezekiah**

Hezekiah was different from most of the other kings of Judah. Even in the face of great adversity he put his total trust in God.

Knowing it was only a matter of time before his city of Jerusalem would be attacked by the great nation of Assyria, Hezekiah became proactive, ordering that a tunnel be made to divert Jerusalem's water so it would not be available for the encamped Assyrian army. In addition, he rebuilt parts of the wall that were needed for defense.

Hezekiah encouraged his army by reminding them that the Assyrian king had only an earthly army, but Israel had the Lord God on their side (II Chron. 32:8).

When the attack came, the Lord defended the city with an angel who destroyed most of the Assyrians and forced the king to retreat home.

—Martin R. Dahlquist.

Scripture Lesson Text

I THESS. 4:13 But I would not have you to be ignorant, brethren, concerning them which are asleep, that ye sorrow not, even as others which have no hope.

14 For if we believe that Jesus died and rose again, even so them also which sleep in Jesus will God bring with him.

15 For this we say unto you by the word of the Lord, that we which are alive and remain unto the coming of the Lord shall not prevent them which are asleep.

16 For the Lord himself shall descend from heaven with a shout, with the voice of the archangel, and with the trump of God: and the dead in Christ shall rise first:

17 Then we which are alive and remain shall be caught up together with them in the clouds, to meet the Lord in the air: and so shall we ever be with the Lord.

18 Wherefore comfort one another with these words.

5:1 But of the times and the seasons, brethren, ye have no need that I write unto you.

2 For yourselves know perfectly that the day of the Lord so cometh as a thief in the night.

3 For when they shall say, Peace and safety; then sudden destruction cometh upon them, as travail upon a woman with child; and they shall not escape.

4 But ye, brethren, are not in darkness, that that day should overtake you as a thief.

5 Ye are all the children of light, and the children of the day: we are not of the night, nor of darkness.

6 Therefore let us not sleep, as do others; but let us watch and be sober.

7 For they that sleep sleep in the night; and they that be drunken are drunken in the night.

8 But let us, who are of the day, be sober, putting on the breastplate of faith and love; and for an helmet, the hope of salvation.

9 For God hath not appointed us to wrath, but to obtain salvation by our Lord Jesus Christ,

10 Who died for us, that, whether we wake or sleep, we should live together with him.

NOTES

A New Understanding

Lesson Text: I Thessalonians 4:13—5:10

Related Scriptures: I Corinthians 15:12-23; Romans 14:7-9;
Mark 13:30-37; II Peter 3:9-14

TIME: A.D. 51   PLACE: from Corinth

GOLDEN TEXT—"I would not have you to be ignorant, brethren, concerning them which are asleep, that ye sorrow not, even as others which have no hope" (I Thessalonians 4:13).

Introduction

As human beings, we are confined to the moment. We can remember the past, but we cannot change it. We can plan for the future, but we cannot know it—or can we?

According to a recent market research report, individuals as well as companies in the United States spend a total of two billion dollars a year on psychics, astrologers, fortune-tellers, mediums, and the like. Yet all that money does not help anyone except those who are preying on the curiosity and worries of people desperate to know the future, hoping that somehow everything will work out well for them, their loved ones, and the world. They could save themselves a great deal of money and actually learn what the future holds by simply opening and reading the Bible.

Granted, we cannot know with assurance what the future holds for us individually in terms of specific events—health issues, relationships, career success, and so on. But the Bible is filled with infallible prophecies of things still to come. Those coming events are certain to occur. For Christians, the prophetic Scriptures are a source of great comfort and encouragement.

LESSON OUTLINE

**I. HOPE FOR THE DEAD—
I Thess. 4:13-18**

**II. HELP FOR THE LIVING—
I Thess. 5:1-10**

Exposition: Verse by Verse

HOPE FOR THE DEAD

I THESS. 4:13 But I would not have you to be ignorant, brethren, concerning them which are asleep, that ye sorrow not, even as others which have no hope.

14 For if we believe that Jesus died and rose again, even so them also which sleep in Jesus will God bring with him.

15 For this we say unto you by the word of the Lord, that we which are

alive and remain unto the coming of the Lord shall not prevent them which are asleep.

16 For the Lord himself shall descend from heaven with a shout, with the voice of the archangel, and with the trump of God: and the dead in Christ shall rise first:

17 Then we which are alive and remain shall be caught up together with them in the clouds, to meet the Lord in the air: and so shall we ever be with the Lord.

18 Wherefore comfort one another with these words.

Assurance of hope (I Thess. 4:13).

Paul's letters to the Thessalonian church cover a number of topics. Ray Stedman, however, makes an interesting observation: "A striking feature about the Thessalonian letters is that each chapter in both letters ends with a reference to the coming of the Lord" (*Waiting for the Second Coming,* Discovery House). This great hope of the church is the dominant theme of the letters.

It seems clear that Paul had given the Thessalonians instruction concerning the return of Christ. It is equally clear, however, that there was some lack of understanding about how the Lord's return related to those who were "asleep." Sleep is used here as a euphemism for death (cf. Matt. 27:52; John 11:11-13; Acts 7:60).

Apparently, the Thessalonians were fearful that their brethren who had died would miss out on the blessed hope of Christ's return and "miss the blissful reunion, or at least come behind those who lived" until His coming (Hiebert, *The Thessalonian Epistles,* Moody). Paul was anxious to address their ignorance in this matter so that they would not sorrow as those who have no hope. For unbelievers, there is no sure hope beyond death; there is only unrelieved sorrow when a loved one dies.

Reason for hope (I Thess. 4:14-17).

In addressing the confusion among the Thessalonian congregation, Paul goes back to the death and resurrection of Christ. It is the resurrection in particular that gives every Christian hope (cf. I Cor. 15:12-20). If we believe Christ rose from the dead, there is no reason to hopelessly grieve over believers who have died.

The resurrection of Christ guarantees the resurrection of all who have died in Him (cf. I Cor. 15:21-23). This means that when Jesus returns, those who have fallen asleep in Him (that is, died) will come back with Him in resurrected bodies (vs. 52).

Paul was confident of this because it was the "word of the Lord" (I Thess. 4:15). By the revelation of God, this had been revealed to him. God revealed that the bodies of the dead in Christ will be raised, and they will return with the Lord. Furthermore, those who remain alive at the time of "the coming of the Lord shall not prevent them which are asleep." "Prevent" simply means "precede." In other words, the dead in Christ will be glorified before living believers.

Paul then goes on to outline the order of events at Christ's return. It is important to understand that the return of Christ, while one event, has two phases. The first phase is what is commonly called the rapture. This is the coming of Christ in the clouds to gather His people to Himself forever. At a later time, He will return to the earth as conquering King to establish His righteous kingdom (Rev. 19:11—20:6).

Associated with Christ's return is a time of terrible tribulation and divine judgment on earth (cf. Dan. 12:1; Rev. 4—19). The chronology seems to be that the rapture occurs first, followed by seven years of tribulation on earth before Christ returns to earth to reign as King for a thousand years.

It is the rapture, the first phase of Christ's return, that is in view in

I Thessalonians 4:16-17. This event can happen at any time. Paul describes Christ's descent from heaven as being accompanied by a shout, the voice of the archangel, presumably Michael (cf. Jude 1:9), and the trumpet of God (cf. I Cor. 15:52). These phenomena announce in a powerful and authoritative way the Lord's coming.

At these heavenly sounds, the dead in Christ will be the first to rise from the dead. Much as Lazarus rose to life at the voice of Jesus (John 11:43-44), the bodies of departed believers will be raised to join the Lord. At death the spirits of believers immediately enter the presence of the Lord (cf. II Cor. 5:8; Phil. 1:23). At the rapture, their bodies will be resurrected and transformed.

After the resurrection of dead believers, living believers will immediately be "caught up together with them in the clouds, to meet the Lord in the air" (I Thess. 4:17). In this instant, the bodies of living Christians also will be transformed (I Cor. 15:52-53). While the dead will precede the living, all this will occur in the "twinkling of an eye," and from that moment on, all believers will live in the presence of the Lord forever.

Comfort of hope (I Thess. 4:18). The great truth of Christ's coming and our being caught up to be with Him forever was a great comfort to the Thessalonians who were concerned about their departed brethren. The hope of His return is a great comfort to us as well. In fact, as Paul indicates, we should often recall these truths and encourage one another with them.

In spite of all the suffering and death experienced in this life, and in spite of the frightening things still to come upon this earth, we can take comfort in knowing that God has a special plan for us. We can look forward with anticipation to the imminent return of our Lord, the resurrection of the dead, and being with Him forever.

HELP FOR THE LIVING

5:1 But of the times and the seasons, brethren, ye have no need that I write unto you.

2 For yourselves know perfectly that the day of the Lord so cometh as a thief in the night.

3 For when they shall say, Peace and safety; then sudden destruction cometh upon them, as travail upon a woman with child; and they shall not escape.

4 But ye, brethren, are not in darkness, that that day should overtake you as a thief.

5 Ye are all the children of light, and the children of the day: we are not of the night, nor of darkness.

6 Therefore let us not sleep, as do others; but let us watch and be sober.

7 For they that sleep sleep in the night; and they that be drunken are drunken in the night.

8 But let us, who are of the day, be sober, putting on the breastplate of faith and love; and for an helmet, the hope of salvation.

9 For God hath not appointed us to wrath, but to obtain salvation by our Lord Jesus Christ,

10 Who died for us, that, whether we wake or sleep, we should live together with him.

Be informed (I Thess. 5:1-3). With chapter 5 Paul begins to address another matter related to Christ's return, namely, when these events will occur. Undoubtedly, the Thessalonians wondered whether they themselves would live to see the return of the Lord or would be among the dead in Christ when He returns.

The apostle states that there was no need to write about "the times and the seasons" (cf. Acts 1:7). "Times" refers to quantity of time, while "seasons" speaks of the character, or nature, of time. These matters the Thessalonians already knew quite well enough. In particular, they knew that the Day of the Lord was going to arrive like a thief in the night.

Clearly, Paul connects the rapture (I Thess. 4:13-18) with the "day of the Lord" (5:2). The Old Testament uses of this expression form the basis for its use here and in other New Testament passages. In the Old Testament, "day of the Lord" was used with reference to a coming locust plague (Joel 1:15; 2:1, 11), as well as the judgments of the end times (Joel 2:31; Mal. 4:5). It is also used of the fall of Samaria (Amos 5:18, 20) and similar judgments (Isa. 13:6, 9). In each case, it refers to a time of divine judgment.

In the New Testament, "day of the Lord" refers to the judgments of the end times—specifically, the climax of the tribulation, which follows the rapture (Acts 2:20; II Thess. 2:2; II Pet. 3:10), and the "consummation judgment which closes the annals of earth's fallen history (2 Pet 3:10-13)" (Mayhue, *1 & 2 Thessalonians,* Christian Focus). While the return of Christ offers comfort to believers, it means judgment for unbelievers and the world.

The Thessalonian Christians understood this. They also understood that the arrival of this day, starting with the Lord's return in the clouds to resurrect and rapture His saints, will come "as a thief in the night" (I Thess. 5:2). This fact should have made it clear to them that there is no need to speculate about the timing of this day. The time of judgment will come unannounced, like a thief who sneaks into a house at night when people are sleeping.

The Day of the Lord will also come unexpectedly. In fact, people will be lulled into thinking there is peace and safety, and then suddenly "destruction cometh upon them" (vs. 3). The destruction here probably points to the hopeless situation of those suffering under the divine acts described in Revelation 16.

Furthermore, Paul describes the Day of the Lord as coming like the labor pains that beset an expectant mother. The figure pictures intense pain that cannot be reversed. Once one is caught up in the Day of the Lord, there is no stopping it and no escape from it.

Be prepared (I Thess. 5:4-8). The contrast between the "they" in verse 3 and the "ye" in verse 4 makes it clear that the focus returns at this point to the readers of this epistle, the Thessalonian Christians. They stand in contrast to those who will not escape the destruction of the Day of the Lord. And unlike those of the last days who are in the darkness of sin, they, like all followers of Christ, will not be overtaken as if by a thief in that day.

The contrasts continue in verse 5 and following. Paul describes his readers as being "children of light" and "children of the day." "Children of light" are simply Christians, who reflect their Father, who is light (I John 1:5). This description, along with that of "children of the day," speaks of the righteousness of believers. They have been delivered "from the power of darkness" and "translated . . . into the kingdom of [Christ]" (Col. 1:13).

Paul then switches to "we" (I Thess. 5:5) in describing all believers as "not of the night, nor of darkness." That is, Christians are not characterized by sin. They live in the realm of truth and seek holiness.

As such, believers are not to "sleep" as unbelievers do but to "watch and be sober" (vs. 6). In anticipation of the coming Day of the Lord, we are not to sleep, meaning to be inattentive and spiritually and morally lax. This is another way of saying we are not to be spiritually unprepared for what is coming. We are to be prepared for the Lord's coming, actively watching for it with a sober, calm attitude.

This perspective on the coming Day

of the Lord is again contrasted to that of unbelievers who "sleep in the night" and are "drunken in the night" (vs. 7). These are simply statements of fact. Night is the time for sleep and also, for many, the time for drunkenness. Paul is illustrating the point that it is only natural for unbelievers to be indifferent to spiritual truth and lacking in self-control (and thus fall into unwatchfulness), for they live in spiritual "darkness" and "night" (vs. 5).

As believers, we are "of the day" (vs. 8; cf. vs. 5) and should conduct ourselves accordingly. We will not suffer the same fate as unbelievers, but we must still guard against adopting their attitudes.

Again, there is a call to be "sober" (vs. 8; cf. vs. 7). As we await the Lord's return, we are to be in complete control of our senses. Such a sober attitude is assured by clothing ourselves with faith and love and the hope of salvation. These virtues are couched in military terms (cf. Eph. 6:11-17). Like a soldier's breastplate and helmet, they protect us from worldly attitudes and prepare us for Christ's coming. Our faith is in God, our love is to be expressed toward others, and our hope in this life is for eternal salvation.

Be encouraged (I Thess. 5:9-10). There is great encouragement for God's people in Paul's instruction regarding the Day of the Lord. We are "not appointed . . . to wrath," he writes. Certainly it is true that we who have trusted in Christ will not suffer eternal wrath but rather will enjoy the full measure of salvation, which was purchased by Christ's death for us. Salvation is fully realized when all believers "live together with him," whether we die or live till His coming.

The wrath mentioned here may also refer to the wrath of God poured out in the Day of the Lord. If this is the case, I Thessalonians 5:9 offers assurance that God's children will not suffer the judgments of that day but will be delivered by rapture before they come.

There is a clear distinction between believers and unbelievers in this passage. Unbelievers have no assurance regarding the future. They live in anxiety and a self-indulgence that seeks to hide the empty hope that somehow everything will work out to their favor. As believers, we must strive to be sure our lives are filled with faith, hope, love, and the calm assurance that comes from knowing our Lord will return in glory to take us to Himself.

The future is not to be feared, for God has revealed all we need to know about it. And in that divine revelation there is comfort and the means of edifying, or building up, one another in the body of Christ (I Thess. 4:18; 5:11).
—Jarl K. Waggoner.

QUESTIONS

1. What aspect of the Lord's return concerned the Thessalonians?
2. What guarantees that those who have died in Christ will be raised?
3. What phenomena will accompany Christ's coming in the clouds?
4. What is the order of events with regard to the rapture?
5. What did the Thessalonians already have sufficient knowledge about?
6. To what does "Day of the Lord" refer in the New Testament?
7. What figures does Paul use to describe the arrival of the Day of the Lord?
8. What contrasts are made between Christians and unbelievers?
9. What should characterize believers as they await Christ's return?
10. What makes the truth of Christ's return a comfort to Christians?
—Jarl K. Waggoner.

Preparing to Teach the Lesson

This week we learn that when we get the new teaching from our Lord Jesus, we also receive a new understanding of what it means to follow Him. We learn that Jesus is our ultimate hope.

TODAY'S AIM

Facts: to show how Jesus will return to gather His own to Himself.

Principle: to remember that Jesus will come again to give us fresh hope.

Application: to live as Christians who know that our Lord has promised to take us home.

INTRODUCING THE LESSON

Hope is a word that gives us something to look forward to. It infuses us with new life. Without hope, we cannot go forward. Hope allows us to see that some things will change for the better in the future. That is hope. I can remember as a young child that one day my father, who was on outstation duty, would come home. It was something that the future would bring. Waiting was not easy, but it was worth it because I would see my daddy again, and he would bring gifts with him.

It was the same with the Lord Jesus and His followers in the years that followed His crucifixion. Paul reminded his readers that Jesus did not leave them without hope because He promised to come again for them.

DEVELOPING THE LESSON

1. The gift of hope (I Thess. 4:13-14). It is obvious that when a loved one dies, we will be saddened by their passing. That is a common human response. But we do not mourn as those in the world who do not know Jesus. We mourn with the promise of hope because Jesus promised that when He comes back, He will gather those believers who have died before us.

Have the class share about those believers they have loved dearly who have died. Help them to understand that they will see them again along with Jesus. This is the essence of Christian hope because it is based on the promises of God Himself.

2. The bringing of hope (I Thess. 4:15-18). Notice the specifics given to us in this passage. Paul does not leave us clueless. Jesus had revealed to him that those believers who die before us will rise first to meet Him in the air before those who are still alive. It will be a glorious event with all the glory that is attributed to a King. Jesus will come when the archangel shouts and the trumpet blows loudly, signifying the call of God to the world.

The Word tells us that at the return of Christ the Christian believers who have died will rise from their graves and meet Christ. These will then join the army of the faithful with Jesus and be caught up in the clouds to meet Jesus in midair. This will be a permanent reunion. We will never again be separated from our Lord for whom we have waited so long.

Help the class to see that our hope will then become real, and that we are to keep encouraging each other till these things happen. We do know that when Jesus comes it will renew our hope in Him.

3. The day of hope (I Thess. 5:1-3). It is interesting that Jesus did not tell us when He will come again. In His human limitations, He did not know (Mark 13:32). Paul reminds us that the day will come without warning like a thief in the night. The Thessalonian believers had been taught about this. Jesus will return at a time when many will be complacent and unprepared. Disaster comes when we are least prepared. There will be no time to escape when it happens.

Paul gives us the analogy of a woman who gives birth. While there may be time to prepare, the birth itself happens suddenly. Encourage the class to take the Word seriously here and be prepared for Jesus' coming. It will happen suddenly and will also bring hope to believers in Him. Notice the urgency of Paul's message here. We should also feel this sense of urgency. Though we ourselves do not save people, Jesus commissioned us to spread His truth.

4. Preparation for hope (I Thess. 5:4-10). Paul reminded the Thessalonian believers that they had been taught about this. So they were to take heed. They were not to be taken by surprise when Jesus comes like a thief, without warning. Paul calls them "children of the day" who do not sleep but are ever prepared and ready for the great event. This is a call for us too to be ready. We are to be awake and sober, eagerly awaiting our hope.

Help the class to see that this takes deliberate preparedness on our part as Christians. At night people sleep and get drunk, but that is not the case with the children of the day. We are to think clearly and put on our spiritual armor. Notice that this armor has the breastplate of faith and love and the helmet of salvation. These are the prerequisites for receiving the hope that is near. Ask the class if they are prepared and ready.

Point out to the class that without hope, all of us will face God's anger. But Jesus died for us to give us hope that we may live with Him forever. We must be ready for Him whenever He comes.

BELIEVERS HAVE HOPE

JESUS IS COMING AGAIN

ILLUSTRATING THE LESSON

We have hope because Jesus is coming again for us. Without this eternal hope, we face the anger of God.

CONCLUDING THE LESSON

It is so clear through this passage that our Lord does not want us to live without hope. He is our hope, and He made it possible for us to receive this hope for ourselves through His promises down through the ages. He promised to come again to take us to Himself so that we can remain with Him forever and ever. Is that not something to shout about?

Encourage the class to take this urgent need to be prepared for Jesus' coming very seriously. We have now been warned about the details and suddenness of His coming. We have been called to be prepared and ready. It will be a day of hope when He comes.

ANTICIPATING THE NEXT LESSON

Next week, we begin a new unit called "New Growth." We learn how we can be a confident people even in difficult times because of our faith in Jesus.

—A. Koshy Muthalaly.

PRACTICAL POINTS

1. Christian loved ones who have breathed their last breath are now with God (I Thess. 4:13-14).
2. Christians who have passed away will not miss the second coming of Christ (vs. 15).
3. At the appointed time, God will call us to be forever in His presence (vss. 16-18).
4. We do not need to know precisely when the Lord will return (I Thess. 5:1-3; cf. Acts 1:7).
5. We should live godly lives, knowing that the Lord could return at any moment (I Thess. 5:4-6).
6. We must live with vigilance as we await Christ's return (vss. 7-10).

—Charity G. Carter.

RESEARCH AND DISCUSSION

1. Why do we grieve our departed Christian loved ones who are "asleep" (I Thess. 4:13)?
2. How can we take comfort in Paul's words about being "caught up together with [the dead in Christ] in the clouds" (vs. 17)?
3. Movies typically display robbery scenes in the dark of night with thieves wearing black. With that in mind, consider what it means when Paul says that the day of the Lord will come like that (5:2).
4. How does being children of the light prepare us for the coming of the Lord (vs. 5)?
5. Why take on the armor of God as we prepare for the last days (I Thess. 5:8; cf. Eph. 6:13-17)?

—Charity G. Carter.

ILLUSTRATED HIGH POINTS

Sorrow not, even as others

There were three pots of boiling water. In the first was placed a potato, in the second, an egg, and in the third, ground coffee beans. After a while the potato grew soft and fell apart, the egg got harder, but the beans became coffee and got stronger. Their aroma filled the room.

When the heat is turned up in life, how do people respond? Some are potatoes, they fall apart. Others are eggs, they harden their hearts. Believers are more like the coffee beans. They look to God and just grow stronger. The heated waters of life do not destructively change them, unlike the potato and egg. On the contrary, the beans change the water. The believer changes his environment and becomes a pleasant aroma to the Lord.

Let us not sleep, as do others

William Booth, the founder of the Salvation Army, spoke of his disturbing vision of the modern church. Here are some highlights:

1) A dark, stormy ocean is filled with the lost and dying.
2) Many of the lost make it to a platform at the base of a mighty rock.
3) Many of the rescued quickly find amusements on the platform.
4) They also listen to sermons and pray for their own needs.
5) Jesus is in the water calling for them to help Him rescue the perishing.
6) Some, at great risk to themselves, dive in to help, but most do not.
7) While Jesus cries for them to come to Him, they cry for Him to come to them instead.

Could it be that we are asleep on the Rock while the lost perish around us?

—Therese Greenberg.

Golden Text Illuminated

"I would not have you to be ignorant, brethren, concerning them which are asleep, that ye sorrow not, even as others which have no hope" (I Thessalonians 4:13).

Paul wrote an encouraging message on a difficult topic to the young Thessalonian church. His hope in doing so was that a new understanding would bring some measure of comfort as their loved ones passed away.

Death is not something that most people care to talk or think about, yet since sin infected the human race through Adam, it has been a reality we all must face (Rom. 5:12).

Death certainly has some degree of mystery, and what follows it is often surrounded with misinformation and, therefore, confusion. This was true for the early church (cf. I Cor. 15:12-19) and is true for people today.

Just think for a moment of some of the ways people try to control death because of their fear of it. Some people attempt to look into the future to avoid the forboding portent of death. Others consult mediums or other dark sources, attempting to contact deceased loved ones for information about the afterlife. How ridiculous, not to mention dangerous (cf. Deut. 18:9-12)!

In the golden text we find that Paul did not want the Thessalonian church to lack accurate knowledge concerning their loved ones who had died.

Although God certainly expects believers to grieve loss, as even Jesus grieved when Lazarus died (John 11:35-36), we are not left to sorrow inconsolably. We are not without hope and, in fact, have much to look forward to.

Though it is difficult to experience, as death separates believers from one another physically, it cannot separate us from God's love (Rom. 8:38-39) or God's presence (cf. II Cor.5:8). These two promises alone give great comfort to those grieving loss.

Also, there is the promise of being reunited with loved ones in heaven someday (I Thess. 4:16-17). We can remind ourselves of the certainty of Psalm 23:6; our believing loved ones are at home with the Lord, and eventually we will be with them again.

Paul taught the doctrines of the resurrection and the second coming of Jesus Christ (I Thess. 4:14-16), both of which give courage and comfort to Christians when death occurs. Furthermore, both of these precious promises belong to every believer.

As the Thessalonians embraced this new understanding of what was in store beyond the grave, they could better comfort one another in their loss (I Thess. 4:18).

There is another group of people that Paul mentioned: "Others which have no hope." Who could be in such a tragic category? Ephesians 2:12 tells us it is those without Christ, without God, who have no hope beyond the grave.

What great news, however, that our compassionate God promises eternal life to all those who will turn to Him in repentance; He will be faithful to make them new in Christ (II Pet. 3:9). Hallelujah!

Maybe you have gained a new understanding of death, the resurrection, and Christ's return. If so, comfort someone who may be grieving, and share Christ with the lost.

—*Christine M. Morrison.*

Heart of the Lesson

Have you ever wondered about the splendors of heaven? No one living has experienced heaven, but most people have ideas about this majestic land. The Scriptures give a glimpse of its glory and splendor but leave our imaginations to fill in the gaps. Still, there are aspects of heaven that even the most educated scholars cannot fathom. Paul gives us a small impression of this glorious realm in his message to the Thessalonians.

1. The believer's assurance (I Thess. 4:13-18). The Apostle Paul wanted the Thessalonians to have an understanding about the afterlife of a Christian. Loved ones should view a saved person's death as a sign of hope, not sorrow. When Christ returns, He will take all who have received salvation back to glory with Him. Believers who have already died will be the first to join the Father. Christians who are still alive will then rise to meet Christ in the air.

People today still speak of the time when Christ will return to earth. Paul's description of this event begins with the voice of God calling the righteous forth from the grave. When a loved one dies, we often sorrow at his or her passing. However, if the deceased person was a disciple of Christ, the bereaved should be rejoicing. Although they are temporarily parted from their loved one by death, they will be reunited when Christ returns. This should bring comfort and reassurance.

2. The believer's watch (I Thess. 5:1-8). Christ's return will happen, although no one is certain about the time. The "day of the Lord" will come unexpectedly, just like a thief. When this moment does come, there will be no time for the unsaved to repent or hide. Therefore, Paul warned the Thessalonians to be vigilant. There will be signs indicating that day's approach. Even though it did not happen in their time, Paul's readers were to be ready by arming themselves with faith, love, and salvation.

Today people live as though the end of time will never happen. Even believers think that Christ is slow in making His earthly appearance. Nevertheless, Christ has made a promise that He will fulfill. His return is imminent, even though no one knows the day or the hour. Many people are noticing signs that suggest the time may be drawing near. Therefore, it is wise for people, especially believers, to be on the lookout for Christ's return.

3. The believer's hope (I Thess. 5:9-10). We know that the Lord wants all people to come to salvation rather than face condemnation (I Tim. 2:4). God desires to save everyone from eternal destruction. Believers should be comforted, knowing they will enjoy everlasting life. Encouraged by this promise, they should also build up fellow believers. Inspiring words can give a believer the confidence to continue living for Christ.

Christians must then desire to see the lost saved, reassuring them that if they trust in Him, they too will live forever with Christ instead of in an eternity of torment. Then the saved can gladly sing the words of Eliza Hewitt's hymn, "When We All Get to Heaven":

> When we all get to heaven,
> What a day of rejoicing that will be!
> When we all see Jesus,
> We'll sing and shout the victory.
> —*Catherine Moore.*

World Missions

The little girl came into the clinic. Her father was an alcoholic. He mistreated her mother and siblings. She asked those working there, "Do you have any pills that would give me hope?"

Hope. Something our world desperately needs. Google saw four million searches for hope on the internet one year. Millions of people in America try to fill their emptiness with alcohol or drug addictions. Around seven percent of the American population live in the darkness of depression, and in 2013 alone 41,149 people ended their own lives. This was just in the United States.

Death, the common denominator for all people, is the greatest source of fear for many, and it should be. However, the thought of death, or a medical scare, can be the catalyst God uses to bring to mind the eternal and a person's need of a Saviour.

One man fell into a machine at a steel mill and knew that it would kill him. When someone shouted, "Call nine-one-one!" he cried back, "No! No! Tell me about God. I'm dying and I don't know God."

The recognition of spiritual need during times of great physical need is one of the reasons medical missions can be so vital to the cause of Christ.

At the mission hospital in one restricted country, a missionary doctor had to tell a Hindu woman that she was dying of liver cancer. She was told of her spiritual need, but she did not want to hear about it then. That night, however, she stared at the Bible verses displayed on the hospital walls. In the morning, she said she was ready to receive Jesus as her Saviour. She died five hours later.

Another Muslim patient trusted in Christ during the night hours after talking with a national nurse. Many Muslim converts fear telling their family and friends about their new faith because of possible persecution, but this man, knowing he was dying soon, joyfully told his immediate and extended family about his decision.

Having spent time in the ICU, I know that thoughts of death are close companions in such settings. I also know that there was a drastic difference in my nurses between believers and those who were not. Working in the medical field affords many opportunities to shine the light of Christ, in both words and in actions.

But one does not have to work in the medical field to make a difference among the sick and dying. Physical struggles can have an impact on the thoughts of the sufferer. A believer who visits a friend in the hospital might find that person much more open to spiritual discussion than they normally would be.

"Showing compassion validates your message," said a nurse. "God is a God of compassion and caring. In a land like this, where compassion is such a rarely seen quality, it gives more authority to your message."

In our own country too, compassion is becoming rare, and those facing death often do so wrapped in loneliness. Helping another find Christ before death means taking away that sorrow without hope and replacing it with unspeakable joy.

We can do kingdom work by supporting medical missions, praying for opportunities for friends in the medical field, and visiting the sick with the hope of everlasting life.

—*Kimberly Rae.*

The Jewish Aspect

Persecution and false teachings were prevalent in the church at Thessalonica, and Paul's letters addressed the discouragement of the new believers. They had suffered much and had given up much for the sake of Christ. Many of their fellow believers had died, and those who remained alive worried about their eternal fate. False teachers had said that those who died before Jesus' return would not have a part in that day. Paul addressed this concern and told the Thessalonians to encourage one another with the hope of future reunion with their loved ones who had died in the Lord.

"Belief in the eventual resurrection of the dead is a fundamental belief of traditional Judaism. It was a belief that distinguished the Pharisees (intellectual ancestors of Rabbinical Judaism) from the Sadducees," (Rich, "Olam Ha-Ba: The Afterlife," www.jewfaq. org). The prophet Daniel said, "And many of them that sleep in the dust of the earth shall awake, some to everlasting life, and some to shame and everlasting contempt" (12:2). Resurrection is "the doctrine that in a future age the dead will rise from their graves to live again. This doctrine appears frequently in Jewish eschatology, where it is associated with the doctrine of the Messiah and the immortality of the soul," (Jacobs, *The Jewish Religion: A Companion,* Oxford University Press).

Paul encouraged the new believers with his teachings about those who die in Christ. "For if we believe that Jesus died and rose again, even so them also which sleep in Jesus will God bring with him" (I Thess. 4:14). Paul said that Jesus had inaugurated the age to come, however it had not arrived in its fullness and that this age had not yet come to an end. After the destruction of the First Temple in Jerusalem, several of the Hebrew prophets, including Isaiah, Amos, and Hosea, began forecasting a better future for their people. "The day of the Lord" referred to the whole period of the Lord's climactic judgment upon the earth, resulting in the setting up of His Kingdom (Isa. 13:6, 9). "The resurrection of the dead will occur in the messianic age, a time referred to in Hebrew as the Olam Ha-Ba, the World to Come, but that term is also used to refer to the spiritual afterlife," (Rich).

Paul, in his teachings to the early church in Corinth, taught that Christ, the firstfruits raised from the dead, was the guarantee for all those who share in his resurrection.

"But now is Christ risen from the dead, and become the firstfruits of them that slept. . . . But every man in his own order: Christ the firstfruits; afterward they that are Christ's at his coming" (I Cor. 15:20, 23). "The offering of the Firstfruits of the harvest occurs in the week of the Passover/Unleavened Bread festival and is a ceremony performed which commences the marking off of time to the Feast of Firstfruits, which is called Shavuot or Pentecost. This was instituted as a memorial of Moses (a type of Messiah) presenting Israel as an offering to the Father after he had completed the work of delivering them from the dominion of the enemy (Pharaoh of Egypt). They went out from Egypt into the wilderness and held this feast. (Exodus 3:18; 5:3; 8:17; 12:17, 41; 13: 20-22). . . . Everything on the earth, both man and beast, was to be presented before Yahweh God as a first fruits offering to Him," ("Hebrew Roots/Holy Days/Firstfruits," www. wikibooks.org).

—Deborah Markowitz Solan.

Guiding the Superintendent

Doctrine has its consequences. What someone believes will affect how he or she behaves. The great doctrines of the New Testament have a direct relationship to how a believer is to live. The doctrine of the second coming of Christ is no exception.

The Apostle Paul had been in Thessalonica for only a very brief time. Nevertheless, he had taught them several great facts about the return of Jesus Christ.

But now the people in the church were concerned. It seems that some of their loved ones had died since Paul left. What would happen to them? Paul wrote to encourage them not to despair, but to continue in hope. The death of any believer is not the end but only the beginning.

Belief in the return of Jesus Christ should produce these results in the believer's life.

DEVOTIONAL OUTLINE

1. Hope (I Thess. 4:13-18). The future return of Jesus Christ should give hope to believers in the present.

Belief in the bodily resurrection of Jesus Christ carries with it the corollary belief in the future bodily resurrection of believers who have died (in Paul's terms: those who sleep) and that they will return when Jesus returns. This idea is not something that Paul invented. It comes directly from Jesus himself!

The return of the Lord will be accompanied with great rejoicing; the Lord, the trumpet, and the archangel will all sound. When this happens, those who are dead in Christ will be resurrected to join the Lord. They will then be reunited with believers who are still alive at that time.

"So shall we ever be with the Lord" (vs. 17). Knowledge of these future events should bring comfort to believers in the present.

2. Watchfulness (I Thess. 5:1-10). The future return of Jesus Christ should lead to a watchful attitude among believers.

The text switches focus from how the Lord will return to what His coming will mean for both unbelievers and believers.

The return of the Lord will come as a total surprise to unbelievers. It will happen so fast that the Apostle Paul likens His return to the suddenness of a thief or the labor pains of a pregnant woman.

This should not frighten believers. Believers are not in the dark, but in the light. Paul calls believers to sober watchfulness that is characterized by faith, love, and hope.

CHILDREN'S CORNER

text: **Jeremiah 26:1, 4-15**
title: **God's Servant Jeremiah**

Time was running out for the nation of Judah. For centuries the people had lived their lives in defiance of the Lord God.

For one last time, God sent one of His servants, the prophet Jeremiah, to speak to the people of Jerusalem. His message was very clear—unless Judah and Jerusalem started to obey the prophets that God had sent, He would destroy the city.

The message was not received very well. Jeremiah was treated as a traitor and threatened with death. He would not be deterred. If they did kill him, he told them they would be shedding innocent blood and God's message would still be the same.

—*Martin R. Dahlquist.*

Scripture Lesson Text

II THESS. 1:1 Paul, and Silvanus, and Timotheus, unto the church of the Thessalonians in God our Father and the Lord Jesus Christ:

2 Grace unto you, and peace, from God our Father and the Lord Jesus Christ.

3 We are bound to thank God always for you, brethren, as it is meet, because that your faith groweth exceedingly, and the charity of every one of you all toward each other aboundeth;

4 So that we ourselves glory in you in the churches of God for your patience and faith in all your persecutions and tribulations that ye endure:

5 Which is a manifest token of the righteous judgment of God, that ye may be counted worthy of the kingdom of God, for which ye also suffer:

6 Seeing it is a righteous thing with God to recompense tribulation to them that trouble you;

7 And to you who are troubled rest with us, when the Lord Jesus shall be revealed from heaven with his mighty angels,

8 In flaming fire taking vengeance on them that know not God, and that obey not the gospel of our Lord Jesus Christ:

9 Who shall be punished with everlasting destruction from the presence of the Lord, and from the glory of his power;

10 When he shall come to be glorified in his saints, and to be admired in all them that believe (because our testimony among you was believed) in that day.

11 Wherefore also we pray always for you, that our God would count you worthy of this calling, and fulfil all the good pleasure of his goodness, and the work of faith with power:

12 That the name of our Lord Jesus Christ may be glorified in you, and ye in him, according to the grace of our God and the Lord Jesus Christ.

NOTES

A Growing Confidence

Lesson Text: II Thessalonians 1:1-12

Related Scriptures: Ephesians 4:11-16; I John 2:28-29;
Luke 21:32-36; Jude 1:14-21

TIME: A.D. 51   PLACE: from Corinth

GOLDEN TEXT—"We are bound to thank God always for you, brethren, as it is meet, because that your faith groweth exceedingly, and the charity of every one of you all toward each other aboundeth" (II Thessalonians 1:3).

Introduction

Suffering produces various responses. Some people are not very good at tolerating pain of any sort. They grumble and complain and blame God. They cry out for immediate relief. And if it does not come, they fall into despair and hopelessness.

Others endure suffering much longer, determined to "win" and show themselves strong and self-reliant. Even if they see no sign of relief, they hold out for the sake of being seen as brave. Yet even such self-will is limited, and eventually despair often sets in, along with the charges against God for allowing such affliction.

There are others, however, who endure tremendous suffering and pain and do so without despairing of life or charging God with injustice. They seem to grow closer to Him, become more thoughtful and wise, and even see benefit in their suffering.

The great difference, of course, is faith. Those who know and trust the Lord can endure anything because they have hope. And hope comes from their confident belief that God is just and that His justice ultimately will be served.

The Bible affirms that while justice might be elusive in this life, God will one day set all things right. He will vindicate His righteousness and avenge His oppressed people.

LESSON OUTLINE

I. **PRAISE FOR THE FAITHFUL—II Thess. 1:1-4**

II. **JUDGMENT FOR THE WICKED—II Thess. 1:5-10**

III. **PRAYER FOR THE AFFLICTED—II Thess. 1:11-12**

Exposition: Verse by Verse

PRAISE FOR THE FAITHFUL

II THESS. 1:1 Paul, and Silvanus, and Timotheus, unto the church of the Thessalonians in God our Father and the Lord Jesus Christ:

2 Grace unto you, and peace, from God our Father and the Lord Jesus Christ.

3 We are bound to thank God always for you, brethren, as it is meet, because that your faith groweth exceedingly, and the charity of every one of you all toward each other aboundeth;

4 So that we ourselves glory in you in the churches of God for your patience and faith in all your persecutions and tribulations that ye endure.

Greeting (II Thess. 1:1-2). Second Thessalonians was written shortly after the first letter to that church. In his second letter, Paul addresses issues in the church that had recently come to his attention. There was still confusion about the Lord's return (I Thess. 4:13), exacerbated by the introduction of false teaching (II Thess. 2:2). And the need for honest and diligent work (I Thess. 4:11-12) had become a more serious matter (II Thess. 3:11-12). The apostle begins, however, with the ongoing persecution of the church and the proper perspective on it.

The opening greeting (II Thess. 1:1-2) is almost identical to the one in I Thessalonians (1:1), the only difference being that "the Father" in the first letter is changed to "our Father" in the second letter. Paul again includes Timothy and Silas (Silvanus) in his greeting and emphasizes the church's standing in "God our Father and the Lord Jesus Christ." Paul's desire for the church to fully know God's grace and peace—typical of his letters—is also present.

Thanksgiving (II Thess. 1:3). Also quite common in Paul's letters is an expression of thanksgiving for his readers. Here he, along with Timothy and Silas, feels "bound," or obligated, to offer thanks for the Thessalonian believers. He says this was "meet," or right. "Bound" probably emphasizes the divine side of the obligation and "meet" the human side (Robertson, *Word Pictures in the New Testament,* Baker).

Paul and his companions were thankful for the continuing growth of the Thessalonians' faith and love (charity) toward one another. This church had been known for both their faith and their love (cf. I Thess. 1:3), but it was Paul's desire and prayer that they increase and abound in both (3:10, 12). Paul now expresses his thanks to God that this had indeed been the case.

Commendation (II Thess. 1:4). The result of the Thessalonians' growing faith and love was that Paul and his friends were able to "glory," or boast, about them among the "churches of God." Particularly, they praised the church for their patience and faith amid persecution and trials. Their faith had not faltered but grown, even during persecution, and this was evidenced by their patience.

The Greek word for "patience" is composed of two elements that literally mean "remain under." It describes steadfastness and endurance under difficult circumstances. For the Thessalonian church, those circumstances involved persecution and "tribulations," which refer to pressures from all directions. The present tense of "endure" indicates the trials were continuing even as Paul wrote this letter. The church had its problems that needed correction, but their faith and love were not among them. And where faith and love are present, there is every hope that doctrinal and practical shortcomings can be corrected.

JUDGMENT FOR THE WICKED

5 Which is a manifest token of the righteous judgment of God, that ye may be counted worthy of the kingdom of God, for which ye also suffer:

6 Seeing it is a righteous thing with God to recompense tribulation to them that trouble you;

7 And to you who are troubled rest with us, when the Lord Jesus

shall be revealed from heaven with his mighty angels,

8 In flaming fire taking vengeance on them that know not God, and that obey not the gospel of our Lord Jesus Christ:

9 Who shall be punished with everlasting destruction from the presence of the Lord, and from the glory of his power;

10 When he shall come to be glorified in his saints, and to be admired in all them that believe (because our testimony among you was believed) in that day.

Evidence of God's judgment (II Thess. 1:5). What is the clear "token," or indication, of God's righteous judgment mentioned in verse 5? It is not the persecutions and tribulations the Thessalonians endured but rather the patience and faith with which they endured them, and this was something only God could instill in them. "The very fact that God rewards his children with fortitude indicates that he is a righteous God, who, accordingly, will also manifest this righteousness in the final judgment" (Hendriksen, *Thessalonians, Timothy, and Titus,* Baker).

The believers' steadfast faith in the midst of suffering not only was a token of God's righteous judgment but also gave assurance that they were genuine followers of Christ. As such, they would be counted (or declared) worthy of God's kingdom when they stand before Him.

Nature of God's judgment (II Thess. 1:6-8). Having mentioned God's righteous judgment in verse 5, Paul now begins to describe the nature of that judgment and what it meant for his readers. We should keep in mind that "Paul is not writing a detailed, precise, or even chronological prophetic treatise here but rather is wanting to give the Thessalonians hope that, in the end, God's righteousness would

prevail for them and for their tormentors" (Mayhue, *1 & 2 Thessalonians,* Christian Focus).

The apostle states that God will in fact judge those who were persecuting the believers in Thessalonica. It is right that He should repay them with "tribulation," or affliction, for this is in accordance with the divine principle that people reap what they sow (Gal. 6:7).

The coming judgment upon the wicked would bring rest for the persecuted Christians in Thessalonica (II Thess. 1:7). The idea is that both the Thessalonians and Paul and his companions would experience rest. Clearly this is not immediate and temporal rest but eternal rest. While we can enjoy spiritual rest in Christ now, free of condemnation, we have no promises that we will be free of suffering in this life. In fact, just the opposite is the norm (cf. II Tim. 3:12).

The time when the wicked are judged and the righteous are delivered from affliction and given rest is the glorious manifestation of the Lord Jesus from heaven, accompanied by His mighty angels. This is not at the Lord's coming in the clouds (the rapture) described in I Thessalonians 4:13-18. Rather, it refers to Christ's coming to earth in judgment at the end of the time of tribulation. Angels will accompany Him and help carry out His righteous judgment (Rev. 19:11-21; cf. Matt. 13:37-43, 49-50; 25:31-46).

Furthermore, Christ's coming in judgment is described as being "in flaming fire" (II Thess. 1:8). If this phrase is taken with what follows, it would indicate that fire is the means of judgment. However, "it is more natural to connect this phrase with what has gone before as a further description of the returning Judge" (Hiebert, *The Thessalonian Epistles,* Moody).

The preincarnate appearances of the Lord in the Old Testament were often marked by fire (cf. Exod. 3:2; 19:18; 24:17; Dan. 7:9-10), and Revelation 19:12 describes the returning Lord as having eyes like a "flame of fire" (cf. 1:14). Fire is symbolic of God's presence and of divine judgment (cf. Zeph. 1:18; Mark 9:43; Heb. 12:29).

Finally, the coming judgment is described as divine vengeance (II Thess. 1:8). This is just payment for evil deeds. The Bible says that vengeance is God's (cf. Deut. 32:35; Ps. 94:1; Rom. 12:19), yet here it is Jesus Christ who avenges His people, reminding us that Jesus is in fact fully God.

The objects of Christ's vengeance are those who do not know and do not obey the gospel. These are not two separate groups. Rather, those who do not know God personally by faith are simply defined by their rejection of the gospel.

How did this information about future vengeance on the wicked help the Thessalonians, and how does it help Christians today who are suffering persecution? It assures all followers of the Lord that suffering is not purposeless and that there is ultimate moral justice. Those who suffer for the sake of Christ will be vindicated, and those who persecute God's people will suffer the judgment of God. Knowing that God is sovereign and will not forever tolerate evil helps us patiently endure suffering in faith.

Results of God's judgment (II Thess. 1:9-10). Verse 9 speaks of the abiding results of the judgment on those who do not know God or obey the gospel. The divine vengeance they suffer is described as punishment "with everlasting destruction." "Everlasting" is the same word used for God's eternality (cf. Rom. 16:26) and the believer's eternal life (cf. John 3:16).

While we are accustomed to thinking of destruction as the end of something, the destruction, or ruin, of unbelievers is unending. The Greek word is never translated "annihilation."

The eternal destruction of the un-saved is further described as being away "from the presence of the Lord, and from the glory of his power" (II Thess. 1:9). One of the great horrors of eternal punishment is unending separation from the presence of the Lord. The hopelessness that marks the lives of so many people in this life will be the lot of all the unsaved in eternity, where they will be excluded from the Lord's presence with no hope of their destiny ever changing. This is the exact opposite of the promise for believers Paul pointed to in I Thessalonians 4:17— that they *will* forever be with the Lord.

The unsaved will also be separated from the glory of the Lord's power. This is a further description of separation from God. The emphasis here again may be on the utter hopelessness of those who are judged, for they will be forever banned from the presence of the One who possessed the power to save them from such punishment.

The return of Christ will be a time of judgment for unbelievers but a time of glorification for Christ Himself. He will be glorified in the presence of His saints at that time. The parallel thought, that He will be marveled at by all who believe, gives us a clear picture of all believers (saints, or holy ones) bringing honor to Christ.

The preposition "in" can mean either in the saints or among them. Probably both ideas are present. The Lord Jesus will receive glory "when it is openly displayed what He has wrought in His saints, now assembled with Him in glorified bodies and perfected in spirit" (Hiebert).

In a brief aside, Paul makes this whole scene very personal to the Thessalonian Christians. They will be among those saints who bring glory to Christ at His coming because they believed the testimony of Paul and the other missionaries. The believers in Thessalonica could endure the trials they were facing because they had believed in Christ and could look forward to His coming, knowing justice would be done and God would be glorified in them.

PRAYER FOR THE AFFLICTED

11 Wherefore also we pray always for you, that our God would count you worthy of this calling, and fulfil all the good pleasure of his goodness, and the work of faith with power:

12 That the name of our Lord Jesus Christ may be glorified in you, and ye in him, according to the grace of our God and the Lord Jesus Christ.

Paul concludes by assuring his Thessalonian brethren of the missionaries' prayers on their behalf. Their prayers were in light of the persecution the Thessalonians were enduring but also in light of the justice of God that will be fully revealed at Christ's coming.

The constant prayer of Paul and his fellow missionaries focused on two things. First, they prayed that God would count the Thessalonian Christians worthy of their calling. In II Thessalonians 1:5, Paul speaks of their being counted worthy to enter God's kingdom. In verse 11, "he prays that God would count them worthy or affirm that they had lived up to the purpose of their salvation" (Mayhue). The emphasis here is on the practical outworking of their faith, especially in the midst of persecution.

Second, they would indeed be counted worthy if they fulfilled "all the good pleasure of his goodness." The Greek could be more smoothly translated "every desire for good." Thus, the prayer was for God to bring to fruition the desire to do good that He had instilled in the believers. This would be seen outwardly in "the work of faith," that is, the work that is produced by faith.

The constant prayers of Paul and his friends were for the Thessalonians to demonstrate the change God had worked in their lives. God had implanted new desires in them, but they could be realized only as the Thessalonians trusted God and relied on His power.

The goal of the missionaries' prayer was that Christ would be glorified in the Thessalonians. "Name" in verse 12 refers to the Lord's Person and character. The goal of all believers should be to live in a way that brings honor to Christ by revealing His character in our lives. Amazingly, when we do this, He also brings glory to us. This mutual glorification is enacted solely by His grace, for it is not within our power to exalt Him as He deserves.

Let us thank God for His grace, which allows us to fulfill His purpose for us and to properly exalt Him even in times of suffering.

—Jarl K. Waggoner.

QUESTIONS

1. How does Paul's greeting in II Thessalonians compare to his greeting in I Thessalonians?

2. What did Paul thank God for in regard to the Thessalonians?

3. What did the missionaries boast among the churches?

4. How did the church's patience and faith amid persecution point to God's righteous judgment?

5. Why is it right for God to repay the persecutors of believers?

6. What does "flaming fire" signify (II Thess. 1:8)?

7. How would God's coming judgment encourage the Thessalonians?

8. How is the divine punishment of unbelievers described?

9. How is Christ glorified at His coming (vs. 10)?

10. For what did Paul and his companions pray regarding the Thessalonians?

—Jarl K. Waggoner.

Preparing to Teach the Lesson

We are now in a new unit of lessons under the heading of "New Growth." In our lesson this week, we learn that as Christians we can have a growing confidence because of our faith in Jesus.

TODAY'S AIM

Facts: to show that while Christians are called to suffer, we also can look forward to the blessings when Jesus returns.

Principle: to realize that suffering and increased confidence grow side by side.

Application: to know that when we suffer, we can also expect to grow spiritually as Christians.

INTRODUCING THE LESSON

Many a parent has given comfort to a child after they have fallen and skinned their knees. As followers of Jesus, we receive our comfort through the Spirit of God, who in our times of difficulty and persecution for our faith becomes our singular source of comfort. In our lesson this week, we learn of the comfort that comes from the promises of God. Jesus promises to come again and give us relief from our suffering. It gives confidence and hope to the Christian believer.

DEVELOPING THE LESSON

1. Christians belong to God (II Thess. 1:1-2). We see that Paul is joined by two others as he pens this second letter to the church in Thessalonica. These friends were Silvanus (Greek for Silas) and the young pastor Timothy. Paul identifies the Thessalonian believers as those who belonged to God the Father and to the Lord Jesus. God called them His very own people. What a comfort it is to know that our God calls His children His very own. We have a new identity.

Discuss with the class how God would address us as a body of Christians if a similar letter was being written to us today. The Apostle Paul goes on, in typical Pauline fashion, to offer grace and peace from God our Father and our Lord Jesus. It is a salutation that will get your attention. Compare this greeting with the way we begin our letters (or e-mails) today. How can we approach others in a way that shows we are followers of our Lord Jesus?

2. Endurance is rewarded (II Thess. 1:3-10). Word had reached Paul that the little congregation in Thessalonica was being persecuted. But they grew stronger in their confidence and in their faith. They loved each other even more. Their suffering brought about a change in their attitude for good. Paul goes on to say that he told other churches about them and used them as a much appreciated example of endurance and faithfulness.

Our local churches need to encourage each other in this same manner and grow in faith as a result. Paul shows us that we are not alone in suffering. God can use our suffering as a means to show His justice. He does this by punishing the persecutors and providing rest to the persecuted. Our God is a just God and will be on the side of those who follow Him.

At times this divine justice may be delayed, but our God is always on time. He sometimes brings about this justice through His servants, the angels, with swords of flaming fire on those who trouble us. Angels are often portrayed in the Bible as God's servants (Heb. 1:14). We have no reason to worry, because God always wins in the end. God's retribution or vengeance is taken on those who do not know Him or believe His good news.

The persecutors will be cut off from the presence of God when Jesus comes again. They will be sentenced to everlasting destruction while His children, who were set apart for Him, will give Him praise and glory. There will be weeping in one camp and rejoicing in the other when Jesus comes. Ask the class in which camp will they be. Those who will praise our Lord Jesus when He comes will be those who believed the gospel that the Apostle Paul preached.

3. Paul prays for the believers (II Thess. 1:11-12). The Apostle Paul expresses two major concerns in his prayers for these Christians. First, that God would make them worthy of the calling to which He had called them. Second, that God would honor their good intentions, provoked by their faith, which would show up in their powerful good deeds; that when others looked at them, they would give honor to the Lord Jesus because of them and that they in turn would be rewarded and recognized by him.

If we remain as faithful Christians, we will always be rewarded, even if we go through difficult times. It might be hard for us right now, but our Lord Jesus does not leave us without hope. Endurance during times of suffering is possible only because our Lord showers His grace upon us. The Christians in Thessalonica certainly experienced this and have set us a good example to follow.

ILLUSTRATING THE LESSON

Endurance in suffering leads to increased growth in faith and love.

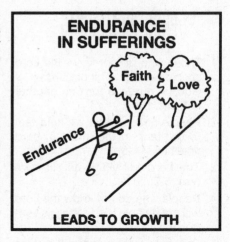

CONCLUDING THE LESSON

As Christians we must remember that we are never forgotten by God. In our most difficult times, our God is still with us. We will see our rewards even as we know that we can show the world how to endure by putting our faith in Jesus. It is He who must be honored. By believing the good news, we have committed ourselves to the power of the gospel and to following our Lord faithfully to the very end.

Leave the class with the clear thought that it is worth enduring suffering for Jesus. He does not give up on us. We will receive the reward if we endure. Those who trouble us will also get their reward. This will happen because our God is a just God and loves His children, giving them the courage to endure suffering for Him. This increases our confidence and our faith and love toward others.

ANTICIPATING THE NEXT LESSON

Next week we learn about the importance of the imminence of our Lord's return for us. We also learn that before that happens the wicked one will be revealed. We are encouraged to be ready for His coming and our deliverance.

—A Koshy Muthalaly.

PRACTICAL POINTS

1. Those who do not know the Lord should be able to spot children of God by our love for one another (II Thess. 1:1-3).
2. People notice when we hold fast to our faith in the midst of hard times (vss. 4-5).
3. The Lord will vindicate His own (vss. 6-7).
4. People who do not know the Lord will not be able to escape His vengeance (vs. 8).
5. Failure to acknowledge Jesus as Lord will result in eternal punishment (vss. 9-10).
6. Our heart's desire should be to glorify God in everything that we do (vss. 11-12).

—Charity G. Carter.

RESEARCH AND DISCUSSION

1. Explain why God's people should feel obligated to give thanks for one another (II Thess. 1:3).
2. Why is it especially commendable to hold fast to our faith in the midst of "tribulations" (vs. 4)?
3. How should knowing that God punishes people who wrong us with "recompense tribulation" alter our attitude toward vengeance (vs. 6)?
4. Sometimes it is easy to understand why God would take vengeance on those who reject His commands and willfully disobey Him. Explain why those who do not know Him will receive that vengeance (vs. 8).
5. How does God make us worthy of His calling (vss. 11-12)?

—Charity G. Carter.

ILLUSTRATED HIGH POINTS

Faith groweth exceedingly

Biologists identify six signs of life. And what of our churches? Do we demonstrate the six signs of life?

1) A highly complex structure
Believers compare spiritual things with spiritual (cf. I Cor. 2:12-13).

2) The maintenance of a chemical composition distinct from their surroundings
Believers do not blend with the world (cf. Rom. 12:2).

3) The ability to take in, transform, and use energy from their environment
Believers spend time in God's Word and are transformed (cf. Heb. 4:12).

4) A response to outside stimuli
Believers are moved to action by God's presence, His Word, the cry of the lost, and the promptings of the Spirit (cf. Acts 18:25).

5) The ability to reproduce
Believers multiply (cf. Acts 6:7).

6) The capacity to grow and develop
Believers start as babies and develop into teachers, leaders, and evangelists (cf. II Peter 1:5-8).

Admired in all them that believe

Wrapped in brown paper, hidden in a closet for 20 years, and marked "Pollock (1946-49)," the 32 overlooked paintings might have been worth 40 million dollars. Although they seemed to be originals to the trained eye of Pollock scholars, it was decided to put them to more scientific scrutiny. The paintings failed the test. The pigments used did not exist until after Pollock's death.

When Jesus comes, many counterfeit Christians will claim authenticity, but the penetrating light of Jesus will reveal whose works are genuine.

—Therese Greenberg.

Golden Text Illuminated

"We are bound to thank God always for you, brethren, as it is meet, because that your faith groweth exceedingly, and the charity of every one of you all toward each other aboundeth" (II Thessalonians 1:3).

Most believers, at some point or another, face some level of ridicule and persecution for their faith from those who do not know the Lord. As such, if there is no end in sight to the opposition or it is extreme, feelings of discouragement, confusion, and fear can set in.

At its worst, affliction can begin to erode a believer's faith and confidence in his future. He may start to question the promises of God or wonder if God sees the sin of those who hurt him simply for trying to live for the Lord.

Christians today are not immune to difficulties caused by the actions or words of others, nor are they immune to the havoc that false teachers can potentially wreak on their spiritual lives (cf. Eph. 4:14). The early church faced these same issues.

In Paul's second letter to the young Thessalonian church, he offered encouragement to help them stay hopeful in the midst of persecution. He also told them how they could safeguard themselves from falling prey to false doctrines.

As the church applied Paul's wisdom and practical steps, they experienced a growing confidence in the promises of God and a growing anticipation of Christ's return. Remarkably, new growth developed despite the negativity the Thessalonians faced.

Prior to the events of the golden text, Paul, Silas, and Timothy had prayed to God about their beloved brethren in Thessalonica (I Thess. 3:10). The golden text begins with their grateful response to God for having answered that prayer. The three men's thanksgiving was the appropriate response.

Since they were aware of the believers' persecution and their potential, Paul and his helpers were surely relieved by the church's steadfast faith. The fledgling believers' trust in God had actually grown exceedingly. They demonstrated abounding charity and love for one another!

Christians that persevere and grow despite daunting circumstances give evidence to the wonderful truth that God is at work (II Thess. 1:5). It is a visible attestation of God's invisible strength and presence.

It was important to Paul that the church continued to grow in their faith. He knew that a growing faith would inevitably lead to a growing confidence that God was in control and that, furthermore, God would repay those who troubled them (II Thess. 1:8-10).

A deeper knowledge of the things of God would also lessen their risk of being deceived and led into sin (cf. Eph. 4:14-15). Many of God's people are badly hurt by lack of knowledge (cf. Hos. 4:6).

As we draw closer to the Lord's return and troubles increase, may we be like the Thessalonians, growing in faith and love. We would do well to remember the many promises of Scripture, including Psalm 34:15: "The eyes of the Lord are upon the righteous, and his ears are open unto their cry."

You too can enjoy a growing confidence. Stay in the Word!

—*Christine M. Morrison.*

Heart of the Lesson

Have you ever been ridiculed for not conforming to the world's standards? Maybe your clothes do not imitate modern fashions or you do not use obscene language. Society may label you as behind the times. However, while you enjoy a heavenly eternity, such taunters will rue their unbelieving scorn as they suffer an everlasting existence in hell.

1. Paul's greeting (II Thess. 1:1-2). Paul probably wrote this second letter to the Thessalonian church a short time after the first. He sent greetings to the Thessalonians from himself, Timothy, and Silas. In his greeting Paul included the words "grace" and "peace."

Unbelievers continue to search for peace in various ways. They do not realize that grace and peace can come only through the Heavenly Father and His Son. What a better place this world would be if more people obtained this knowledge!

2. Paul's thanks (II Thess. 1:3-4). In his previous letter, Paul prayed that the Thessalonians' faith and love would increase, so he was thankful that both had intensified. This was an answer to prayer, so he praised the Lord. Afflictions had mightily increased the Thessalonians' faith.

Believers in Christ still suffer today. While no one likes troubles, everyone has them. God sends trials to develop a Christian's faith. The believer should realize that God uses tests to produce a confidence in the believer that the Lord keeps His promises. Also, earthly trials are often essential in equipping a Christian to help someone else deal with the same issue later.

3. God's judgment (II Thess. 1:5-10). The judgment of God will come eventually. Because He is just and fair, God will mete out His punishment of eternal flaming fire on the unsaved when He returns. At the same time, Christians who have endured suffering at the hands of oppressors will not suffer anymore. Since the Thessalonians had placed their trust in the Heavenly Father, they would live in heaven with Him.

Christians today are still suffering for the name of Christ. While America was founded on Christian principles, the respect for these principles has diminished. Public prayer was removed from the schools years ago. "Merry Christmas" is no longer a permitted greeting in some stores. False religions are prospering. One day all these tormentors will regret the deeds they have performed against Christ on this earth. However, it will be too late for them to ask for forgiveness. The ones who have suffered in this world for Christ's sake, though, will enjoy life everlasting.

4. Paul's prayer (II Thess. 1:11-12). Paul continually kept the Thessalonians in his prayers. He wanted them to live a life pleasing to God and asked Him to shower them with His power. With the confidence of their hope in God, the Thessalonians would be able to serve the Lord boldly and then exalt Him when He returns to claim His children.

All those of us who believe in Christ should have the same desire. Knowing that we have no strength on our own, we must rely on the might and strength of the Almighty. This should give us the confidence to believe that God always keeps His promises. Then we can leave this world knowing we have an eternity of blessedness awaiting us. What a glorious day that will be!

—*Catherine Moore.*

World Missions

The Thessalonians, with their patience and faith through trials and suffering, were believers Paul was happy to boast about.

Today around the world, there are still believers who are enduring suffering through great difficulty. They are worth boasting about here, because by doing so we are truly boasting about God and His grace.

Some are well known, like Kim Phuc, famous worldwide as the Vietnamese girl running, covered in burns, from her village in the 1972 photo that won a Pulitzer Prize. She endured seventeen operations and still lives with pain. After years of hate and anger, she found Christ and chose the difficult task of forgiveness. She is now a wife, mother, goodwill ambassador for the United Nations, and founder of a charity that helps child war victims like she was.

Others worth boasting about are not so well known, such as JoAnne, a seventy-year-old woman with macular degeneration who makes evangelistic dolls. Volunteers help sew the dolls, and JoAnne paints the faces, nearly eight thousand by now. One missionary who took a thousand dolls to Kenya said it was the best outreach tool he had ever had. One of the doll-making volunteers, at age seventy-eight, prayed that she would be able to share her faith with one thousand people before she died. She realized over time that her group made that many dolls and more. Each person who makes the dolls, carries them overseas, or distributes them, is worth boasting about.

In the tribal hills of a certain restricted country, believers' lives draw attention for all the right reasons. A national Christian said, "I saw that the tribal people are not like other Christians. They are faithful to God, devoted, prayerful, and hospitable to their guests. They keep themselves away from all kinds of wickedness." What a testimony for those believers, and what a negative testimony concerning the other Christians this man knew!

This national asked one of the tribal Christians, "What is the revival?"

The man answered, "You have to control your head, mind, eyes, ears, legs, stomach, and physical hunger and give yourself to God. Then there will be change in you."

How different this testimony is from what a pastor in America heard after witnessing to a man. The lost man told the pastor that at a gas station one of the deacons from his church told a joke so inappropriate it almost embarrassed him. "I don't need your God," the man said. "Being a Christian is no different than being anyone else."

If Paul were writing a letter about your church, would he have reason to boast? Would you personally be one who stands out as a beacon of faith through difficulty? Would your testimony inspire others to endure with patience and hope?

Many of us hope and pray for comfortable lives free of sickness and suffering, but those who are comfortable rarely do great things for the kingdom. They are too busy enjoying their rewards here on earth. Jesus wants us to die to ourselves in this life and set our affections on the eternal (Col. 3:1-2). To walk such a path is hard; it will include afflictions (II Tim. 3:12). But what a crown waits for those who dare choose it! Can there be a greater goal than to be someone God Himself will boast about in heaven one day?

—Kimberly Rae.

The Jewish Aspect

Paul, in his second letter to the church at Thessalonica, expressed a deep thanksgiving for the faith and love they had for one another, which, he said, was growing "exceedingly" (a metaphor for luxurious plant growth). The Psalmist David used a similar term—flourishing—when he said, "The righteous shall flourish like the palm tree: he shall grow like a cedar in Lebanon. Those that be planted in the house of the Lord shall flourish in the courts of our God" (Ps. 92:12-13). Paul wanted the Thessalonians to know that their patience and love were providing a growing confidence for many new believers.

Paul said that God would one day punish their persecutors and provide rest for all those who had suffered at the hands of the ungodly (II Thess. 1:4-9). David also found comfort in God as the avenger of his enemies. "And of thy mercy cut off mine enemies, and destroy all them that afflict my soul: for I am thy servant" (Ps. 143:12).

A fundamental principle in traditional Judaism is that God demonstrates justice to all people. David said, "Let the floods clap their hands: let the hills be joyful together before the Lord; for he cometh to judge the earth: with righteousness shall he judge the world, and the people with equity" (Ps. 98:8-9). Another foundation of the Jewish faith is that God ultimately rewards good and punishes evil. "He is the Rock, his work is perfect: for all his ways are judgment: a God of truth and without iniquity, just and right is he" (Deut. 32:4).

Paul condemned the ungodly who were troubling the church at Thessalonica. He said they would be punished with everlasting destruction (II Thess. 1:9). "Traditional Judaism firmly believes that death is not the end of human existence. . . . The Torah indicates in several places that the righteous will be reunited with their loved ones after death, while the wicked will be excluded from this reunion. . . . Certain sins are punished by the sinner being 'cut off from his people.' See, for example, Gen. 17:14 and Ex. 31:14. This punishment is referred to as kareit . . . (literally, 'cutting off,' but usually translated as 'spiritual excision,'), and it means that the soul loses its portion in the World to Come" (Rich, "Olam Ha-Ba: The Afterlife," www.jewfaq. org).

Paul prayed that God would count the Thessalonians worthy of their calling (II Thess. 1:11). "This prominent biblical term [call, calling] is used with particular theological significance in three ways: in connection with worship, with election, and with vocation. . . . The fact of God's call, and the destiny it involves, has moral consequences now. Believers are called to be holy (Rom. 1:7; 1 Cor. 1:2), and must act worthy of their calling (Eph. 4:1). Peter twice uses the phrase 'to this you were called' with reference to the meekness Christians must show their opponents, following the example of Jesus (I Pet. 2:21; 3:9)" (Elwell, ed., *Baker's Evangelical Dictionary of Biblical Theology,* Baker).

Paul thanked God for the great love that the Thessalonians had for one another and told them to walk in humility and gentleness. "In the Jewish tradition, humility is among the greatest of the virtues, as its opposite, pride, is among the worst of the vices. Moses, the greatest of men, is described as the most humble: 'Now the man Moses was very meek, above all the men that were on the face of the earth' (Num. 12:3)" (Jacobs, *The Jewish Religion: A Companion,* Oxford University Press).

—Deborah Markowitz Solan.

Guiding the Superintendent

The church in Thessalonica was born in persecution (Acts 17:1-9). Shortly after establishing the church in the town, Paul and company were forced to leave. As soon as he was able, Paul wrote a letter of encouragement to the struggling church, giving some details about the second coming of the Lord Jesus Christ, who would deliver them forever from their suffering and struggles.

Sometime after that first letter was written by Paul, a forged letter claiming to come from Paul appears to have arrived at the church (cf. II Thess. 2:2). This letter apparently asserted that their persecution was a sign that the Lord had already returned. Paul's second letter was written to encourage the church in the midst of their suffering.

DEVOTIONAL OUTLINE

1. Thankful for persecution (II Thess. 1:1-4). Paul's writing style is always affirming. He began his second letter by telling the Thessalonians how much he appreciated that their faith was continuing to grow. He was thankful that God was watching them.

They were indeed growing day to day in the Lord. But growth always has its challenges. This caused him to brag to the other churches about how they were persevering in the face of their struggles.

2. Encouragement in the face of persecution (II Thess. 1:5-10). Paul had taught them that one day Christ would return and deliver them from persecution. This had caused many to think that this return would be very soon. In the meantime they were confused by their persecution.

Paul reminded them that all suffering is not a result of sin. In fact, it might be an indication of God's love and purpose for them.

God is just and will one day come and judge all the wicked in the world. Those who are persecuted will then "be punished with everlasting destruction from the presence of the Lord" (vs. 9).

3. Prayer for the persecuted (II Thess. 1:11-12). Knowing all this, Paul told his readers how he was praying for them in the midst of their suffering. First, Paul prayed that they would live in a way that made them worthy of God's calling.

Second, Paul prayed that ultimately and in spite of their suffering the name of the Lord Jesus Christ would be glorified in them.

Do not be surprised when suffering comes your way. Suffering is a part of God's plan to enable the believer to mature.

CHILDREN'S CORNER

text: **Esther 4:7-17**
title: **God's Servant Esther**

Word had just got out that the Persian king had agreed to an order by the Jew's archenemy, Haman, to totally destroy all the Jews in his kingdom. The order gave Haman and his henchmen the authority to kill every Jew in the empire and plunder their goods.

Enter Mordecai, the uncle of Queen Esther. By God's sovereign plan, Mordecai's Jewish cousin was the queen. He was able to persuade Esther to appeal to the king for the Jews' safety.

Esther was determined to appear before the king, even though to do so uninvited could mean her death. Esther had uttered the famous words, "If I perish, I perish" (Esther 4:16).

Esther was truly a great servant of God, for she put her people ahead of her personal safety.

—*Martin R. Dahlquist.*

Scripture Lesson Text

II THESS. 2:1 Now we beseech you, brethren, by the coming of our Lord Jesus Christ, and by our gathering together unto him,

2 That ye be not soon shaken in mind, or be troubled, neither by spirit, nor by word, nor by letter as from us, as that the day of Christ is at hand.

3 Let no man deceive you by any means: for that day shall not come, except there come a falling away first, and that man of sin be revealed, the son of perdition;

4 Who opposeth and exalteth himself above all that is called God, or that is worshipped; so that he as God sitteth in the temple of God, shewing himself that he is God.

5 Remember ye not, that, when I was yet with you, I told you these things?

6 And now ye know what withholdeth that he might be revealed in his time.

7 For the mystery of iniquity doth already work: only he who now letteth will let, until he be taken out of the way.

8 And then shall that Wicked be revealed, whom the Lord shall consume with the spirit of his mouth, and shall destroy with the brightness of his coming:

9 Even him, whose coming is after the working of Satan with all power and signs and lying wonders,

10 And with all deceivableness of unrighteousness in them that perish; because they received not the love of the truth, that they might be saved.

11 And for this cause God shall send them strong delusion, that they should believe a lie:

12 That they all might be damned who believed not the truth, but had pleasure in unrighteousness.

NOTES

A Growing Awareness

Lesson Text: II Thessalonians 2:1-12

Related Scriptures: Matthew 24:6-14; II Timothy 3:1-9;
I John 2:18-19; John 12:39-41

TIME: A.D. 51   PLACE: from Corinth

GOLDEN TEXT—"Then shall that Wicked be revealed, whom the Lord shall consume with the spirit of his mouth, and shall destroy with the brightness of his coming" (II Thessalonians 2:8).

Introduction

The future is an area of continuing interest for people. Investors want guidance on economic decisions, government leaders try to anticipate political movements and international trends, and business leaders seek to determine what consumers will want or demand in the years ahead.

The desire to know as much as possible about what awaits us has kept astrologers and fortune-tellers in business, but it has also given rise to a new and more reputable occupation—that of futurist. Futurists are people who analyze various trends, past and present, and explore future possibilities from multiple perspectives in an attempt to visualize what the future holds and how people and societies can best prepare for it. Futurists often come from science backgrounds, and their books and advice are highly valued by corporations, governments, and academics.

Most individuals' interest in the future, however, is driven by curiosity or perhaps more so by fear. Futurists can offer them little in the way of specifics and nothing to allay their fears.

The only infallible guide for the future is the prophetic Scriptures. But these need to be studied carefully, for they are often misunderstood. Indeed, even the Apostle Paul had to correct those who had misunderstood his teaching regarding the end times.

LESSON OUTLINE

I. **ERROR CONCERNING THE DAY OF THE LORD**—II Thess. 2:1-2

II. **CORRECTION CONCERNING THE DAY OF THE LORD**—II Thess. 2:3-12

Exposition: Verse by Verse

ERROR CONCERNING THE DAY OF THE LORD

II THESS. 2:1 Now we beseech you, brethren, by the coming of our Lord Jesus Christ, and by our gathering together unto him,

2 That ye be not soon shaken in mind, or be troubled, neither by

spirit, nor by word, nor by letter as from us, as that the day of Christ is at hand.

The first chapter of II Thessalonians speaks of coming judgment upon unbelievers. The emphasis is on the vindication of God's righteousness and rest for God's people. While the future judgment is described, the chronological details of the end times are not dealt with. As chapter 2 reveals, timing was still a point of confusion for the Thessalonians.

Paul had corrected the Thessalonians' misunderstanding regarding the rapture and the resurrection of dead believers (I Thess. 4:13-18) and assured them that this event and the divine judgments of the Day of the Lord that follow it were still future (5:1-10). Yet sometime between the apostle's first and second letters to the church, further confusion had arisen regarding the Day of the Lord.

Paul's approach to the Thessalonians' error was to plead with them not to become unsettled by spurious reports about "the coming of our Lord Jesus Christ, and . . . our gathering together unto him" (II Thess. 2:1). This refers to a single event, namely, the first phase of Christ's return—the rapture. What Paul had already taught them about this event (I Thess. 4:13-18) should have been sufficient to answer their concerns about the coming Day of the Lord.

The issue the Thessalonian church was dealing with at this point had caused them to be "shaken in mind" or "troubled" (II Thess. 2:2). "Shaken" refers to agitation and is used elsewhere of an earthquake (Acts 16:26) and a reed blown in the wind (Matt. 11:7). "Troubled" indicates a "state of alarm, of nervous excitement" (Hiebert, *The Thessalonian Epistles,* Moody), and the tense suggests this alarm was continuing.

The cause of this emotional turmoil was the teaching that the Day of the Lord had arrived. The word "Christ" in II Thessalonians 2:2 is "Lord" in most Bible versions, and the context of future judgment makes it clear it refers to the Day of the Lord, that time of divine judgment that is connected with the return of Christ. The specific error the Thessalonians were entertaining was that the Day of the Lord had already begun.

Such an idea conflicted with Paul's previous teaching and thus produced great confusion, but apparently it had been promoted by a teaching in some form or other that supposedly came from Paul and his companions. "Spirit" would indicate a claimed supernatural revelation concerning this matter. "Word" suggests a message taught by someone who claimed Paul as the source of his teaching. Another possible source of this error was a forged letter purporting to be from Paul.

Regardless of where the teaching came from, it was false and must not be allowed to sway the Thessalonians from the hope of which Paul had assured them. They were suffering persecution (1:4-5), but this did not mean they were in the Day of the Lord.

CORRECTION CONCERNING THE DAY OF THE LORD

3 Let no man deceive you by any means: for that day shall not come, except there come a falling away first, and that man of sin be revealed, the son of perdition;

4 Who opposeth and exalteth himself above all that is called God, or that is worshipped; so that he as God sitteth in the temple of God, shewing himself that he is God.

5 Remember ye not, that, when I was yet with you, I told you these things?

6 And now ye know what withholdeth that he might be revealed in his time.

7 For the mystery of iniquity doth already work: only he who now

letteth will let, until he be taken out of the way.

8 And then shall that Wicked be revealed, whom the Lord shall consume with the spirit of his mouth, and shall destroy with the brightness of his coming:

9 Even him, whose coming is after the working of Satan with all power and signs and lying wonders,

10 And with all deceivableness of unrighteousness in them that perish; because they received not the love of the truth, that they might be saved.

11 And for this cause God shall send them strong delusion, that they should believe a lie:

12 That they all might be damned who believed not the truth, but had pleasure in unrighteousness.

Reminder of teaching (II Thess. 2:3-5). Paul emphatically stated that the Day of the Lord had not begun. This was proved by the fact that certain prophesied events that mark that day had not yet occurred.

There are several things we should keep in mind here. First, Paul's teaching in I Thessalonians (4:13—5:11) on the timing of the rapture and the Day of the Lord suggests that the rapture comes first and delivers the saints from the time of tribulation. The apostle did not repeat that argument here, though it seems to be implied.

Second, "Day of the Lord" here refers primarily to the last half of the seven years of tribulation, when the judgments of God are most severe upon the earth. This is just prior to the return to earth of Christ the King.

Third, a number of the truths Paul set forth in II Thessalonians 2:3-13 are found only here in Scripture. As such, this passage is extremely important to our understanding of the end times.

"That day," the Day of the Lord, will not come until there is first a "falling away" (vs. 3). The Greek word is *apostasia,* from which we get our word "apostasy." The Day of the Lord will be preceded by a massive defection from the true faith. While apostasy sadly occurs in every generation and is sometimes very widespread, the context suggests that what is in mind is ultimately related to the worship of the "man of sin." A great falling away from the faith by those who once professed Christ will lead up to and culminate with the revelation of the man of sin and his almost universal worship.

The "man of sin" is also called the "son of perdition," or son of destruction. Like Judas, who was identified with the same phrase (John 17:12), he is one who destroys. This end-times figure is readily and properly equated with the "prince that shall come" (Dan. 9:26), the "beast" (Rev. 13:1), and "antichrist" (I John 2:18).

The antichrist is described as one who opposes God and exalts "himself above all that is called God, or that is worshipped" (II Thess. 2:4). Indeed, he will sit "in the temple of God," claiming to be God (cf. Dan. 9:27; Matt. 24:15), and he will be worshipped as God (Rev. 13:4). While the temple of the true God does not exist today in Jerusalem, it will be rebuilt and claimed by the antichrist.

Since these things had not occurred, the Thessalonians were clearly not in the Day of the Lord. Paul reminded them that he had taught them about these matters when he was with them. There is a clear hint of rebuke in Paul's words, for the Thessalonians had entertained teaching that contradicted Paul's faithful instruction.

Even today, with the completed Bible, many professing Christians are quick to abandon what they have been taught and have learned from Scripture. Our first line of defense against getting sidetracked by errant ideas is to remind ourselves of what the Bible clearly teaches.

Removal of restraint (II Thess. 2:6-7). Paul said that his readers knew what was withholding the revelation of the antichrist, the man of sin, for they had been instructed about this. For us, it is not quite as clear. What is clear is that some restraint has been put in place that prevents the appearance of the antichrist until "his time." God is in complete control of this evil person, and He will permit his lawless reign only when He desires.

The thought is continued in verse 7, where Paul refers to "iniquity," or lawlessness, as a "mystery" that is already at work. Lawlessness has been present in the world since the Fall, "but lawlessness remains a mystery in the sense that it has not yet been fully revealed or manifested in its worst, unchecked form" (Mayhue, *1 & 2 Thessalonians,* Christian Focus). The full revelation of evil will be seen when God removes the restraint upon it and the man of sin is unveiled.

Only when "he who now letteth [restrains]" is "taken out of the way" will the antichrist be revealed and freed to carry out his satanically inspired plan.

Who or what is the restrainer? We might wish we had the advantage of the Thessalonians, who had been instructed regarding this. We do not, however, and many answers have been offered, including the church, the Roman Empire, the preaching of the gospel, and the Holy Spirit.

The arguments are many and sometimes complicated, but the simplest answer is that the restrainer is God, and perhaps specifically God the Holy Spirit. God alone is more powerful than Satan and can restrain him and his ruler. The Holy Spirit is not taken from the world but rather removes His restraint on sin and the lawless one. Many see this removal of God's restraint as being connected with the rapture of the church since the Holy Spirit works through the church to accomplish God's purposes on earth.

Revelation of the antichrist (II Thess. 2:8-10). Though the restraint on the antichrist will be withdrawn, the Apostle Paul is quick to note the ultimate end of this wicked one. The Lord will "consume [him] with the spirit of his mouth." The word here does not mean "consume" in the sense of "kill" but rather "overthrow." The Greek word for "spirit" is also the word for "breath." Jesus, the returning King, will overpower the antichrist with a mere word.

The phrase "destroy with the brightness of his coming" adds to the picture. The very appearance of Jesus in His glorious return will spell doom for the antichrist.

The punishment of the antichrist, or beast, is described in Revelation 19, where Jesus is depicted with a sharp sword coming from His mouth (vs. 15). He will defeat His enemies and cast the beast alive into the lake of fire (vss. 19-20).

Before Christ brings the reign of antichrist to an end, however, he will be empowered by Satan to produce "signs and lying wonders" (II Thess. 2:9). Through counterfeit miracles and the superhuman power of Satan, he will convince the world to follow and worship him.

"All deceivableness of unrighteousness" (vs. 10) simply means wicked deception. It points to various means beyond the signs and wonders the antichrist will use to deceive people. This will undoubtedly include oratorical, intellectual, and political skills. These means and others will be effective among those who are perishing. Because they "received not the love of the truth, that they might be saved," they are easily manipulated and deceived by satanic skills and deeds.

Delusion of unbelievers (II Thess. 2:11-12). "For this cause" points back to the rejection of the truth by the unbelievers mentioned in verse 10.

Divine judgment is the consequence of this rejection and their willing embrace of the antichrist. Those who have been deceived will be confirmed in their deception. God will actually "send them strong delusion, that they should believe a lie" (vs. 11).

This is the condemnation of God on "the countless millions on earth who have maneuvered themselves into the position of accepting a false messiah by rejecting the true Christ" (Hoyt, *The End Times,* BMH). At some moment known only to God, rebellious sinners reach a point of no return, and He turns them over to that which they love and have already chosen.

In this case, God's removal of restraint allows the lies of Satan to go unchecked. "In other words, Satan will be, for a time, totally free to give people exactly what they want to believe . . . the lie" (Mayhue).

The end result of the delusion God sends is stated in verse 12: "That they all might be damned [judged]." "All" refers to those who refused to believe the truth but instead took delight in unrighteousness. Their rejection of the truth and their pleasure in their sin mark them as unsaved. God simply confirms this by allowing them to fulfill their evil desires and make their judgment greater, as well as obvious and fair in the sight of all.

The delusion God sends does not trap innocent people into condemnation. Rather, it confirms sinners in the unbelief and wickedness they have already chosen. We see this same principle in Romans 1:24-32, where God releases vile sinners to sin more and to sin more wickedly, bringing greater judgment upon themselves (2:5-6).

The Thessalonians were confused. Though Paul had taught them otherwise, their own suffering, coupled with false teaching, was swaying them toward the belief that they had entered the end-time Day of the Lord. Their confusion gave Paul the opportunity to explain in detail why this was not the case. In the process, he revealed important details about the end times, the coming antichrist, and God.

These great truths make clear that the Thessalonians were not in the Day of the Lord; nor are we. Though that day approaches, we can rest in Him, knowing He is fully in control of our future as well as our present. No matter how much wickedness dominates our world, God's justice will prevail, and we who truly follow Christ will be saved from the wrath to come (I Thess. 1:10).

—Jarl K. Waggoner.

QUESTIONS

1. What prior teaching of Paul should have answered the Thessalonians' concern?

2. What error had infiltrated the church?

3. What proved that the Day of the Lord had not yet begun?

4. Who is the "man of sin" (II Thess. 2:3)?

5. How does the Apostle Paul describe this future person?

6. In what sense is lawlessness a "mystery" (vs. 7)?

7. Who or what prevents the revelation of the man of sin?

8. When and how will Jesus deal with the man of sin?

9. How will the antichrist convince people to follow and worship him?

10. What delusion will God send on unbelievers on the Day of the Lord? Why will He do this?

—Jarl K. Waggoner.

Preparing to Teach the Lesson

This week we learn that believers in Jesus will have a growing awareness about the way in which the Lord will destroy the wicked one who will emerge in the last days.

TODAY'S AIM

Facts: to show some of the events related to the antichrist that will take place before the Lord Jesus returns to earth.

Principle: to realize that as the church becomes aware of the rise of the antichrist to power, they have the promise of victory over him through Jesus.

Application: We have no reason to be afraid because our Lord will defeat the man of sin.

INTRODUCING THE LESSON

Down through the ages we have all heard conversations about the "man of sin," otherwise referred to as the antichrist (cf. Rev. 13). Right now we do not know who this person is, but the Bible reminds us that when he comes and assumes power we will know who he is, for he will not keep his promises to his people. Our Lord Jesus will be the One who will defeat him and utterly destroy his power.

It is certainly encouraging to those of us who put our faith in our Lord Jesus that He will never let us down and will be with us at the time when we will need Him the most. The Bible does not leave us in darkness about these times, but lets us know in no uncertain terms things that will happen before this takes place, so we can be ready and prepared. In this week's lesson we learn about some of these very important events that must take place before that time.

DEVELOPING THE LESSON

1. Jesus is coming soon (II Thess. 2:1-3a). The coming of our Lord Jesus should be a source of hope for all of us. Paul reminds the Thessalonian church and us that we can be encouraged with the promises of the Word. He wants us to know the things that will take place before this hope takes concrete shape when Jesus comes. Believers in Jesus will be gathered together to meet the Lord.

We are not to be troubled in spirit or in our minds about the evil of the end times. We are not to be fooled by those who tell us that this period of time has begun because when it does, we will know it. The Thessalonians were not to be fooled by those who told them otherwise either. Some claimed to have a revelation or a vision from God; others would say that they had even received a letter from Paul. We are reminded that we are not to be fooled by those who do not know our Lord.

2. The man of sin will be revealed (II Thess. 2: 3b-6). We are clearly told that before Jesus comes there will be a great rebellion against God. The world will deteriorate in its morals and move away from God. Jesus warned us about this falling away (cf. Matt. 24). It is at such a time that the "man of sin" (II Thess. 2:3) will be revealed to the world. He will be the one to usher in an age of spiritual ruin. That is what the word "perdition" refers to.

It is interesting that the Bible tells us that the antichrist will attempt to destroy all that represents God. We can safely assume here that all forms of worship, good and bad, will be demolished because he will establish his own form of false religion. He will proclaim Himself as God and take over the temple at Jerusalem and sit where God Himself was present. Jesus Himself alluded to this in Matthew 24:5.

Paul reminded the Thessalonian church that when he had visited them earlier, this was something that he had already talked about with them. Now he was telling them again of this. The Holy Spirit is the restraining force to evil in the world. When the time comes, the Spirit will move away and the antichrist will take control. Ask the class to talk about what they feel as they read about this "man of sin." They may be sad about the concept of judgment. They may even be fearful of the end times and the antichrist. However, hope comes as we realize Jesus will come in victory.

3. The Antichrist will be destroyed (II Thess. 2:7-12). Paul warns us here of the evil of these days. The antichrist will work evil behind the scenes until it is time for the Spirit to move out of the way and have him manifested. Then Jesus will come with the breath (spirit) of His mouth and destroy the antichrist with the brightness of His coming. Evil cannot stand in the bright presence of holiness. The glory of divine purity will take over in victory.

Help the class to see that Jesus is no longer the helpless baby of Christmas but the King of kings who will usher His children into an era of peace. But the world still has to go through this dark time first. Jesus gives us hope.

The "man of sin" is also described here as a man of deception. He will do Satan's evil work with signs and miracles. Help the class to see that Satan is a deceiver because he can become an "angel of light" (II Cor. 11:14). He will deceive many. Many who refuse to believe the truth of Jesus will be destroyed as they follow this man of sin.

God gives us free will to choose whom we will follow even if it is a "strong delusion" (II Thess. 2:11).

God will never lead us astray or condemn us. Those who follow this man of sin will ultimately be condemned because they have cast aside the truth that was shown them through Jesus. They also will love unrighteousness.

ILLUSTRATING THE LESSON

While the antichrist will deceive many, Jesus will destroy him with the breath of His mouth.

CONCLUDING THE LESSON

We live in dark times where God is pushed aside and evil takes His place. We often run after things that ultimately deceive us. We are called to stand firm and follow our Lord as we become aware of what the Bible tells us is coming. We dare not lose sight of the fact that Jesus is the One who will destroy the man of sin. So let us follow our Lord.

ANTICIPATING THE NEXT LESSON

Next week we learn that the path to victory is to follow what is taught to us in God's Word.

—A. Koshy Muthalaly.

PRACTICAL POINTS

1. Even strong spiritual leaders cannot pinpoint the Second Coming (II Thess. 2:1-2).
2. Very specific events will take place before Christ's return (vss. 3-4).
3. The one who will exalt himself against God will not do so until the appointed time (vss. 5-6).
4. We have no reason to fear the wicked one because Jesus will defeat him (vss. 7-8).
5. Those who refuse to be saved from their sins are under the influence of Satan (vss. 9-10).
6. Eventually, people who refuse to accept the truth will be condemned forever (vss. 11-12).

—Charity G. Carter.

RESEARCH AND DISCUSSION

1. How should we respond when people say that they know when the world will end or when Christ will return (II Thess. 2:1-2)?
2. Why must the man of sin opposing God occur before Christ returns (vs. 4)?
3. What can we do to ensure that we do not forget the wise counsel of our spiritual mentors when we are no longer with them (vss. 5-6)?
4. How is the mystery of iniquity already at work in the world (vs. 7)?
5. What is the significance of the Lord consuming the wicked one (vs. 8)?
6. We know that God loved the world so much that He sent His Son to die for our sins. Explain why those who refuse to believe in Him are subject to damnation (II Thess. 2:12; cf. John 3:16).

—Charity G. Carter.

ILLUSTRATED HIGH POINTS

Our gathering together unto him

"Scatter/gather" is a process used by coders. This method breaks up and disperses data from a single stream to multiple containments with a single word, "read." This is the scattering part. Then, with another word, "write," the data is recovered. This is the gathering part.

Scatter/gather is also God's operating principle (cf. Eccles. 3:5). It is how God deals with His church. First, He went about gathering followers. Then, with a command, "Go," He scattered them throughout the world. Finally, with another single command, a shout this time, He will gather them again to Himself (cf. I Thess. 4:16).

Shewing himself that he is God

"Woo, too, yoo," repeated the owl. A couple moles, moving stealthily along the ground, heard "you" and then "you two." Believing the owl was all-knowing, they scurried off to tell the other critters they had found a god. The secretary bird decided to confirm this for himself and went to visit. "How many claws am I holding up?" asked the bird. "Two." Okay then, "Why does a beau call on a maiden?" "To woo." The bird was convinced and told the others a god had come amongst them.

He came on a bright afternoon. Nearly blinded by the sun, he walked down the highway toward their gathering. "He's a god, he's a god," they all shouted. As a truck came speeding toward them, they enquired, "Aren't you afraid?" Unable to see the truck, the owl said, "Who?" Taking courage from this, they cried again, "He's a god." Beguiled by misguided faith, they continued their praise till the truck ran them down.

Oh, how perilously ready mankind is to make a false god of anyone!

—Therese Greenberg.

Golden Text Illuminated

"Then shall that Wicked be revealed, whom the Lord shall consume with the spirit of his mouth, and shall destroy with the brightness of his coming" (II Thessalonians 2:8).

Though the exact time of Christ's return is unknown (Matt. 24:36-44), God's Word does provide us with signs that can give us a growing awareness of the day's drawing near.

Believers must continue to grow in knowledge and faith as well as remind one another of the truths concerning the latter days. In doing so, they will not be easily deceived by false teachers or swayed to live as the world does (cf. Matt. 24:4-14).

In the Apostle Paul's second letter to the Thessalonian church, he reminded them of some significant future events (2:5) that would signal the second coming of the Lord.

The new believers apparently needed a reminder of these truths, as many of them thought they had missed the return of the Lord (vss. 1-2). Paul's letter assured them they had not missed Christ's return; the apostle reminded them that they should be looking for specific events to unfold.

First, a great rebellion against God will take place (II Thess. 2:3; cf. Matt. 24:11-12). The character traits of unrepentant mankind are listed in II Timothy 3:1-9. Although there has always been the presence of sin since the Fall, the prominence and intensity of evil will increase to such a degree that it will be very difficult not to notice.

Then another event will occur; a person empowered by Satan (II Thess. 2:9) will arise. The "Wicked," that is, the lawless one, will exalt himself, sit in the temple, and even claim to be God (vss. 2-4)! Many will be destroyed for believing his lies (vss. 10-12).

The golden text tells us that this event (when the lawless one is revealed and let loose along with his destructive and deceptive influence) will happen at God's divinely decreed moment. Until then, the lawless one will be restrained or limited in his power (vss. 6-7).

The golden text also reveals, with great and reassuring certainty, the lawless one's fate. The Lord shall consume (utterly destroy) him with the spirit of His mouth. God's spoken word brought creation into being (Gen. 1), and God's very breath can destroy those who oppose Him (Isa. 11:4). From these Scriptures, we know that God has the power to overthrow the lawless one.

Finally, God will destroy the lawless one with the brightness, or splendor, of Christ's coming. God is so holy and pure that even His most faithful followers cannot look upon Him (cf. Exod. 33:20-23). Imagine what doom awaits the lawless one and his followers when Jesus returns (Rev. 19:20-21)!

The Thessalonian church surely found comfort in Paul's letter once they realized they had not missed the Lord's return. They could continue to grow in faith and therefore grow in awareness of the times in which they lived.

Perhaps all this talk of the latter days and the lawless one is making you anxious. Relax! Stay in the Word and take comfort! Though you may have a growing awareness that our world is becoming darker, this world is not our home. Likewise, you have not missed Jesus' return! So pray and keep watch, for He is coming!

—*Christine M. Morrison.*

Heart of the Lesson

Have you ever been deceived into believing a rumor? With strong conviction, you thought something was genuine that really was not. Only later did you realize the truth. Unfortunately, you had convinced others to believe the falsehood too, but now it was too late to persuade those people that the fabrication was not accurate.

In Paul's second letter to the Thessalonians, he addresses a lie that Satan had persuaded the church to believe about Christ's return.

1. False teaching (II Thess. 2:1-2). In the first chapter of I Thessalonians, Paul had spoken to the church about the second coming of Christ. In our present text, he explains that believers should not be anxious about the end of time. Apparently, some people had filled their heads with false concepts about Christ's return. Paul just wanted them to know the truth.

Today there are individuals who falsely convince others that Christ's return has already happened. Others say that Jesus will perform numerous activities before He returns. A believer in the Lord should not worry about such false rumors but should realize that Christ will not make His earthly entrance prematurely or in disguise. The Christian needs to be continuously aware of false teachings.

2. False pretense (II Thess. 2:3-6). Before Christ returns, two things will happen: man will rebel against God, and the "man of sin" will reveal himself. He will claim he is God and take over God's throne in the temple. Paul had already warned the Thessalonians about this event.

Many individuals have claimed to be God and, in the process, have acquired followers. This deceitfulness has led to the deaths of untold numbers of people. No man or woman who makes such a claim should ever be given the time of day. While this country has quickly become a rebellious nation, unprecedented lawlessness will reign at the end of time.

3. False hope (II Thess. 2:7-10). The man of sin will rebelliously destroy all goodness. Although Satan is already working to demolish Christianity, he will continue his destruction until the wicked one (the antichrist) comes. This deceiver will trick people into believing he is God. By the time his followers learn the truth, it will be too late.

Unfortunately, people today are easily deceived by Satan. He has individuals believing that all dead people go straight to heaven. However, this is not what the Bible teaches. John 3:16 explains that a person must believe in Christ to be able to receive salvation and live eternally with Him.

4. False belief (II Thess. 2:11-12). God will allow people to believe the lies of the wicked one. Paul says that these people under a "delusion" will be judged fairly for believing a fabrication and pursuing the pleasures of sin.

No false deed goes unpunished; all actions have consequences. Men believe that they should be allowed to do as they please. However, God sees all and will faithfully punish those who do not believe in Him. The punishment includes an eternal inferno. Therefore, everyone should repent from sin and receive salvation through God's grace. Only then can a person live eternally in paradise. Where will you spend eternity—heaven or hell?

—Catherine Moore

World Missions

As the end times draw near, the wicked wax worse. God's people are called to carry His light throughout the world, into the darkest places, turning what was meant for evil into good (cf. Gen. 50:20).

God Himself is leading the way, overruling and directing even in matters concerning ISIS. The atrocities committed by this militant Islamic group are horrific, but their evil doings are one of the reasons more Muslims are coming to Christ in this generation than ever before. Some Muslims are seeing the bloodshed and recognizing that violence is at the core of their religion. They are turning away from it looking for a better way. They find it in Christ.

For many, choosing Christ means persecution or even death. "One group of converts in Central Asia said they tell each other: 'If you're persecuted just thank God that you haven't been beaten, if you've been beaten, thank God you haven't been thrown in prison, if you're in prison, thank God you haven't been killed, and if you've been killed, thank God that you're with Jesus in heaven'" (christiantoday.com).

Families in Iraq are pouring into refugee camps and facing all the heartaches that come with being homeless and afraid. Samaritan's Purse has sent people there with blankets, shoes, and other help the refugees will need to get through a long winter in a cold and muddy camp. Among their chaplains and workers are believers who are refugees themselves. One said, "We bring Jesus to the people. We have hope in God. Here in Iraq, we've suffered a lot. Each family has plenty of bad news. But in God, there is joy and peace."

War-torn Bosnia, full of children traumatized and impoverished, was the spark that started Operation Christmas Child. Since its beginnings over one hundred million shoeboxes have been given to children in countries all over the world. Great multitudes of children have trusted in Christ, families have come to Christ, and churches have been planted.

God's Word says that times will be very bad for Christians as the end draws near. But Matthew 24:14 gives hope: "And this gospel of the kingdom shall be preached in all the world for a witness unto all nations." God will make a way for the world to hear.

In China, one missionary group that fought sex trafficking was asked to throw a special dinner, not for the victims, but rather for the perpetrators of this evil. That night, the leader of the missionary group was told that something unprecedented had happened. The government had planned a crackdown on the commercial sex industry, so the brothel owners and mafia lords were all taking the evening off, laying low. Many of them—gang members, pimps, the worst of the worst—ended up at the dinner.

A man spoke of how God had turned his life around from evil to good. The hotel staff were all so stunned that at times they forgot to wait on the tables. Through a translator, this speaker invited people to pray after him for salvation. When he finished and asked how many had prayed, all over the room hands went into the air! At the leader's table alone, eight criminals had turned to Christ!

One day all evil will be cast down, and God will make all things right. Justice will reign. Until then, with hope in that promise, we can carry light into the darkest of places, knowing our God goes before us. He is the God who is Himself the Light of the World.

—*Kimberly Rae.*

The Jewish Aspect

The believers at Thessalonica were being influenced and troubled by false teachings regarding many things, including that the return of Christ had already occurred (II Thess. 2:2). Paul reminded them that several things had to happen before the Lord returned, including a falling away and the man of sin—the son of perdition—being revealed (II Thess. 2:3). He said that many would not believe the truth of God and that their lives would be filled with ungodliness. "For men shall be lovers of their own selves, covetous, boasters, proud, blasphemers, disobedient to parents, unthankful, unholy" (II Tim. 3:2). "Young people will not respect the old, and governments will become godless. This is why the Midrash [ancient commentary of the Hebrew Bible] says, 'One third of the world's woes will come in the generation preceding the Messiah," (Kaplan, *The Handbook of Jewish Thought,* Moznaim Publishing).

"According to the Talmud, as the Messianic era approaches, the world will experience greater and greater turmoil: Vast economic fluctuations, social rebellion, and widespread despair. The culmination will be a world war of immense proportion led by King Gog from the land of Magog. There will be a war the likes of which have not been seen before. This will be the ultimate war of good against evil in which evil will be obliterated" (Kaplan).

The prophets Isaiah, Jeremiah, and Ezekiel wrote about events that will happen in the end days. Daniel had visions of the end days (9-12), and Zechariah spoke of the end of days when all the people of the earth will be gathered against Jerusalem (12:3). "In Judaism, the main textual source for the belief in the end of days and accompanying events is the Tanakh or Hebrew Bible. In the Five Books of Moses, references are made in Deuteronomy 28-31, that the Jews will not be able to keep the Law of Moses in the Land of Israel and will be subsequently exiled but ultimately redeemed. The books of the Hebrew Prophets elaborated and prophesied about the end of days" ("Jewish Eschatology," www.wikipedia.org).

Paul also spoke about the working of Satan with all power and signs and lying wonders (II Thess. 2:9). Although Satan does not occupy a prominent role in Judaism, it would be incorrect to say that he is entirely ignored. "Satan is the Devil, the prosecuting angel. . . . In the book of Zechariah (3:1-2), the angel whom God rebukes for his evil designs upon Jerusalem is 'the Satan'. . . . In subsequent Jewish literature, Satan is personification of both a demonic power outside man and the urge to do evil in the human psyche," (Jacobs, "Satan, the Adversary," www.myjewishlearning.com).

Paul said the son of perdition would sit in the temple of God, claiming to be God (II Thess. 2:4). "According to the Hebrew Bible, Solomon's Temple, also known as the First Temple, was the Holy Temple, . . . (Beit HaMikdash) in ancient Jerusalem before its destruction by Nebuchadnezzar II after the Siege of Jerusalem of 587 BCE and its subsequent replacement with the Second Temple in the 6th century BCE," ("Solomon's Temple," www.wikipedia.org). The second temple was also later destroyed. The temple mount is the holiest site in Judaism. It is where Abraham was to offer his son Isaac as a sacrifice. Currently, some Jews are making preparation for the third temple to be built.

—Deborah Markowitz Solan.

Guiding the Superintendent

During his first visit to Thessalonica, Paul had taught the believers a considerable amount of truth, especially about the future. Unfortunately, they had since jumped to some wrong conclusions that required clarification.

In his first letter to these believers, Paul dealt with some concerns about the future of deceased loved ones. Now, in his second letter Paul had to correct some misgivings about their own future.

DEVOTIONAL OUTLINE

1. Confusion (II Thess. 2:1-2). It seems the church in Thessalonica had come under some extreme persecution that had confused the people. They thought they were now experiencing the judgments associated with the Day of the Lord. The Day of the Lord is an expression used to describe that part of the Second Coming when God will directly judge human sin.

Some type of report had come to the believers in Thessalonica, by Paul, that had unsettled and alarmed them. According to the report, the suffering they were experiencing was an indication that the Day of the Lord had already come.

Paul denied that he had sent any such report. He would go on to explain that certain events must happen before the judgments of the Day of the Lord would begin.

2. Clarification (II Thess. 2:3-12). Several things must first happen before the Day of Lord is ushered in.

First, there must come a time of great rebellion, or apostasy, in which many will deliberately turn from the faith.

Next, there needs to be the revelation of the "man of sin" (vs. 3). This individual is better known by the name given by the Apostle John (I John 2:18-19)—the antichrist. He will oppose God; in fact, he will set himself up in the temple as God himself!

There is still more to come. The one holding back the man of sin must be withdrawn from the world (II Thess. 2:5-7). Paul had told them the restrainer's identity but, unfortunately, he did not identify him in this letter.

This will be followed with the man of sin working all kinds of miracles under the power of Satan. All this will lead to a great delusion of all those who refuse to accept God's truth and turn to Christ.

People will refuse God's truth and instead accept Satan's lies with total abandon.

CHILDREN'S CORNER

text: **Matthew 12:9-21**
title: **God's Chosen Servant**

For several lessons we have been looking at a few of God's chosen servants from the Old Testament. We now start to look at God's ultimate chosen Servant—Jesus Christ.

To prove that He was indeed God's chosen Servant, Jesus healed a person who had a withered hand. This upset the religious leaders of the day because Jesus did this against their rules, since it was done on a Sabbath day.

Jesus pointed out to His critics that they had provisions in their rules for helping a stranded sheep on the Sabbath. His reasoning was simple: "How much then is a man better than a sheep?" (Matt. 12:12).

Matthew not only proved that Jesus was God's chosen Servant by what He did; the apostle also quoted Isaiah 42:1-4 to indicate who Jesus was.

—Martin R. Dahlquist.

Scripture Lesson Text

II THESS. 2:13 But we are bound to give thanks alway to God for you, brethren beloved of the Lord, because God hath from the beginning chosen you to salvation through sanctification of the Spirit and belief of the truth:

14 Whereunto he called you by our gospel, to the obtaining of the glory of our Lord Jesus Christ.

15 Therefore, brethren, stand fast, and hold the traditions which ye have been taught, whether by word, or our epistle.

16 Now our Lord Jesus Christ himself, and God, even our Father, which hath loved us, and hath given us everlasting consolation and good hope through grace,

17 Comfort your hearts, and stablish you in every good word and work.

3:1 Finally, brethren, pray for us, that the word of the Lord may have free course, and be glorified, even as it is with you:

2 And that we may be delivered from unreasonable and wicked men: for all men have not faith.

3 But the Lord is faithful, who shall stablish you, and keep you from evil.

4 And we have confidence in the Lord touching you, that ye both do and will do the things which we command you.

5 And the Lord direct your hearts into the love of God, and into the patient waiting for Christ.

NOTES

A Growing Resolve

Lesson Text: II Thessalonians 2:13—3:5

Related Scriptures: Ephesians 1:4-5; I Corinthians 15:54-58;
I Peter 1:3-8; Revelation 3:10-12

TIME: A.D. 51   PLACE: from Corinth

GOLDEN TEXT—"Brethren, stand fast, and hold the traditions which ye have been taught, whether by word, or our epistle" (II Thessalonians 2:15).

Introduction

Solomon wrote that we should not despise the Lord's chastening. The correction of the Lord is always for our benefit and thus is a reflection of His love for us.

The same should be true of parents' correction of their children (cf. Heb. 12:7-9). A loving parent disciplines for the child's benefit.

Yet even loving discipline can be misunderstood if the discipline seems more for the parent's benefit than the child's, and this can give rise to bitterness and despair. It is so important that words of encouragement accompany correction.

The Apostle Paul spent most of II Thessalonians correcting his readers concerning doctrinal (1:5—2:12) and practical (3:6-15) matters. In the midst of this correction, however, he wisely took time to encourage his readers.

LESSON OUTLINE

I. **THANKS FOR THE THESSALONIANS**—II Thess. 2:13-14

II. **EXHORTATION TO THE THESSALONIANS**—II Thess. 2:15

III. **PRAYER FOR THE THESSALONIANS**—II Thess. 2:16-17

IV. **REQUEST OF THE THESSALONIANS**—II Thess. 3:1-2

V. **CONFIDENCE IN THE THESSALONIANS**—II Thess. 3:3-4

VI. **PRAYER FOR THE THESSALONIANS**—II Thess. 3:5

Exposition: Verse by Verse

THANKS FOR THE THESSALONIANS

II THESS. 2:13 But we are bound to give thanks alway to God for you, brethren beloved of the Lord, be- cause God hath from the beginning chosen you to salvation through sanctification of the Spirit and be- lief of the truth:

14 Whereunto he called you by

our gospel, to the obtaining of the glory of our Lord Jesus Christ.

Paul had just completed a lengthy description of the end-times antichrist and the doom that awaits both him and those who believe and follow him (vss. 3-12). This is now followed by a "wonderful passage of comfort and assurance, signaled by that pivotal word *but*" (Stedman, *Waiting for the Second Coming,* Discovery House).

The apostle reminded the Thessalonian Christians that despite their confusion and even questioning of Paul's previous teaching, he was grateful for them. In fact, he stated the very thing he had said at the beginning of his letter (1:3). He and his missionary companions were "bound" (2:13), or obligated, to thank God always for them because of what God had done in their lives.

The author described his readers as "beloved of the Lord." They were clearly objects of the special love of Christ, and this was evident because God had chosen them to salvation. This, their election "from the beginning," again reflects Paul's earlier statement in his first epistle (I Thess. 1:4).

This speaks of God's role in choosing those who are saved, and it looks back to the beginning of everything, even before the beginning of the world (cf. Eph. 1:4). Election is a gracious work of the sovereign God that remains, in large part, a mystery to human minds.

The salvation of the chosen is effected through the sanctifying work of the Holy Spirit and through faith in the truth. Here Paul set side by side the divine and human perspectives on salvation. On the divine side, the Holy Spirit sanctifies, or sets apart, believers for salvation (cf. I Cor. 6:11; I Pet. 1:2). Sanctification here refers to the position in which believers stand in Christ, having been made saints (holy ones) through the work of the Spirit (cf. I Cor. 1:2).

Salvation, of course, is never apart from "belief of the truth" (II Thess. 2:13). The Greek word for "belief" is the common word for faith. The human side of salvation is faith that believes the truth. The truth here refers to the truth of the gospel.

The Thessalonians were called to the truth through the preaching of the gospel (vs. 14). They had responded in faith and were saved. The end result of salvation is "the obtaining of the glory of our Lord Jesus Christ." The Thessalonians, like all Christians, will share in the honor and glory of Christ when He returns (cf. 1:10).

There is a great deal of theology packed into these first two verses of our lesson text. In the Thessalonians' salvation, Paul saw much for which to be thankful. While we might have our disagreements and even disappointments with fellow believers, we have much we can thank God for in relation to all who know and follow our Saviour.

EXHORTATION TO THE THESSALONIANS

15 Therefore, brethren, stand fast, and hold the traditions which ye have been taught, whether by word, or our epistle.

The great truths related to salvation under gird Paul's exhortation to his readers to "stand fast, and hold the traditions" they had been taught. Salvation brings with it an obligation to stand firm in the truth.

We usually think of traditions as merely helpful human inventions and teachings. Here, however, the term refers to God-given truths conveyed either by Paul and others or through his written correspondence. This was an appropriate exhortation for the Thessalonians, for "a continuation in basic Christian doctrines would have alleviated the instability and alarm that prompted the writing of this letter" (Barker and Kohlenberger, eds., *The Expositor's Bible Commentary— Abridged Edition,* Zondervan).

To claim Christ as Lord is to submit to His written Word, the Bible. What it teaches will often go against the grain of society, but it alone is divinely inspired truth and the source of stability for our lives.

PRAYER FOR THE THESSALONIANS

16 Now our Lord Jesus Christ himself, and God, even our Father, which hath loved us, and hath given us everlasting consolation and good hope through grace,

17 Comfort your hearts, and stablish you in every good word and work.

Paul now turns from exhortation to prayer. His prayer for the Thessalonians expresses his recognition that they could not continue firm in the faith without divine help.

The prayer is addressed to "our Lord Jesus Christ himself, and God, even our Father" (vs. 16). The whole construction equates the two as God. It also points out the appropriateness of addressing our prayers to Jesus, the Son, as well as to God the Father.

Paul goes on to describe God in terms of what He has done. Paul uses "our" and "us" here because he is describing God's work on behalf of all believers. All who follow Christ can rejoice that God has loved us. This was demonstrated at the cross, when Jesus died in our place and for our sins (cf. I Cor. 15:3; II Cor. 5:21; I Pet. 3:18).

Through Christ's death, we have been given "everlasting consolation and good hope through grace" (II Thess. 2:16). "Consolation" is comfort or encouragement. Hope looks to the future with absolute assurance, for

our hope is based on the promises of the faithful God. Here the hope probably focuses on the coming of Christ and our being with Him for eternity. The unending comfort and hope we enjoy are gifts of God's grace. They are ours no matter what we might suffer or what doubts might occasionally arise, for God has given them to us.

Because of who God is and what He has done for those who believe in Christ, Paul could confidently pray for the Thessalonian believers. The current situation in the church (vs. 2) certainly made the prayer for comfort appropriate. Paul wanted their hearts, their inner beings, to be encouraged in this time of turmoil.

The apostle also prayed that God would "stablish," or strengthen, them "in every good word and work" (vs. 17). His desire and prayer was for the Lord to bring the Thessalonian church to maturity in their faith. Such maturity would be reflected in words (speech) and works (actions) that were truly good— God-honoring and beneficial.

While the establishment of Christians in a firm, stable faith is the work of God (3:3), He uses the ministry of His servants (I Thess. 3:2) and our faithful prayers for one another (I Thess. 3:13; II Thess. 2:17) to accomplish this work. Paul's prayer for the Thessalonians is a worthy prayer for us to offer for one another.

REQUEST OF THE THESSALONIANS

3:1 Finally, brethren, pray for us, that the word of the Lord may have free course, and be glorified, even as it is with you:

2 And that we may be delivered from unreasonable and wicked men: for all men have not faith.

"Finally" in II Thessalonians 3:1 marks the transition to a new section of the epistle, which deals with another issue that required Paul's correction—namely, the failure of some in the church to live orderly, productive lives (vss. 6-15). Interestingly, this section begins much as chapter 2 ended, with an emphasis on prayer, the establishment of the Thessalonian church, and encouragement for them.

Paul had just offered his prayer for his readers (2:16-17). Now he asks them to pray for him and his fellow missionaries. Though Paul spoke with authority as an apostle and the spiritual father of the churches he wrote to, he never presented himself as a self-sufficient spiritual giant. In fact, he often asked others to pray for him (cf. Eph. 6:18-20; Col. 4:2-4).

Paul had asked for the prayers of his brethren in Thessalonica in his first letter to them (5:25); now he asks them again for their prayers. The verb tense he uses suggests that the request is "continue to pray for us," or "pray constantly for us" (Hendriksen, *Thessalonians, Timothy and Titus,* Baker).

Paul's request reminds us that our prayers are a crucial element in the work of God. Even if we are young in the faith and still greatly lacking in biblical knowledge, we can share in God's work through our prayers for other servants of the Lord. And if we are older in the faith and perhaps serving in very visible roles in the church, we should be reminded that we do not serve alone or in our own power. We desperately need the prayers of fellow Christians.

Paul did not just ask for prayer in a general sense. He asked his readers to pray specifically for two things. First, he wanted them to pray that the "word of the Lord" would have "free course" (II Thess. 3:1). The "word" is the gospel message in particular. "Free course" literally means "to run freely or quickly." Paul's desire was that the gospel would spread quickly and "be glorified."

The picture is that of a race, with the gospel of Christ swiftly running along and being honored as people accept it and are transformed by it. In other words, the apostle wanted the gospel to go forward swiftly and with success, even as it did in Thessalonica.

Second, Paul sought the prayers of the Thessalonians that he and his colleagues would be "delivered from unreasonable and wicked men" (vs. 2). "Unreasonable" refers to out of place, or perverse, people. They were also "wicked," actively pursuing that which is evil. Paul probably had in mind those who were presently opposing him in Corinth (cf. Acts 18:1-17).

The apostle's prayer requests were for the gospel to be successful and the messengers of it to be protected. These are worthy prayers for us to offer on behalf of the Lord's servants today. In fact, they are needed because, as Paul notes, not all people are believers, or have faith.

CONFIDENCE IN THE THESSALONIANS

3 But the Lord is faithful, who shall stablish you, and keep you from evil.

4 And we have confidence in the Lord touching you, that ye both do and will do the things which we command you.

While not all people have faith, the Lord Himself is faithful (vs. 3). He is faithful to His children and to His promises. As such, Paul could assure his Thessalonian brethren that the Lord would establish them and keep them from evil. "Evil" could be translated "evil one," and thus be a reference to Satan. It was Paul's prayer that they be established, or strengthened, in their faith (2:17), and he was sure the Lord would do this. He was also certain the Lord would protect them from Satan and those through whom Satan worked (cf. 3:2).

Paul's assurance was based on the nature of the Lord Himself as the faithful Lord. It was also based on his certainty regarding the Thessalonians' faith (cf. I Thess. 1:3-5; II Thess. 1:4; 2:13).

The work that God begins in His people will be completed (Phil. 1:6). This does not mean believers are entirely passive, however. We are continually enjoined to obey all the Lord has commanded us (cf. Matt. 28:20). When the power of God is joined with the obedience of believers, God's unique work is brought to completion.

Paul was confident the Thessalonians would continue to obey the commands of the Lord he gave them. "The missionaries were not relying on their readers' inherent power to do what was right; their confidence was that since the believers were in Christ, the Lord would work in them to react favorably to this epistle" (Walvoord and Zuck, eds., *The Bible Knowledge Commentary,* Cook).

PRAYER FOR THE THESSALONIANS

5 And the Lord direct your hearts into the love of God, and into the patient waiting for Christ.

The Apostle Paul then uttered another brief prayer on behalf of his readers. While he was confident of their continued obedience, that obedience would come only as their hearts were directed "into the love of God." The phrase "love of God" can refer either to their love for God or God's love for them. It is likely that both ideas are present. As they contemplated and fully appreciated God's love for them, they would grow in their love for Him and their desire to obey Him. This is what Paul prayed for.

The word for "patient waiting" is simply translated "patience" in 1:4. It refers to endurance or steadfastness amid hardship. Paul prayed that the Thessalonians might consider Christ's steadfastness in suffering and be inspired to continue their own steadfast endurance as they suffered.

Paul expressed thanksgiving for his readers and confidence in the Lord's work in their lives. He prayed for them and asked them to pray for him. And he encouraged them to stand firm in the faith. He was about to offer them rebuke and correction, but his humility, love, and confident expectation prepared them to accept his words and act on them. Paul's desire was not to exalt himself or punish his readers. It was to honor Christ and help them do the same. This should be our constant desire as well.

—Jarl K. Waggoner.

QUESTIONS

1. For what did Paul give thanks regarding the Thessalonians?

2. What is the divine side of salvation? What is the human side?

3. What did Paul exhort the Thessalonian Christians to do?

4. To whom was Paul's prayer for the Thessalonians addressed?

5. What does the apostle say Jesus Christ and God the Father have given us?

6. What did he ask God to do for his readers?

7. For what did Paul ask the Thessalonians to pray for him and the other missionaries?

8. What was Paul confident the Lord would do for the Thessalonian church?

9. What was he confident they would do?

10. What is meant by "love of God" in II Thessalonians 3:5?

—Jarl K. Waggoner.

Preparing to Teach the Lesson

New growth involves some new resolutions. This week we learn of Paul's encouragement to the church in Thessalonica to stand firm and strong in what they were taught. For us it can be said that the unsullied faith of our faithful ancestors is still worth holding on to today.

TODAY'S AIM

Facts: to show that we must hold fast to the ancient truths of the Word of God.

Principle: to realize that when we trust in the Bible, we can never go wrong.

Application: to make a decision to stay strong in the faith and hold on to what was taught to us from God's Word.

INTRODUCING THE LESSON

There is no shortage of the distortions of Bible teaching today. They all claim to have God's Word as their basis. Most of us have free access to social media and broadcast media. It is important that we search the Scriptures to see if what is said in the media is really true. What sounds true does not have to be true to get our attention. This is where we need to use discernment. Only God's Spirit can guide us into truth.

DEVELOPING THE LESSON

1. Chosen by God (II Thess. 2:13-14). Paul thanked God for the church at Thessalonica and its faithful believers. He reminded them that it is God who initiated their salvation. However, they had to accept that very precious gift. They were some of the very first to do this among the early Christians.

Two things had to take place for salvation to materialize. First, they needed the work of the Spirit within them. Second, they had to believe the truth that they had been taught. This is the same for us today. Help the class see that salvation is initiated by the Spirit of God, who leads us to exercise faith.

Paul reminded the Thessalonians that He and his companions (Silas and Timothy) had shared the gospel with the faithful there, but it was they who resolved to accept the saving message as truth. The result was they could now share in the glory of the Lord Jesus as part of His church. What a blessing this was!

We are called to share in all that the Lord Jesus has. This is the inheritance of the believer in Christ. Ask the class what it means to share in the glory of God.

How will this change our lives?

2. Stand firm in God (II Thess. 2:15-17). In Paul's day, there were many voices crying out to be heard. It was hard to tell the truth from error. Paul encouraged the believers in Thessalonica to hold firm to the truth that they were taught in person and through Paul's letters.

Today also we hear of many teachings claiming to be true, so we have to be careful to discern truth from error. We must study the Word to avoid heresy.

When we stay close to God we will experience His daily divine comfort. We will know that He loves us and that this allows us to experience His presence that gives us hope for the day. It is this special favor that gives us the resolve to say and do the right things in every situation. Help the class to see that we experience His comfort through the promises in His Word.

Through God's comfort, we know that His presence is with us. We can stand strong.

Discuss with the class some of the deviations from the truth of the gospel that they hear today. Identify clear steps to help them stay strong in the truth in such situations. Stress why this is important.

3. God is faithful (II Thess. 3:1-5). It is Satan that brings distortion to the truth of the gospel. We see here Paul's resolve to pray for steadfastness in his spiritual children at Thessalonica. He calls them his brethren (an intimate term for both brothers and sisters). He first seeks prayer for himself. This brings us the idea that even leaders can go astray if they are not careful.

Paul also asks that the church pray that the powerful gospel message will spread everywhere and that people will respond to it wherever it is preached, just as they first did. He also calls for protection for the church from those who are evil.

We have today those in our world who work hard to wipe out the Christian message. This is not going away, and we must pray for protection. The gospel will always be under attack because it is the ultimate truth.

Help the class to understand that if they receive the gospel of truth, they will always be a target of those who do not believe in this truth. Help them identify the risks, then show them that they are to stay close to the truth as our lesson teaches us. Truth often arouses opposition.

Our protection against the enemies of the gospel lies in our Lord Jesus, who is faithful. He gives us strength and sustains us as long as we are practicing the truth that was taught to us, just as the Thessalonian church did. We are told to expect to suffer for the gospel, but the Lord will help us endure. Paul ended his prayer by praying that they would understand the deep love that God has for them and that they would patiently wait for their deliverance when Jesus comes again. This is a message of hope for those who stay close to the truth that we were taught.

ILLUSTRATING THE LESSON

You will stay in the truth as long as you stay with what you are taught from God's Word.

THE WORD OF GOD

CONTINUE TO STUDY IT

CONCLUDING THE LESSON

We all know the dangers of the many false gospels around us. They often look very much like the truth but will lead us away from Jesus. So it is important that we stay grounded in the Word of God. Ask your class whether they think what they believe is directly from the Word or whether they believe some things that could lead them astray. Help the class resolve to read His Word daily and diligently.

ANTICIPATING THE NEXT LESSON

Next week, we begin a new unit that reminds us of the true gospel of our Lord Jesus.

—A. Koshy Muthalaly.

PRACTICAL POINTS

1. God saved us so that we might bring glory to His name (II Thess. 2:13-14).
2. Biblical Christian traditions have great value and should be honored (vs. 15).
3. God's comfort fills us with peace and confident assurance (vss. 16-17).
4. We should pray before embarking on any new work for the Lord (3:1-2).
5. We have no reason to fear that evil will overtake us. God will establish and protect us (vs. 3).
6. The Lord will only direct us to do what will enable us to showcase His love (vss. 4-5).
   —Charity G. Carter.

RESEARCH AND DISCUSSION

1. Why should we "stand fast, and hold the traditions" we have been taught (II Thess. 2:15)? What kind of tradition is Paul referring to?
2. How can we be certain that we are equipped t do God's work (vs. 17)?
3. Explain the importance of lifting our leaders up in prayer when they prepare to minister to others (3:1-2).
4. Think of a time when you or family members were kept from evil (vs. 3). How did you know that the Lord was protecting you?
5. Do those in authority over you have confidence that you will do as you have been taught (vs. 4)? How do you know?.
   —Charity G. Carter.

ILLUSTRATED HIGH POINTS

Word of the Lord have free course

The king placed a boulder in the middle of the road and hid to watch the people pass by. What would they do with the boulder? First, there came a group of wealthy advisers who spent much time debating. They began to complain that the king should take better care of the kingdom. Still debating, they walked around the boulder.

Then, a pauper, carrying a load of vegetables, approached the boulder. Laying aside his personal burden, he proceeded to push the boulder out of the way. Just under the rock he found a small purse filled with gold coins and a note from the king. It said that the gold was for the person who was willing to move the obstacle.

Our King knows there are obstacles to the preaching of His gospel. With prayerful struggle, we can move the impediments and discover the most precious treasure beneath—souls.

Confidence in the Lord

It is difficult to leave children in the care of others. A blogger wrote about a special teacher. Here are a few excerpts.

"You chose to get up early and stay up late, to be underpaid and rarely thanked. . . . to give my kids . . . second, third, fourth and fortieth chances. . . . to care even when the kids didn't. . . . You hugged them when they fell . . . and I wasn't there. You talked them down when they were fighting. You drew them out when they were quiet. You cheered the loudest."

Paul had to leave the Thessalonians early, but he left them in excellent hands—God's. He had confidence in the Lord concerning them.
   —Therese Greenberg.

Golden Text Illuminated

**"Brethren, stand fast, and hold the traditions which ye have been taught, whether by word, or our epistle"
(II Thessalonians 2:15).**

Believers are declared holy and without blame before the Lord and adopted as God's children (Eph. 1:4-5). We also have a lively hope because we have been promised an inheritance in heaven and the ongoing protection of God (I Pet. 1:3-7)!

These foundational truths, given to every believer, are truly amazing. Yet if Christians are not diligent to guard what they believe, they become subject to Satan's wiles (cf. Eph. 6:11-12). Then discouragement and erroneous doctrine can begin to erode, and even replace, previously embraced truth.

The Apostle Paul, therefore, wrote to the Thessalonian church, urging them to guard those precious truths they had already been taught. This would help them avoid the traps of the sinful culture they lived in, and the confusion resulting from false teachers (cf. II Thess. 2:2).

As we see in the golden text, Paul instructed his brothers in the Lord to be immovable, firmly rooted in what they had learned. They were not to be swayed by various strange teachings (Heb. 13:7-9), regardless of the popularity of these ideas.

The Thessalonians had not only listened to Paul's preaching but had also observed his lifestyle, which was modeled by Silas, and Timothy as well. The believers knew that these men were truly committed to living lives pleasing to the Lord (I Thess. 2:10-11). That made Paul and his helpers trustworthy examples to be imitated.

In addition, the church received written letters, or epistles, from Paul. These too helped the young believers understand biblical doctrine and how the Christian faith, when applied practically to daily living, would help them live righteous lives.

Regardless of whether the church heard Paul's message by word of mouth, directly from his sermons, or through his written letters, the charge was the same: "Stand fast."

Paul knew the young church would continue to mature only if they resolved to hold on to the truthful traditions they had already embraced. However, they also needed to remain teachable in order to experience further growth in God's Word.

As we consider the traditions we have been taught, we must seriously consider the credibility of the ones who are leading and teaching us before accepting their doctrines.

For Christ followers who study the Scriptures, it is reassuring to know that our teacher is the Spirit of Truth (John 16:13). The one we imitate, though of course falling short, is Jesus Christ, the perfect Son of God.

We also have access to countless audio and visual teachings by trusted Christian ministries. These can reinforce what we have already learned, as well as add to our knowledge.

If you find yourself subjected to different teachings than you initially believed—or if you are drifting spiritually—repent and return to what God had you doing when you were first saved. You will be revived (cf. Rev. 2:5).

May we always stand firm on the truths from the Word of God. Then, as we build on that sure foundation, new growth can flourish!

—*Christine M. Morrison.*

Heart of the Lesson

Do you realize that you have been specifically chosen by God? He has a definite purpose for your life and designed a plan for you before you were ever conceived. Are you following His plan for your life? Paul illustrated this point in his second letter to the Thessalonian church; he wanted them to understand that no matter what happens in life, God is and has always been in control.

1. Thanking God (II Thess. 2:13-15). Paul, along with Timothy and Silas, was constantly thanking God because He had clearly chosen the Thessalonians for salvation. God selected the citizens of Thessalonica to receive the good news. Paul desired that they would stand strong in the Lord and not let false teachings influence their beliefs.

God has individually chosen each person (Eph. 1:4). He knows when each person will enter this earth, who will receive salvation, and when everyone will exit this earth. Knowing that God is in control even before anyone is conceived should convince everyone to dedicate his or her lifetime to serving the Lord.

2. Blessing the Thessalonians (II Thess. 2:16-17). Paul explained that God gave the Thessalonians hope through His grace. Paul desired to see them thrive and do good in both word and deed. He did not want this church to be led astray with false teachings.

Believers need to stand firm for the Lord. One never knows what impact he or she will have on another. Even a seemingly trivial offense may prevent someone from receiving salvation. Who wants to stand before God and answer for this on Judgment Day? Therefore, followers of Christ should always be aware of their conduct before others. Believers also need to be scholars of God's Word in order to discern when a speaker is spouting untruths about the gospel. A few wrong words may lead another believer astray.

3. Praying for Paul (II Thess. 3:1-2). Primarily, Paul wanted the good news to flourish. Then he asked the Thessalonians to pray for his safety. Paul had repeatedly suffered for preaching the gospel, and there were still individuals who wanted to destroy him and prevent his good works.

Anyone who proclaims the gospel needs individuals who will pray for him constantly. Satan is continually attempting to silence the gospel, so those who proclaim it need followers who will ceaselessly intercede on their behalf. Believers should also give verbal encouragement to pastors and evangelists who preach the good news. A few words of inspiration can greatly embolden a minister.

4. Building confidence (II Thess. 3:3-5). In verse 3, Paul wrote that the Lord is faithful and will keep believers from evil. Paul had faith that the lessons he taught were being followed. He wanted the Thessalonians to have an understanding of the love of God and to be patient in waiting for God's timing.

How many people today say they believe in God but then demonstrate their unbelief by not fully trusting that God will do everything He says? Believers need to exhibit their faith by expectantly waiting for Him to answer their prayers. Patiently waiting for an answer may influence another person to do the same. Numerous instances of waiting for an answer to my prayers has given me the ability to recognize the Lord's faithfulness in all things.

—Catherine Moore.

World Missions

A distant friend convinced Kamlai to leave her village in Thailand in search of a better life. Tiny Hands International met Kamlai at an airport in South Africa and, on hearing her story, were fairly certain Kamlai was in the process of being trafficked.

They shared this concern with her, but Kamlai did not believe them. She wanted the better life she was offered. They had to let her go, but they gave her information on whom to call if she found herself in trouble.

Kamlai was, indeed, trafficked, and her life became a nightmare. Her passport was taken. She was told she owed her trafficker thousands of dollars and would be forced into prostitution if she could not pay.

Kamlai's story is representative of the lost person's experience. Satan uses the world to set forth his lies, saying a life of sin is good and fun and everything to be hoped for. Believers may warn them, but ultimately the choice is their own, and unless the Spirit illumine them, they will remain blinded. Once on the wrong path, people soon find themselves in a place far from what they dreamed, but how are they to escape? The debt of sin is too great to pay.

For Kamlai, her freedom came because she met people who knew the lies of the traffickers, understood what was happening to her, and offered her hope despite her wrong choices at the time. Kamlai contacted the Tiny Hands team, and they were able to rescue her. They got her home, opened a legal case against her trafficker, and provided ways to help heal her trauma.

As we as believers encounter the lost, we can follow the example of Tiny Hands. Even if a person does not listen to our message the first time, we can offer the information they need to turn back when they realize they are on the wrong path. We can give them our personal number or a church to contact or a specific portion of the Bible (along with a Bible) to read.

Kamlai's story is unusual in that she escaped fairly quickly. Statistics say a trafficked victim will try to escape and return an average of seven times before truly finding freedom.

This "seven times" statistic is similar to what victims in an abusive relationship face. They are psychologically and emotionally trapped even when they are not physically enslaved.

There is no deeper slavery than the ownership Satan has over a lost person. He tries to keep them trapped in any way possible, using lies to hold their minds and hearts captive.

As it happens, in the Scriptures seven is the number of completion. When it appears our message is rejected, we can still hope, knowing that God is not finished with that person yet. Perhaps it will take seven, or more, times of hearing the gospel before they break free of Satan's grasp and are saved. We should never give up.

What would have happened to Kamlai had someone not been there to warn her of what was about to happen and offer a way out? She might well still be enslaved today.

Millions around us are trapped in spiritual slavery. Will we intervene, even if our message might be rejected at first? Will we offer a way of escape, of hope?

Leave the tract, give the Bible, share the truth. Nothing done for Christ is wasted. Stand fast. Your labor is not in vain in the Lord.

—*Kimberly Rae.*

The Jewish Aspect

Paul told the Thessalonians that he was thankful to God for them because they had been chosen for salvation through the sanctification of the Spirit (II Thess. 2:13). The Thessalonians would have understood the meaning of sanctification because God had set apart His people for Himself. "And ye shall be unto me a kingdom of priests and an holy nation" (Exod. 19:6). "For I am the Lord your God: ye shall therefore sanctify yourselves, and ye shall be holy: for I am holy" (Lev. 11:44). To sanctify someone or something is to set that person or thing apart. . . . In the theological sense, things are sanctified when they are used for the purposes God intends. . . . The Greek word translated 'sanctification,' . . . means 'holiness.' To sanctify, therefore, means 'to make holy'" (Elwell, ed., *Baker's Evangelical Dictionary of Biblical Theology,* Baker).

Paul instructed the Thessalonians to stand fast upon the traditions that they had been taught. *Stand fast* is a military term that means to have a firm persuasion of mind and a constant purpose of will. The phrases *hold fast* and *stand fast* are used frequently throughout the Hebrew Bible. King Hezekiah trusted in the Lord, the God of Israel, and *held fast* to the Lord (II Kings 18:6).

The traditions Paul referred to were the ordinances, precepts, and teachings that were transmitted through the apostles. God's Word was extolled in Psalm 119, the longest chapter in the Bible. This psalm used eight words—law, word, judgments, testimonies, commandments, statutes, precepts, and word—to describe God's revelations to His people through the Scriptures (www. enduringword.com). The psalmist also wrote, "I have rejoiced in the way of thy testimonies, as much as in all riches. . . . Therefore I love thy commandments above gold; yea, above fine gold" (Ps. 119:14, 127). Paul told the Thessalonians that despite their sufferings, they would be established in every good work by holding fast to the statutes of God. Peter said that the trials of faith are more precious than gold that one day will perish. Gold was a symbol of purity in the Hebrew Bible. Job, in his sufferings, said that he had not gone back on the commandments of God and that when he was tried, he would come forth as gold (Job 23:10).

Paul told the Thessalonians that their resolve would result in their reward of everlasting consolation. He prayed that the Lord would direct their hearts into God's love and Christ's perseverance (II Thess. 3:5). David, as he commissioned Solomon to build a temple for God, prayed that the Lord would direct the hearts of the people towards Him and that Solomon would keep His commandments, testimonies, and statutes to build the palace.

Paul told the early church that by holding fast, they would be delivered from the sting of death, which was swallowed up in victory, and that they would be raised immortal with Christ (I Cor. 15:54-58). The Hebrew prophet, Hosea, told the ancient Jews that they would be ransomed from the power of the grave and redeemed from death (13:14). Isaiah said the Lord would swallow up death in victory (25:8). In the Hebrew Bible, "the concept of victory is more than a military conquest. . . . Victory is ultimately something that comes from the Lord" (Elwell).

—*Deborah Markowitz Solan.*

Guiding the Superintendent

What does one do in the mean time? Paul's teachings and writings about the Second Coming had encouraged many of the people in the Thessalonian church. But his teachings had also left some confused. They were having trouble reconciling the soon return of Jesus with what appeared to be too long a delay. The Second Coming had not happened yet. Paul finished his second letter by urging the Thessalonians to continue doing what they were doing with even more resolve as they waited for Jesus to come again.

DEVOTIONAL OUTLINE

1. Stand firm (II Thess. 2:13-15). Paul reminded the Thessalonians that they were part of his thanksgiving to God. Despite their persecution and difficulties, they were loved by God, who had called and sanctified them. They were to stand firm and hold to those teachings ("traditions") he had passed on to them earlier. This would be the opposite of "shaken" and "troubled" (2:2).

2. Take courage (II Thess. 2:16-17). To build strong resolve in their hearts, the apostle reminded his readers that they were loved very much by both Jesus and God the Father. They had given them love and hope, which should bring them great comfort and establish them in good words and works.

3. Pray (II Thess. 3:1-5). While they were waiting for the Lord's return, there was much work to be done. Paul was a person of prayer, but he also coveted the prayers of others. Paul desired that they would continue to pray that the Lord's work would spread rapidly. He wanted them to pray that he be delivered from wicked men.

Paul believed strongly in the Lord's faithfulness (in contrast to some who were unfaithful) to establish them and protect them from evil. He was confident they would continue to obey the gospel.

Paul prayed that the Lord would direct their "hearts into the love of God, and into the patient waiting for Christ" (vs. 5). It seems that some were growing anxious in the face of the seemingly delayed return of the Lord.

Until the Lord returns, believers are encouraged to maintain their stand for the truth and their prayers for the Lord's work.

CHILDREN'S CORNER

text: **Matthew 21:1-16**

title: **Jesus Honored as God's Servant**

Jesus was heading to Jerusalem and the cross. In preparation for His entrance, He had arranged for a donkey and her colt to be available. Two of His disciples went and got the donkey and her colt, and Jesus then rode the colt into town. This was all planned many years before by God, and was foretold in Zechariah 9:9.

As they arrived at the city gates, the crowds started to spread their cloaks and lay out palm branches to line Jesus' path. It was at this point that the crowds started shouting the words of Psalm 118:26, recognizing Him as the Son of David, the Messiah. He was being honored as God's Son. From there He went to the temple and overturned the tables of those who were making money in the temple. The religious leaders' reaction was the opposite of the crowd. "They were sore displeased" (Matt. 21:15).

—Martin R. Dahlquist.

Scripture Lesson Text

GAL. 1:6 I marvel that ye are so soon removed from him that called you into the grace of Christ unto another gospel:

7 Which is not another; but there be some that trouble you, and would pervert the gospel of Christ.

8 But though we, or an angel from heaven, preach any other gospel unto you than that which we have preached unto you, let him be accursed.

9 As we said before, so say I now again, If any man preach any other gospel unto you than that ye have received, let him be accursed.

MATT. 28:1 In the end of the sabbath, as it began to dawn toward the first day of the week, came Mary Magdalene and the other Mary to see the sepulchre.

2 And, behold, there was a great earthquake: for the angel of the Lord descended from heaven, and came and rolled back the stone from the door, and sat upon it.

3 His countenance was like lightning, and his raiment white as snow:

4 And for fear of him the keepers did shake, and became as dead men.

5 And the angel answered and said unto the women, Fear not ye: for I know that ye seek Jesus, which was crucified.

6 He is not here: for he is risen, as he said. Come, see the place where the Lord lay.

7 And go quickly, and tell his disciples that he is risen from the dead; and, behold, he goeth before you into Galilee; there shall ye see him: lo, I have told you.

18 And Jesus came and spake unto them, saying, All power is given unto me in heaven and in earth.

19 Go ye therefore, and teach all nations, baptizing them in the name of the Father, and of the Son, and of the Holy Ghost:

20 Teaching them to observe all things whatsoever I have commanded you: and, lo, I am with you alway, even unto the end of the world. Amen.

NOTES

Remember the True Gospel!

(Easter)

Lesson Text: Galatians 1:6-9; Matthew 28:1-7, 18-20

Related Scriptures: II Corinthians 11:3-4; Acts 15:1-5;
Romans 2:25-29; Philippians 3:1-3

TIMES: possibly A.D. 48; A.D. 30

PLACES: from Syrian Antioch;
Jerusalem; Galilee

GOLDEN TEXT—"I marvel that ye are so soon removed from him that called you into the grace of Christ unto another gospel" (Galatians 1:6).

Introduction

Orvie Overall, Wildfire Schulte, and Three-Finger Brown—these were names everyone in Chicago knew and celebrated in 1908. These colorfully named characters were just three of the heroes who led the Cubs baseball team to its second straight World Series championship. Their names slowly faded from history, however. It was 108 years before the Cubs won another world championship.

Joy can be forgotten. The resurrection of Christ and the birth and growth of the church brought immense joy to the early believers. Yet within two decades, the church was being chal-

lenged by those teaching a twisted and perverted "gospel." The only antidote to false teaching is to remember, cherish, and cling to the gospel of Christ.

LESSON OUTLINE

I. **THE THREAT TO THE TRUE GOSPEL: FALSE TEACHING—Gal. 1:6-9**

II. **THE BASIS OF THE TRUE GOSPEL: THE RESURRECTION—Matt. 28:1-7**

III. **THE DISSEMINATION OF THE TRUE GOSPEL: THE GREAT COMMISSION—Matt. 28:18-20**

Exposition: Verse by Verse

THE THREAT TO THE TRUE GOSPEL: FALSE TEACHING

GAL. 1:6 I marvel that ye are so soon removed from him that called you into the grace of Christ unto another gospel:

7 Which is not another; but there

be some that trouble you, and would pervert the gospel of Christ.

8 But though we, or an angel from heaven, preach any other gospel unto you than that which we have preached unto you, let him be accursed.

9 As we said before, so say I now again, If any man preach any other gospel unto you than that ye have received, let him be accursed.

Perverting the gospel (Gal. 1:6-7). After a brief and fairly traditional introduction, the Apostle Paul turned to the real issues that necessitated his writing the book of Galatians. The letter is not addressed to a single congregation but to the churches of the province of Galatia. While there is some debate as to exactly what area is meant by "Galatia" (vs. 2), the most common position today is that it was in the southern part of Asia Minor, in what is today Turkey. If this is correct, the letter may have been sent to churches Paul founded on his first missionary journey (Acts 13—14).

The purpose for the letter is quite clear. The apostle was writing to counter certain teachers who were "perverting the gospel of Christ, and . . . attacking the authority and credibility of the apostle Paul" (Benware, *Survey of the New Testament,* Moody).

Paul begins by expressing his astonishment that the Galatian believers were so quickly turning away from the pure gospel of the "grace of Christ" (Gal. 1:6). The tense of "removed" suggests this was a present, ongoing reality. They were in the process of turning away but had not yet fully done so. Paul saw what was taking place and was determined to stop the movement and turn the Galatians back to the truth.

While Paul does not directly touch on the nature of the false teaching at this point, he hints that it was a repudiation of the grace of God. Paul believed the Galatians were genuinely called "into the grace of Christ" and saved. But they were now in danger of embracing what he called "another gospel."

In verse 7, Paul says this false gospel is "not another." It is important to understand that two different Greek words are translated "another" in verses 6 and 7. The word in verse 6 means "another of a different kind," while the word in verse 7 means "another of the same kind." The apostle thus was saying that the new teaching was utterly foreign to the true gospel. It was not a gospel of a similar sort to the truth. In fact, it was not a gospel at all.

The teachers who were troubling the Galatians were preaching a complete perversion of the true gospel. It was not what Paul had taught them, for, as we shall see, they were now being told that "trusting Christ for salvation was insufficient to save them . . . [This] was to pervert the gospel of Christ, for it would change its very character from that of a gift from God to one of merit derived from human works" (Kent, *The Freedom of God's Sons,* BMH).

Preserving the gospel (Gal. 1:8-9). Again, without yet delving into the details of the false teaching, Paul gives instruction on how the true gospel was to be preserved. "Gospel" literally means "good news." The good news of Christ is that He "gave himself for our sins, that he might deliver us from this present evil world" (vs. 4). This glorious blessing is a gift of God's grace. It is received by faith, not merited by our goodness or works.

This is what Paul had preached to the Galatians, and it was the message they had responded to in faith. Now Paul told them that even if he should change his message and preach something else to them, they should reject it. Indeed, even if an angel preached anything contrary to the gospel they had previously received, they must reject it.

The serious nature of altering or perverting the gospel is emphasized by Paul's statement regarding anyone who does this: "Let him be accursed" (vs. 8). Some Bible versions translate this, "Let him be eternally condemned." The word has the idea of being delivered up to divine wrath. Verse

9 repeats the thought. Only the gospel the Galatians originally received, the gospel of Christ, is the true gospel.

THE BASIS OF THE TRUE GOSPEL: THE RESURRECTION

MATT. 28:1 In the end of the sabbath, as it began to dawn toward the first day of the week, came Mary Magdalene and the other Mary to see the sepulchre.

2 And, behold, there was a great earthquake: for the angel of the Lord descended from heaven, and came and rolled back the stone from the door, and sat upon it.

3 His countenance was like lightning, and his raiment white as snow:

4 And for fear of him the keepers did shake, and became as dead men.

5 And the angel answered and said unto the women, Fear not ye: for I know that ye seek Jesus, which was crucified.

6 He is not here: for he is risen, as he said. Come, see the place where the Lord lay.

7 And go quickly, and tell his disciples that he is risen from the dead; and, behold, he goeth before you into Galilee; there shall ye see him: lo, I have told you.

Witnesses to the resurrection (Matt. 28:1-4). The resurrection of Christ is central to the gospel of grace (I Cor. 15:1-4). Paul, in fact, declares that if Christ did not rise from the dead, our faith is vain (vs. 17). His resurrection affirms that Jesus is the Son of God (Rom. 1:4), His sacrifice for sin is sufficient (cf. 4:25), and we who have trusted in Him have the sure hope of resurrection and eternal life (cf. I Cor. 15:21-23).

The historical account of the resurrection actually focuses on the aftermath of that great event—what people saw and how they responded to the realization that Jesus had risen from the dead. The first witnesses were several women. As it began to dawn on Sunday morning, following the Sabbath, Mary Magdalene and Mary the mother of James (Mark 16:1), along with some other women (Luke 24:10), came to Jesus' tomb, bringing spices to anoint His body (23:55—24:1).

Matthew 28:2 tells us that a great earthquake occurred. This was accompanied by the appearance of an angel, who rolled the stone back from the entrance to Jesus' tomb and sat on it. Jesus had already risen from the dead; the angel's action only made it obvious to anyone who came there that the tomb was empty.

The angel's radiant appearance revealed his heavenly origin. His face shone with the brilliance of lightning, and his clothing was "white as snow" (vs. 3). As was normally the case, the appearance of the angel struck fear in people. The first to see the angel were the guards who were stationed at the tomb (cf. 27:63-66). The Bible says that their fear was so great that they shook and became like dead men. This might mean they fainted into unconsciousness. They may well have regained consciousness and fled before the women arrived at the tomb.

Testimony to the resurrection (Matt. 28:5-6). Also before the women arrived, the angel who sat upon the stone had moved into the empty tomb, along with another angel, where they remained unseen until the women entered into it (Luke 24:2-5).

The women found the angels inside the tomb, but they did not find the body of Jesus. They were frightened (Mark 16:5), but the angel who spoke to them told them not to fear. He knew why they were there; they were seeking the crucified Jesus. They should have been looking for the resurrected Jesus.

The angel declared that Jesus was

not there but had risen from the dead. The fact that His resurrection matched what He had previously foretold on a number of occasions may mean that the angel's words were an implied rebuke to the women. Luke 24:8 tells us that with the angel's reminder, the women remembered Jesus' words.

The angel's words were even more of a rebuke to the lack of faith shown by Jesus' disciples, who were not there. They had repeatedly heard Jesus say He would suffer and die and be raised up the third day (Matt. 16:21; 17:22-23). Mark, in fact, states that Jesus said this "openly" (8:32), or plainly.

As further evidence of the Lord's resurrection, the angel invited the women to examine where His body had been placed. These women had seen where He had lain (Matt. 27:59-61; Luke 23:55); now they could plainly see His body was gone.

Confirmation of the resurrection (Matt. 28:7). With the evidence before them, reinforced by the words of the angel, the women could have little doubt that Jesus had in fact risen from the dead. While they were still in amazement and were even fearful (vs. 8), they knew they had to share the good news with the disciples.

The angel made sure they did just that. He told them to "go quickly, and tell his disciples that he is risen from the dead" (vs. 7). Specifically, the women were to tell the disciples that the Lord would go before them to Galilee and meet them there. This was another reminder of something Jesus had told them just a few nights earlier: "After I am risen again, I will go before you into Galilee" (26:32).

Of course, Jesus would appear on several occasions to His followers before they met again in Galilee. But it seems that it was in Galilee, where much of His earthly ministry had centered, that Jesus would appear repeatedly, instruct His disciples, and make a public appearance to more than five hundred brethren at once (I Cor. 15:6).

God made sure that the resurrection was well attested by many witnesses and "many infallible proofs" (Acts 1:3). By any laws of logic, the resurrection meets the standard of verifiable truth. We know, however, that even the most powerful evidence for the resurrection cannot make a person believe. Christian faith stands on historical fact, but it is still a matter of faith, and faith is a moral and personal choice. We can thank God that the Holy Spirit has worked in our hearts to lead us to faith in Christ, and we can pray that He will do the same in those with whom we share the true gospel of Christ.

THE DISSEMINATION OF THE TRUE GOSPEL: THE GREAT COMMISSION

18 And Jesus came and spake unto them, saying, All power is given unto me in heaven and in earth.

19 Go ye therefore, and teach all nations, baptizing them in the name of the Father, and of the Son, and of the Holy Ghost:

20 Teaching them to observe all things whatsoever I have commanded you: and, lo, I am with you alway, even unto the end of the world. Amen.

The power of the gospel (Matt. 28:18). While Jesus did meet with the disciples in Galilee on several occasions (cf. John 21:1-22; Acts 1:3), only one instance is recorded in Matthew. This took place on a mountain and may well have been when "he was seen of above five hundred brethren at once" (I Cor. 15:6).

Jesus declared that "all power," or authority, was given to Him "in heaven and in earth" (Matt. 28:18). He possesses "all power and right to exercise it" (Hendriksen, *The Gospel of Matthew,* Baker). This sovereign authority reflects His deity and was reinforced by the very fact He stood before His followers in resurrected glory. Jesus' declaration here also gave added substance to the commission He was about to give. His command was backed by His authority.

The preeminence of the gospel (Matt. 28:19-20). Verses 19-20 record what is commonly called the Great Commission. It is Jesus' command to His disciples to take the gospel into all the world. This commission is summarized in Mark 16:15: "Go ye into all the world, and preach the gospel to every creature." In Matthew more detail is given. The call is to "teach," or literally "make disciples," of "all nations."

Jesus' command has a worldwide scope. No nation or people group is to be ignored, for all need to hear about Jesus. Also, the work involves much more than simply eliciting verbal decisions from people. Yes, making disciples involves declaring the truth about Jesus Christ and the free gift of salvation He offers to all who believe in Him. But urging people to put their faith in Christ is not where the Great Commission ends; it is where it begins!

To truly carry out Christ's commission, we must make disciples, and this involves at least two actions. First, it involves bringing new believers to an obedient public commitment to Christ through baptism. The uniqueness of this public profession is emphasized in that it is done in the name of the Father, Son, and Holy Spirit, recognizing that the believer is identifying fully with the Triune God revealed in the Bible.

Second, making disciples involves an ongoing process of teaching believers biblical truth. This includes all that Jesus commanded, as well as the obligation to obey God's revealed truth. The Great Commission is given to all the church. As individuals, we might be engaged in one or more of these steps. Some of us are gifted at evangelism—explaining the gospel of grace. Others are better at coming alongside new believers and teaching them about obeying the Lord and following Him daily. But the church as a whole must be engaged in carrying out the Lord's commission. The present-tense verbs indicate it is an ongoing and never-ending process.

Jesus' final words are a great encouragement to all who seek to follow Him and make disciples of all nations. The One who has all power and authority will be with us to empower us and accomplish His work through us. And that promise extends to the very "end of the world" (Matt. 28:20), or more literally, "to the end of the age."

—*Jarl K. Waggoner.*

QUESTIONS

1. To whom was the book of Galatians addressed?

2. What astonished Paul about the Galatian believers?

3. What did the Galatians need to cling to?

4. Who were the first witnesses to Jesus' resurrection?

5. How did the guards respond to the appearance of the angel?

6. Of what did the angels remind the women?

7. What message did the angel give to the women for the disciples?

8. Where did Jesus meet the disciples when He gave them the Great Commission?

9. What must we do if we are to fulfill the Great Commission?

—*Jarl K. Waggoner.*

Preparing to Teach the Lesson

This week we begin a new series of lessons which deal with the meaning of the true gospel of our Lord Jesus. In this lesson we celebrate the risen Lord Jesus and the power of the unique gospel that is to be shared with the whole world.

TODAY'S AIM

Facts: to show how we dare not forget the priceless, true gospel.

Principle: to remember that Jesus called all of us through grace to partake of the true gospel.

Application: to not forget the truth of the gospel, lest we go astray.

INTRODUCING THE LESSON

In our last lesson, we learned that we are to hold fast to the teaching that we received. Our lesson this week shows us that we are to keep this true gospel always before us and never forget what it means to us. There are many voices in the world clamoring for our attention and even our worship, so if we are not careful, it is easy to go astray from the truth. There are many things that we do, even in church, that may not ring true to the gospel. So it is imperative that we be on guard.

DEVELOPING THE LESSON

1. Stay true to the gospel (Gal. 1:6-9). When Paul got reports about the Galatian church, he was shocked that they had so quickly departed from the fundamental gospel that he had taught them. They were now following beliefs and practices that were foreign to Christ's gospel. Help the class see that false gospels sometimes run very close to the true gospel and can therefore be very deceptive.

Help the class identify such teachings around us today. Ask why these are false.

The true gospel is the teaching about Jesus, who loved us so much that He called us into eternal life through His mercy and grace. Paul was upset that the Galatian church was practicing elements of a gospel that was false. They were following a different path that had strayed from the truth. The Christians there were listening to some in the church who were twisting the truth of the good news about Jesus. Paul reminds them that these people are dangerous.

Verse 8 gives us a very strong warning. If anyone teaches any false gospel, they are under the curse of God. A false gospel is defined here as anything that Paul had not taught them about Jesus. He warned them that they were not to listen to anyone, even someone from Paul's team or even an angel, if the original gospel message was distorted in any way. Remind the class that the gospel is the same for all time and will never ever change.

This is how important the truth of the gospel is today. In a world where we hear many distortions, it is important for us to know the fundamental truth of the gospel. There is no other way to be saved from our sins and to inherit eternal life than through the Lord Jesus Christ. The gospel stands out in truth. It is unique!

2. Tell people Jesus lives (Matt. 28:1-7). A gospel that is so precious must be shared with the world. Jesus did this through His disciples first. We read that Mary Magdalene and the other Mary, followers of Jesus, headed to Jesus' tomb early on Sunday morning. Then there was an earthquake, and an angel descended from heaven and sat on the stone that he had just rolled back from the tomb. It was a sign that our Lord Jesus had already risen from the dead.

The angel's appearance is described as being like bright lightning, and his clothes were white as snow. The appearance of the angel made the tomb guards tremble in fear and become "as dead men" (vs. 4). And the angel had the good news message. The women were not to be afraid. They were looking for Jesus, who had been crucified. He was not in the grave, for He had risen! To confirm that, they were invited into the empty tomb to see for themselves the amazing thing that had happened.

What a glorious message of redemption and hope! The gospel truth was being played out before them. They could hardly believe what they were told or what they saw. What Jesus had told them all along had come true! The angel then told the women to go and tell the other disciples what they had experienced. Jesus would be going ahead of them into Galilee. They would see Him there!

Remind the class that such a glorious message cannot be kept to oneself. The angel told the women about this. They were to tell the disciples. We are called to share this message with everyone. It is a great privilege we have been given.

3. Make disciples of all the world (Matt. 28:18-20). Jesus told His disciples that He had all power in heaven and earth. Because we believe in Him, we are to go out into all the world and proclaim this powerful gospel about Jesus Christ. We are to teach and baptize in the name of the Father, Son, and the Holy Spirit. This means that we are to make disciples who will follow everything Jesus taught. He will forever be with us in this global task.

Emphasize to your class the importance of the gospel. God has called us to share it with the whole world. There is no other gospel.

ILLUSTRATING THE LESSON

Jesus is risen from the dead! We are to share this with the world! False gospels will lead us away from salvation.

PROCLAIM THE TRUE GOSPEL

JESUS IS RISEN FROM THE DEAD

CONCLUDING THE LESSON

Leave the class with the idea that the gospel message is unique compared with any other religion in the world. Jesus is God Himself in the flesh. He died and rose again so that we might experience the abundant, eternal life in Him. There is no other message that brings eternal life! False gospels will lead to destruction. Jesus has promised to be with us forever. Challenge the class to remember this true gospel and to share it with the world.

ANTICIPATING THE NEXT LESSON

In our lesson next week, we learn where the Apostle Paul got his gospel. It came to him straight from our Lord Jesus.

—A. Koshy Muthalaly.

PRACTICAL POINTS

1. The Holy Bible is the only written record that inerrantly proclaims the truth of Christ (Gal. 1:6-7).
2. There is no other gospel than the one proclaimed by the Holy Scriptures. Those who claim otherwise will be cursed (vss. 8-9).
3. The Lord has used strange and catastrophic events to accomplish His will (Matt. 28:1-3).
4. The power of God can be completely overwhelming (vs. 4).
5. We should eagerly tell anyone who will listen that Jesus is alive (vss. 5-7).
6. God gives us the power to accomplish what He needs us to do (vss. 18-20).

—Charity G. Carter.

RESEARCH AND DISCUSSION

1. What are possible reasons that some people quickly fall away from following the Lord (Gal. 1:6-7)?
2. Why would people attempt to preach anything other than the gospel as outlined in the Bible (vss. 8-9)?
3. The men guarding the tomb fainted at the sight of angels. Discuss why Mary Magdalene and the other Mary did not faint (Matt. 28:4).
4. Discuss why the angel instructed the women to go quickly and deliver the message to the disciples (vs. 7). Why could they not take their time?
5. Describe how you intend to follow Jesus' command to go, teach all nations, and baptize them (vs. 19).

—Charity G. Carter.

ILLUSTRATED HIGH POINTS

Grace of Christ unto another gospel

They call it "bait and switch hacking." It is the practice of sneaking malicious programs onto the computers of unsuspecting down loaders through switching beneficial programs with nefarious ones. After receiving approval, the hacker advertises his program on a trusted site. Once listed, he then switches the link's destination to a more dangerous version of his program.

Satan is a bait and switch hacker. He is willing to let the gospel of grace be embraced by numerous seekers of righteousness, knowing that he intends to redirect their "link" to the false teachings of a perilous counterfeit: the "gospel" of works. Make very sure that, having subscribed to the true gospel, you have not been switched to a false one along the way.

Angel . . . preach any other gospel

The black crow, as the story goes, was happy and quite satisfied with his lot in life, but as he flew about one day, he happened to spot a beautiful white swan. "You must be the happiest bird in the world," he said to the swan. "You are so white."

"I was feeling I was the happiest bird alive," said the swan, "until I saw a parrot, which has two colors. I think the parrot is the happiest bird in this world."

So, the crow went to visit the parrot, but the parrot only complained that he was not a multicolored peacock. Amazingly, the peacock, in turn, said his beauty had only led to his confinement, and he longed to be as free as a simple black crow.

The gospel of Jesus Christ is plain and simple. It is faith in Christ alone, nothing else.

—Therese Greenberg.

Golden Text Illuminated

"I marvel that ye are so soon removed from him that called you into the grace of Christ unto another gospel" (Galatians 1:6).

A common problem existed in the early church that, unfortunately, continues among believers yet today.

A correct understanding of both grace and law, particularly how they fit together, is vital for living a confident and victorious life as a believer.

Furthermore, an accurate comprehension of the true gospel and the liberty that it brings greatly impacts our witness for Jesus Christ.

In the Old Testament, the law, or commandments, of God served as the system by which people worshipped and approached the Lord. Steeped in those laws and traditions, many Jews had a hard time grasping the gift of grace offered through Jesus Christ (cf. II Tim. 1:9-10).

Some of the Jewish people did accept the gospel; however, they misunderstood how this changed the role of the Law of Moses and their deeply held practices for them and others.

A particularly prominent belief among some was that Gentiles, or non-Jews, had to be circumcised and keep the Law of Moses (Acts 15:5) in order to be accepted by God. A huge debate began over this issue, which resulted in the matter being taken before the Council at Jerusalem to be resolved (Acts 15:1-2, 6).

The Galatian church was being influenced by this false teaching. The Apostle Paul, therefore, wrote a letter to them to clarify and remind them of the true gospel of Christ (cf. Gal. 1:3-5).

The Galatians had previously welcomed both Paul and the gospel he preached, yet they had become confused and began to follow a "different gospel" (cf. II Cor. 11:13). Of course, there is only one true gospel; therefore, their newly adopted beliefs were false and were no gospel at all (Gal. 1:6-7).

The golden text highlights Paul's response to the Galatians' apparent abandonment of the truth. He marvels at his friends' desertion of the God who chose them to inherit the grace and salvation of Christ.

The Galatians, by their own actions, had in a sense rejected God's gift of grace. This is not to suggest that they somehow forfeited the gift of eternal life; rather, this rejection could point to the forfeited rest God offered from their labors (cf. Heb. 4; 9-10).

Although Paul may have been frustrated, he certainly would not have been without empathy toward the struggle that was within the Galatians' hearts. Once he was enlightened by the true gospel himself, Paul lived free from the burden of the law he too once diligently served (Gal. 1:13-14), and he longed for others to do the same.

Jesus had already done everything needed to provide for and secure salvation for all people (Eph. 1:6, 13). How ludicrous it was, not to mention futile, for the church of Galatia to try to earn God's acceptance (cf. Heb. 10:1).

How many of us in the church today would admit to following another gospel? Undoubtedly, not many of us would. Yet, do we sometimes try to follow someone else's or our own spiritual to-do list?

If so, we, like the Galatians, would do well to remember what the true gospel is.

—*Christine M. Morrison.*

Heart of the Lesson

Does speaking to other people frighten you? Are you better at speaking one on one or in front of a crowd? Do you prefer to let someone talk for you? Fear of speaking publicly (stage fright) has been cited by some as the greatest fear in the world. It ranks above death and snakes.

God has commissioned each of us to proclaim the true gospel to all people. Some carry the gospel around the world, while others only voice His message in their neighborhoods. No matter where you are directed to talk about the Lord, there is no need for fear. God will prepare the way, just as He did for Paul and the disciples.

1. The gospel (Gal. 1:6-9). In his letter to the Galatians, Paul expressed concern that this church was turning its back on God. While in Galatia, the apostle had preached the true gospel. However, the Galatians had started to believe a contrary message and were being thrown into confusion and doubt. Too many of them were blindly following erroneous information.

Many of today's so-called Christian leaders distort the Word of God. There are preachers who omit parts of the Scriptures or even add information that suits their lifestyle. Sadly, there are men and women with little knowledge of the true gospel who follow such false teachers. They may be following out of ignorance, but they are still caught in their own sin. Those who lead them further astray, however, incur a much more severe judgment. How much better it is to know God's Word and not be led astray!

2. The fulfillment (Matt. 28:1-7). Mary Magdalene and the other Mary (the mother of James and Joses) arrived at the sepulchre early in the morning to anoint Jesus' body with fragrant oils. They were surprised to find the stone rolled away and an angel sitting on it. The angel explained that Christ was no longer in the tomb. He had risen! Then the angel commissioned them to announce the good news to the Eleven and to advise them to go to Galilee to meet Jesus. This was a fulfillment of what had been foretold in the Old Testament.

God keeps His promises. He fulfilled the messages proclaimed by the prophets of old. He went ahead of the women and provided an angel with a message of hope. He still directs people's lives and goes before them in all situations. God brings comfort and guidance. Individuals need to heed His instructions and call on His name.

3. The commission (Matt. 28:18-20). When Jesus met with the disciples in Galilee, He gave them a commission to preach the gospel to everyone. Previously, God's Word had been available only to the Jews, but now salvation had become accessible to all people through Jesus. While this would be an enormous undertaking, the disciples could step out in faith, knowing that God would guide and direct every step.

God has commissioned each believer to proclaim the good news. Romans 10:14 asks, "How shall they hear without a preacher?" If God directs us to approach someone about the Word of God, we do not need to fear. God is there and will bring to mind His Word to guide us. He can soften the unsaved person's heart to be receptive to the message. While there may not be immediate results, the seed will have been planted. We can continue to pray for that person and trust that there will be openness to the message of salvation in God's perfect time.

—Catherine Moore.

World Missions

Trains can get derailed, and so can people. The Galatians knew the truth, but they were drifting in a dangerous direction due to powerful lies that were infiltrating the church.

Believers are still in danger from the enemy's lies today—not just false ideas about the gospel, but also about ministry. False ideas about ministry can result in burnout, relationship conflict, and misrepresenting Christ to the world.

People can go into ministry for all kinds of reasons. Here are some:

1. They think it will gain God's favor, or even get them into heaven.

2. They hope to gain a higher status in their church, as missionaries and preachers are often placed on spiritual pedestals.

3. They care about making a difference and are drawn to those in need.

4. They are naturally ambitious and want to change the world for good.

5. They are running away from something.

6. They are bowing to pressure from others.

7. Nobody else is doing it.

8. The people who are doing it are not doing it right.

Some of the above motives are obvious derailments, and others are not wrong in themselves. However, just as the absence of the primary motive in any activity is bound to have a negative effect, any work of ministry based only on ourselves or earthly factors is not enough to sustain a genuine, long-term work for God.

Even compassion for others or ambition for God's work are not enough. They might produce results, but what if they do not? What about when the times get hard and the fruit does not show?

The problem with most of our typical motives is that they are based on ourselves—on how we feel or the opinions and circumstances around us. Any personal reason is fragile and subject to change when our feelings or circumstances do not meet our expectations.

Just as there is a true gospel, based on God the Father's gift of salvation through Jesus Christ, there are preeminently good reasons to be in ministry:

1. Obedience. Plain and simple, if God says go, we should go. Giving our lives to ministry out of obedience means we can continue on regardless of results, people's opinions or expectations, or even our own failings and weaknesses. We need not worry about finances or safety, because if God is the one who has directed us, He will be responsible to provide all that is needed for His work.

2. Love. Serving out of love for people is important but not the complete story. People will disappoint us. Going out of love for Jesus Christ and His command to reach the world is enough to sustain us when those around us fall short of our hopes and expectations. Love allows us to give without needing love returned or even a positive response. Love gives us strength to endure through sacrifice, rejection, and even persecution.

Let us examine our own hearts to make sure we are not serving God for the wrong reasons. When we have set aside ourselves (having no confidence in the flesh—Phil. 3:3), we can then ask the Lord to show us His will for us, which we are to obey in love, resulting in ministry that will truly give God glory.

—*Kimberly Rae.*

The Jewish Aspect

In the book of Galatians, Paul addressed the question of whether Gentiles were obligated to follow Mosaic Law to be a part of the Christian community. Justification by faith rather than by the works of the law was being challenged by Jewish legalizers from Jerusalem who insisted that Gentile believers in Christ must keep the law if they expected to be perfect before God. When Paul learned that this teaching had begun to penetrate the Galatian churches, he wrote a letter to reprove the Galatians for their acceptance of this legalistic error.

When he said, "I marvel that ye are so soon removed from him that called you into the grace of Christ unto another gospel" (Gal. 1:6), the word used for "removed" was the Greek word for deserting—*metatithemi.* "The gospel they were turning to was one of 'another kind.' The Greek word used for 'another' (*heteron*) in this instance means another of a different kind. It was not a gospel (good news) at all but another version of works gospel (bad news). It was a gospel from which the good news of free grace had been deceitfully removed (cf. Acts 20:24)" ("J. Gerrish. Galatians: The Letter of Christian Liberty," www.wordofgodtoday.com).

The legalizers said that the Gentile believers needed to be circumcised. The early church had its roots in Judaism, and Paul had circumcised Timothy to incline the Jewish people toward the gospel of salvation through Christ the Messiah (Acts 16:3). Ritual circumcision of male children on the eighth day of life is a ceremony known as *brit milah* in Hebrew. It is a commandment from God that Jews were obligated to follow (Gen. 17:13). The false teaching of the Jewish legalizers was that since circumcision was a sign of the covenant between God and Abraham, all male believers in Messiah needed to be circumcised in order to be a son of Abraham.

The Hebrew Bible, however, spoke of another aspect of circumcision. When the Lord spoke to Moses about the essence of the law, He told Israel to "circumcise therefore the foreskin of your heart, and be no more stiffnecked" (Deut. 10:16). The ancient Jews were told that the Lord would circumcise their heart, and the heart of their seed, to enable them to love Him (Deut. 30:6). Paul reminded the church in Rome, "For he is not a Jew, which is one outwardly; neither is that circumcision, which is outward in the flesh: but he is a Jew, which is one inwardly; and circumcision is that of the heart, in the spirit, and not in the letter; whose praise is not of men, but of God" (Rom. 2:28-29).

Paul told the Galatians that the requirement of physical circumcision for non-Jews was a perversion of the gospel of grace. He said that the Gentile Christians did not need to adhere to all of the Mosaic Law, particularly circumcision. He emphasized the importance of freedom for the non-Jewish believers from many of the ceremonial commandments of the Torah. The Galatians needed to be reminded that the true gospel was that a man is not justified by the works of the law (Gal. 2:16).

Galatians has been called the *Magna Carta* of spiritual emancipation by many Bible commentators. It declares that "Christ hath redeemed us from the curse of the law, being made a curse for us: . . . That the blessing of Abraham might come on the Gentiles through Jesus Christ; that we might receive the promise of the Spirit through faith" (Gal. 3:13-14).

—*Deborah Markowitz Solan.*

Guiding the Superintendent

For centuries Christians have celebrated their faith with two special days—Christmas and Easter. While Christmas celebrates Jesus' birth, Easter is a time to reflect on Jesus' resurrection. The lesson this week will examine the message and the events of Easter.

DEVOTIONAL OUTLINE

1. The message (Gal. 1:6-9). Because the gospel is so simple (believing that Jesus was raised from the dead) many over the years have tried to add something to it. This usually involves adding some type of works to the simple message of the cross.

Not long after Paul had established some churches in Galatia, false teachers were coming into the area and messing with the gospel.

Unfortunately, many apparently were accepting their additions. Paul wrote a letter of extreme concern in which he expressed his astonishment that they had so quickly deserted the gospel.

The gospel is not Paul's invention, but a message from Christ. In the end, any addition to the gospel is bad news, not good news, for it makes the salvation message one of impossible human effort.

2. The event (Matt. 28:1-7). The resurrection of Jesus is presented in its most simple form in Matthew. There was a great earthquake that brought fear to the posted guards.

Two Marys had decided to visit Jesus' tomb. There they were confronted by an angel who told them not to fear but to go tell Jesus' disciples to meet Him in Galilee.

3. The command (Matt. 28:18-20). The disciples did go to Galilee and to the prearranged place to meet Jesus. Jesus had a commission for them. They were to take the message of the resurrection to the world.

Specifically, Jesus commissioned them to go and make disciples of all people. The gospel is a world thing, not just a message for Jewish people. They were to make disciples by baptizing people and instructing them in Jesus' name.

CHILDREN'S CORNER

text: **Matthew 28:1-10, 16-20**
title: **God's Servant Raised to Life**

The greatest proof that Jesus was everything He claimed to be is His resurrection from the dead. The Matthew resurrection account is as sublime as it is simple. It all started when two Marys went early on the Sabbath morning to see the tomb of Jesus.

Suddenly there was a great earthquake, and an angel appeared from heaven and rolled the stone away. This was too much for the guards, who appeared to have been scared unconscious.

The angel encouraged the women not to be afraid and to "come, see" (Matt. 28:6) where Jesus had laid. They were then instructed to go tell the disciples to head to Galilee to see the risen Lord.

With a mixture of fear and joy the women headed out on their task. It was then that Jesus himself appeared to them with the same message: "Be not afraid: go tell my brethren" (vs. 10).

The women went to the disciples, and they soon appeared at the prearranged place in Galilee. Jesus appeared to them and commissioned them with a message. They were to take His message to all nations, baptize people, and teach all that Jesus had taught them.

—*Martin R. Dahlquist.*

Scripture Lesson Text

GAL. 1:10 For do I now persuade men, or God? or do I seek to please men? for if I yet pleased men, I should not be the servant of Christ.

11 But I certify you, brethren, that the gospel which was preached of me is not after man.

12 For I neither received it of man, neither was I taught it, but by the revelation of Jesus Christ.

13 For ye have heard of my conversation in time past in the Jews' religion, how that beyond measure I persecuted the church of God, and wasted it:

14 And profited in the Jews' religion above many my equals in mine own nation, being more exceedingly zealous of the traditions of my fathers.

15 But when it pleased God, who separated me from my mother's womb, and called me by his grace,

16 To reveal his Son in me, that I might preach him among the heathen; immediately I conferred not with flesh and blood:

17 Neither went I up to Jerusalem to them which were apostles before me; but I went into Arabia, and returned again unto Damascus.

18 Then after three years I went up to Jerusalem to see Peter, and abode with him fifteen days.

19 But other of the apostles saw I none, save James the Lord's brother.

20 Now the things which I write unto you, behold, before God, I lie not.

21 Afterwards I came into the regions of Syria and Cilicia;

22 And was unknown by face unto the churches of Judaea which were in Christ:

23 But they had heard only, That he which persecuted us in times past now preacheth the faith which once he destroyed.

24 And they glorified God in me.

NOTES

The Source of Paul's Gospel

Lesson Text: Galatians 1:10-24

Related Scriptures: Matthew 28:19-20; Jeremiah 1:4-5;
I Corinthians 15:1-11; Ephesians 3:1-8

TIME: possibly A.D. 48   PLACE: from Syrian Antioch

GOLDEN TEXT—"But I certify you, brethren, that the gospel which was preached of me is not after man. For I neither received it of man, neither was I taught it, but by the revelation of Jesus Christ" (Galatians 1:11-12).

Introduction

If a church is large and growing, many Christians readily claim that God is "blessing" it. The implication seems to be that a small church does not have God's blessing and is not pleasing to Him. In fact, the size of a church congregation does not in itself say anything about how pleasing it is to God. Whether large, small, or something in between, a church may be honoring to the Lord in its teaching and service, or it may be dishonoring Him with compromise, error, worldly living, and impure motives.

It is a grave error to judge churches or individuals by such superficial standards as size, power, and influence. The real measure of churches and Christians is whether they are true to the gospel of Christ, consistently applying God's Word.

The Apostle Paul told the Galatian believers to cling to the gospel of grace they had received from him and not listen to anyone who taught something different. But how could they be sure the gospel Paul proclaimed was the true gospel? What gave him the authority to declare it so? Such questions were raised by certain teachers who were trying to introduce a different gospel in Galatia.

LESSON OUTLINE

I. PAUL'S AUTHORITY—
   Gal. 1:10-12

II. PAUL'S PAST—Gal. 1:13-14

III. PAUL'S CALL—Gal. 1:15-16

IV. PAUL'S JOURNEY—Gal. 1:17-24

Exposition: Verse by Verse

PAUL'S AUTHORITY

GAL. 1:10 For do I now persuade men, or God? or do I seek to please men? for if I yet pleased men, I should not be the servant of Christ.

11 But I certify you, brethren, that the gospel which was preached of me is not after man.

12 For I neither received it of man, neither was I taught it, but by the revelation of Jesus Christ.

A servant of Christ (Gal. 1:10). Paul's rhetorical questions in verse 10 indicate he was answering accusations made against him. "Persuade" is probably used here in the sense of gaining favor or approval of men. Paul was countering the argument that he was "changing his message to win the favor of whatever audience he chanced to have at the time" (Kent, *The Freedom of God's Sons,* BMH).

Paul's critics, often called Judaizers, were trying to impose the requirements of the Mosaic Law upon Christians, even Gentile Christians, as we will learn. They were probably charging that Paul preached the necessity of the law among Jews but then dropped the Mosaic requirements when preaching to Gentiles in order to win their favor.

"If I yet pleased men, I should not be the servant of Christ," Paul writes. His very strong rejection of those who presented "another gospel" (vs. 6) was evidence that he was not seeking to please anyone but Christ and to uphold His gospel. Paul's allegiance was to Christ as His servant; he felt no obligation to please people for the sake of personal advantage.

Taught by Christ (Gal. 1:11-12). Paul emphatically states that his message was not something people just made up. He preached the gospel not because it was popular but because it was of divine origin. The gospel itself has divine authority, and thus he could preach it with authority and without compromise.

In verse 12 Paul affirms that he did not receive the gospel from man, either by oral tradition ("received") or by academic instruction ("taught") (Ridderbos, *The Epistle of Paul to the Churches of Galatia,* Eerdmans). Rather, it came through direct revelation from Jesus Christ. Paul simply preached what he had received "by the revelation of Jesus Christ."

Paul's experience was unique. The Lord communicated the gospel directly to him. He then, in turn, communicated it to the Galatians and many others. For us the gospel is revealed through the written revelation of God: the Bible. And through the work of the Holy Spirit, faithful teachers have helped us understand it. The point we should always keep in mind, however, is that ultimately the gospel is of divine origin. We are to communicate it to others as Paul did, but we are never to alter it to make it more acceptable to people. Paul certainly did not.

PAUL'S PAST

13 For ye have heard of my conversation in time past in the Jews' religion, how that beyond measure I persecuted the church of God, and wasted it:

14 And profited in the Jews' religion above many my equals in mine own nation, being more exceedingly zealous of the traditions of my fathers.

To bolster his argument that the gospel he preached did not have its source in any man, Paul briefly recounts his past in Judaism. He reminds his readers that they were well aware of his former life in the "Jews' religion" (vs. 13). He had been a relentless persecutor of Christ's church. The word translated "wasted" means "to ruin" or "destroy." It is the same word used of Paul's efforts in Acts 9:21 and translated "destroyed."

Paul's goal had been to utterly destroy the newborn church. This is borne out historically in Acts 9:1-2 and is affirmed by Paul himself elsewhere (cf. I Cor. 15:9; Phil. 3:6).

Furthermore, Paul states that he advanced beyond his peers in his commitment to Judaism and was extremely zealous for the traditions of his forefathers. These traditions probably refer to rabbinic interpretations and additions to the Law of Moses passed down through the generations. They were of primary concern to the Pharisees, of whom Paul was one (Phil. 3:5), but they often brought Jesus' rebuke because they overrode God's commands (cf. Matt. 15:1-9).

Zeal is an admirable quality, but only when it is wedded to the truth. Paul had been zealous for that which came from man, not God. His former deep commitment to Jewish teaching and tradition highlights the fact that the gospel of Christ he now preached had not come from others.

PAUL'S CALL

15 But when it pleased God, who separated me from my mother's womb, and called me by his grace,

16 To reveal his Son in me, that I might preach him among the heathen; immediately I conferred not with flesh and blood.

The outlook and teaching of one so committed to Judaism could be changed only by a direct act of God, and indeed that is what happened when Christ appeared to Saul (as he was then known) on the road to Damascus (Acts 9:3-6). However, Paul recognized that the work of God in his life actually began long before that moment.

The apostle writes that by God's good pleasure, he was "separated" from his mother's womb (Gal. 1:15). This means that God sovereignly chose Paul before he was born and set him apart for a special work, much as He did Jeremiah (Jer. 1:5).

God's plan for us begins before we are born and extends into eternity. Paul speaks of this sovereign, yet mysterious, work of God in Ephesians 1:4-5: "He hath chosen us in him before the foundation of the world, that we should be holy and without blame before him in love: having predestinated us unto the adoption of children by Jesus Christ to himself, according to the good pleasure of his will."

God's unique plan for Paul began

before he was born; it came to fruition on the Damascus road, when God called him through His grace (Gal. 1:15). God's grace, or undeserved favor, was evident in His calling of Paul. He had done—and could do—nothing to merit the gracious salvation of Christ. In fact, he was on the way to persecute Christ's church when the Lord confronted him.

The gospel Paul preached is the gospel of grace. This gospel leaves no room for human merit. No work, no lawkeeping, no human effort, can earn salvation; it is solely of the grace of God humbly received by faith. And this is why Paul was under attack. The Jewish teachers were insisting that keeping the law was necessary for salvation and sanctification.

There on the Damascus road when the risen Christ appeared to Paul, God revealed His Son *in* him (vs. 16). This speaks of the inward revelation to Paul. "Through his outward vision of Christ, he became blind; but in his inward experience, he initially recognized Jesus Christ to be the Son of God" (Gromacki, *Stand Fast in Liberty,* Kress). This was the moment of Paul's rebirth as a believer in Christ. It came by divine revelation, not by human means.

The purpose of this revelation to Paul was not only that he might be saved but also that he "might preach [Christ] among the heathen." The Greek word for "heathen" is the word typically translated "Gentiles," meaning non-Jews. While Paul certainly preached the gospel to his Jewish brethren, and this was part of his commission (Acts 9:15), his ministry was primarily to the Gentiles (Gal. 2:7-9). But his message to both groups was the same pure gospel of grace in Christ.

At this point, the apostle returns to the thought of Galatians 1:12. He had not received the gospel from men. He had been devoutly committed to the Judaism of his day before his conversion and even up until the moment of his conversion. It was only when confronted by the living Christ that the gospel of grace was revealed to him. Furthermore, Paul says that immediately after meeting Christ, he did not confer with "flesh and blood" (vs. 16), that is, people. Nobody instructed him or gave him orders. His message and commission came directly from Christ.

PAUL'S JOURNEY

17 Neither went I up to Jerusalem to them which were apostles before me; but I went into Arabia, and returned again unto Damascus.

18 Then after three years I went up to Jerusalem to see Peter, and abode with him fifteen days.

19 But other of the apostles saw I none, save James the Lord's brother.

20 Now the things which I write unto you, behold, before God, I lie not.

21 Afterwards I came into the regions of Syria and Cilicia;

22 And was unknown by face unto the churches of Judaea which were in Christ:

23 But they had heard only, That he which persecuted us in times past now preacheth the faith which once he destroyed.

24 And they glorified God in me.

Arabia and Damascus (Gal. 1:17). Paul now begins to recount his journeys following his conversion to Christ. First, he says that he did not go up to Jerusalem, where the apostles were. Again, this testifies to the fact that he began preaching the gospel even before meeting the apostles. He did not have their input.

This, of course, is not to say that his teaching differed from that of the apostles. Paul is simply arguing that his authority and his gospel, both of which were being questioned by the Judaizers, came directly from the Lord and were not dependent on the other apostles.

Instead of going to Jerusalem, Paul had gone into Arabia and then returned to Damascus. His time in Arabia is not mentioned in Acts. Some suggest it came between Acts 9:19 and 20 before he began preaching in the Damascus synagogues. Others believe it fits between verses 22 and 23 of Acts 9.

How long Paul was in Arabia or even his precise location is unknown. Arabia could refer to any part of the Arabian kingdom, which extended from the Sinai Peninsula far to the south to near Damascus.

The purpose of Paul's time in Arabia is not stated. It is likely, though, that it was a time of meditation, as he rethought all he had been taught through the Old Testament Scriptures in light of the revelation he received in Christ.

Jerusalem (Gal. 1:18-20). Finally, three years after his conversion, Paul went up to Jerusalem, where he met Peter and stayed with him for fifteen days. His purpose was to visit Peter and become acquainted with him.

Acts 9:26-30 describes this visit. Because of Paul's history as a persecutor of the church, the believers in Jerusalem were suspicious of him at first. Barnabas, however, interceded for him and introduced him to the apostles. Paul even spoke boldly for the Lord Jesus in Jerusalem. There is no hint in Acts that he was looking to be taught by or given apostleship by Peter, and that seems to be the implication in Galatians 1:18.

Aside from Peter, Paul met no other apostles except James. This was not James the disciple of Jesus, but rather the half brother of Jesus. James apparently did not become a believer in Christ until after the resurrection (cf. I Cor. 15:7), but he quickly rose to prominence in the early church (cf. Acts 1:14; 12:17; 15:13; Gal. 2:9).

While James was not one of the

twelve apostles, he may have been considered an apostle in a broader sense. It is unclear whether the wording in Galatians 1:19 is describing James as an apostle or simply as another leader in addition to the Apostle Peter.

Paul briefly pauses here to assert that what he wrote was indeed true. "What Paul has just written was not merely a biographical statement, but was prompted by accusations against him. He has answered the charges by explaining that he had only the most meager contacts with the Twelve up to this time . . . Furthermore, his chief contacts at Jerusalem had been two men whose emphasis was particularly Jewish—Peter and James! They would hardly have provided him with a different gospel which misrepresented the Mosaic Law!" (Kent).

Syria and Cilicia (Gal. 1:21-24). After his brief time in Jerusalem, Paul's ministry shifted far to the north in the provinces of Syria and Cilicia. His hometown of Tarsus was in Cilicia, and it became his chief place of ministry (cf. Acts 9:30).

Again, the apostle emphasizes that he had little contact with Jerusalem and the surrounding area of Judea. In fact, he was unknown to the churches in Judea at that time. All anyone down there heard about him was that he who had persecuted them was now preaching the very faith he had tried to destroy, and they praised God because of him. They could rightly praise God, for Paul preached the same gospel to the Gentiles in the north that the Jewish believers of Judea had embraced.

Paul was under attack, ironically charged with perverting the gospel of Christ by those who were themselves promoting a different gospel by imposing the Mosaic Law on Christians. Paul was forced to defend himself in order to defend the gospel he preached. Those who questioned Paul's authority had to deal with the truth that Christ had supernaturally called him and revealed the gospel to him directly. He had not sought the instruction of the apostles regarding the gospel of Christ, but neither did his teaching contradict that of the apostles.

Warren Wiersbe succinctly states, "In the light of Paul's conduct, his conversion, and his contacts, how could anybody accuse him of borrowing or inventing either his message or his ministry? Certainly he *did* receive his Gospel by a revelation from Jesus Christ. Therefore, we must be careful what we do with this Gospel, for it is not the invention of men, but the very truth of God" (*Be Free,* Cook).

—*Jarl K. Waggoner.*

QUESTIONS

1. Of what was Paul being accused?
2. Who were Paul's critics, and what was the false gospel they were promoting?
3. Where does Paul say he received the gospel?
4. How does he describe his former life in Judaism?
5. How does the apostle affirm God's work in his life even before his conversion?
6. How did Paul come to recognize Jesus Christ as the Son of God?
7. To what specific ministry did the Lord call Paul?
8. Where did Paul first go after his conversion, and why?
9. For what reason did he go to Jerusalem three years after his conversion?
10. How was Paul known to the believers in Judea, and how did they respond to this knowledge?

—*Jarl K. Waggoner.*

Preparing to Teach the Lesson

Last week we talked about the uniqueness of the true gospel. This week we turn to the real source of this Truth, our Lord Jesus Himself, who is the embodiment of all divine truth. If Jesus is our source, then we can never go wrong.

TODAY'S AIM

Facts: to show that the source of Paul's gospel is Jesus Himself.

Principle: to remember that the gospel comes by revelation straight from the heart of God.

Application: to trust in this gospel, because by doing so we cannot go wrong because it reveals God's only way for our salvation.

INTRODUCING THE LESSON

There are many people coming to our doors these days. Many such people are salesmen. It is hard to know whom to trust. We do not know what they are selling, and it is best to always ask for valid identification before dealing with them. In our lesson this week Paul states that the gospel he had come to know is the truth because it came to him directly from our Lord Jesus Christ. This was done through direct revelation to him. Paul knew that this gospel could never be wrong.

DEVELOPING THE LESSON

1. The gospel: direct revelation from God (Gal. 1:10-12). Paul starts off this section by stating that he is not a people pleaser. It is easy for those who are in ministry to compromise because we feel the importance of pleasing people. Paul reminds us that if he had been this way, it would have discredited him as a servant of Christ. We cannot please both people and

God. Our goal must be to please our Lord Jesus as we seek to serve Him daily.

Paul told the Galatian church that the gospel he preached was genuine because it did not come to him through mere human agency but through divine revelation straight from Jesus. The gospel was not taught to him like an academic exercise. It had to be received in his heart as the truth. It came straight from God. God's Spirit regenerates our spirit and makes His truth real to us.

This is a good time to discuss the many ways in which God shows His truth to us. Paul says that he received the gospel "by the revelation of Jesus Christ" (Gal. 1: 12). Talk about what this means. Ask your students to share how they came to know Jesus.

2. The gospel: superior to all religious tradition (Gal. 1:13-14). Paul had tried all the methods of finding favor with God that Judaism offered. Then he discovered the true gospel. He recounted his earlier paths of religious tradition and how he even persecuted the Christians to show his zeal for religion. It would be hard to find another Jew as zealous as Paul was. But he found that following religious traditions did not satisfy the deepest longings of his heart.

Emphasize to the class that ultimately only Jesus can meet our deepest needs. We must turn to the true gospel that He has authored. Help your students to ask whether some have missed the source of the true gospel by relying on religious tradition. Getting to know Jesus personally is the true way to spiritual transformation. We have to trust Jesus personally as Lord and Saviour to have that change happen.

3. The gospel: pointing to the source of transformation (Gal. 1:15-24). Paul declares that Jesus, the source of this gospel, is the one who transformed him. Something miraculous happened on that Damascus road. In His mercy, God set Paul apart from before he was born to serve Him. He called Paul through grace and saved Him. As a persecutor of Christians, Paul did not deserve this commission, but God graciously chose him in spite of this. He is likewise gracious to those whom He chooses today.

Help your students to see the significance of verse 16. God revealed Jesus to Paul in a very special way and assigned him to be a missionary to the Gentiles. Ask the class to identify the verbs in these verses that describe the acts of God toward Paul. Revealing the truth of the gospel is God's work in us.

Paul asserted that he did not consult with anyone—no apostles, church leaders, or others—after his conversion. He took to the desert to be by himself with God to be divinely prepared for his gracious calling. Remind your students that God often uses the most unlikely people for His work.

Three years later, after a time in Arabia, Paul finally met with Peter and James, the brother of Jesus. It was hard for Paul to convince the churches in Syria, Cilicia, and Judea, of his calling because they had not yet seen him after his encounter with the true gospel. He who once persecuted Christians and sought to destroy the faith was now himself proclaiming Jesus! Once they knew the truth, they praised God for Paul. The change in him was indeed real.

Have your students discuss how personally knowing the source of the gospel changes a person from within as it did with Paul. True transformation comes when we meet Jesus face to face and Spirit to spirit.

ILLUSTRATING THE LESSON

The illustration shows that the gospel has been given to us by direct revelation from our Lord Jesus in the Scriptures.

CONCLUDING THE LESSON

Ask your students to think about how God reveals Himself to us deep within our souls to bring about transformation in our lives. Paul knew everything there was to know about formal religion, but it left him empty inside. The gospel is about what Jesus does in our hearts and lives as we respond to what He has already done for us on the cross.

When God speaks to us, we must be open to listening to Him. He speaks to us through His Spirit. The Spirit shows us who Jesus is.

ANTICIPATING THE NEXT LESSON

In our lesson next week, we learn that the true gospel was foretold long before the earthly life of Jesus. It was earnestly looked forward to by those who hoped for salvation from sin.

—A. Koshy Muthalaly.

PRACTICAL POINTS

1. Our aim should be to serve Christ, not please people (Gal. 1:10).
2. The gospel of Jesus has the power to change lives like nothing else can (vss. 11-12).
3. The Lord can use anyone who humbles himself and joins the family of God (vss. 13-14).
4. When God moves upon our hearts, we should quickly respond to His call (vss. 15-17).
5. We should spend time with seasoned believers (vss. 18-20).
6. We should celebrate when people who were strongly opposed to Jesus become His followers (vss. 23-24).

—*Charity G. Carter.*

RESEARCH AND DISCUSSION

1. Why is it not always possible to be a people pleaser and a servant of God simultaneously (Gal. 1:10)?
2. Discuss why it is extremely important for people to know that the gospel being preached is of God and not of man (vss. 11-12).
3. Who could be a modern-day equivalent of Paul before his conversion? Discuss people who are completely outspoken against the church and the things of God (vss. 13-14).
4. Why did Paul take immediate action following his conversion (vs. 16)?
5. Describe what Paul and Peter may have discussed in their two weeks together (vs. 18).
6. How might the Christian community respond if the individuals mentioned in question three came to know the Lord (vs. 23-24)?

—*Charity G. Carter.*

ILLUSTRATED HIGH POINTS

Do I seek to please men?

Consider the father and son who walked happily down the road to market with their faithful donkey in tow. Along the way, they met a couple who inquired, "Why are you walking when you have a perfectly good donkey?

So they put the boy on the donkey and continued. After a while, they met another couple, who chided the boy for his "selfishness." "Shame on you," they scolded, "let your tired old father ride."

With this, they switched. Soon, however, another traveler reproached the father for being "lazy," whereupon the boy climbed up with his dad.

The next traveler criticized the duo for "cruelty to animals," so they dismounted and began to carry the donkey, provoking only laughter when they arrived to market. Spooked by the laughter, the donkey bolted.

Living to please men is a self-destructive, spiritually ill-advised undertaking (cf. Luke 6:25; John 15:19).

Conferred not with flesh and blood

Alexander Dumas, author of the highly-regarded novel "The Three Musketeers," took it upon himself to rid France of a creation which he considered to be an eyesore, waste of government resources, and national embarrassment. To this end, he circulated the following indignant petition: "We, the writers, painters, sculptors, architects and lovers of the beauty of Paris, do protest with all our vigor and all our indignation, in the name of French taste and endangered French art and history, against the useless and monstrous Eiffel Tower."

The opinions of men are constantly shifting. But the opinion of God is pure and incorruptible.

—*Therese Greenberg.*

Golden Text Illuminated

"But I certify you, brethren, that the gospel which was preached of me is not after man. For I neither received it of man, neither was I taught it, but by the revelation of Jesus Christ" (Galatians 1:11-12).

One thing is certain: if the Apostle Paul were living among us today, he would not be known as a people pleaser. In other words, he would not overly concern himself with gaining the approval of others.

There was only one that Paul was committed to pleasing (Gal. 1:10): the God who loved and gave himself for him. Once converted, Paul lived a life of deep gratitude and humility that flowed from a transformed heart touched by grace (cf. I Cor. 15:3-4, 9-10).

Before Paul was converted, he was known as Saul, and he lived in a dramatically different way (cf. Acts 9:13-14; Gal. 1:14). Blinded by pride and separated from God, Saul immersed himself in the study of and strict adherence to the laws and traditions of the Jewish faith.

Though Saul sat under some of the most reputable religious teachers of that time (Acts 22:3) and worked hard to live up to the law's demands, his life was still lacking the fulfilling purpose for which God created him (cf. Gal. 1:15-16).

Then, in God's perfect timing, He revealed Himself to the zealous young persecutor (Acts 9:3-6; Eph. 3:1-8). Saul became a chosen vessel of the Lord!

The true gospel radically changed Paul's life, something that mere intellect and outward behavior never had done.

Having already preached to the Galatian church with a positive response, Paul knew that the believers nonetheless were hearing false reports. Many were attacking his credibility.

Therefore, Paul wrote a letter to the church, contrasting his former life with his new life (Gal. 1:13-16). His dramatic transformation in itself bore witness to the fact that the source of his message could only be explained by revelation from Jesus Christ!

Fully convinced in his own heart of the message he received from the Lord, Paul never went to others for their opinion about what he was told (Gal. 1:16-17). He simply obeyed without hesitation.

The golden text tells us that Paul wanted to prove to his fellow believers that the good news he preached was not given to him through flesh and blood; it was not a message that was created by another man and then given or taught to him. It was given by God Himself.

Why did it make such a difference for Paul to point out the source of his gospel?

Think about that question in your own life. What makes you want to listen to a particular pastor or Bible teacher? The most essential thing surely is that what he says lines up with what the Bible says.

All believers have been given spiritual illumination, that inner testimony from the Holy Spirit regarding the true gospel (Rom. 8:16). Beware of teachers who depart from biblical truth.

If people tell you that the gospel is not enough to transform someone or grant eternal life, tell them they need to consider the credibility of their source. Merely human ideas cannot stand against God's truth. Jesus makes all things new (II Cor. 5:17)!

—*Christine M. Morrison.*

Heart of the Lesson

God has placed a calling on every Christian's life. All believers have a work to do for the Lord, whether it is preaching the Word or sweeping the floor. One individual I knew rang the bell at the start of each church service. He diligently made sure the bell rang at the precise time—not one second before or after. Like this man, Paul faithfully heeded the call that was given to him by Jesus Christ.

1. Paul's testimony (Gal. 1:10-14). Paul posed a rhetorical question: Should I please man or God? He went on to say that his knowledge and his calling came directly from Jesus Christ. Previously, Paul had tormented Christians. He was well schooled in the Jewish religion and had been a diligent student of the law with no equals. God had completely changed his life so that he now ministered to his previous foes—the believers.

Whom do Christians seek to honor—man or God? Matthew 6:24 says, "No man can serve two masters." If your master is man, you will always fall short. Man places restrictions on all things and often provides no forgiveness. God, on the other hand, is loving and kind. While man makes mistakes, God is unerring in His judgment and will always welcome the repentant sinner home. His arms provide comfort and shelter.

2. Paul's travels (Gal. 1:15-19). After Paul received his calling, he needed time alone to contemplate his mission. He probably spent many hours communing with the Lord. Therefore, he traveled to Arabia and then back to Damascus. Three years later, he went to Jerusalem to see Peter. The only other apostle he saw during this time was Jesus' brother James.

When God calls someone to a ministry, each individual deals with the issue differently. Some like to consult with others who have great experience or knowledge. Others like to emulate Paul and spend time alone communing with God. Neither is wrong. It is good to confer with Bible scholars and persons of faith, but it is equally important to spend time alone with God. While God ultimately provides our vision and direction, He uses educated, godly servants to mentor and provide insight. Finding the best balance is an individual decision. However, it is essential to accept the call and follow God's direction.

3. Paul's transformation (Gal. 1:20-24). Paul wanted the Galatian church to realize that he was presenting the true gospel. He did not want to be mistaken for a false teacher. Eventually, he came to Syria and Cilicia, where no one recognized him, although they knew about his persecution of the Christians. These citizens immediately realized that he was a changed man and praised God for the new Paul.

When a person trusts in Christ as Saviour, there will be a change. Even the vilest individual feels compelled to alter his or her lifestyle. Persons acquainted with a repentant sinner may have difficulty believing that the person has transformed, but seeing the new believer living a noticeably different life should cause friends and neighbors to realize that they are dealing with a new person.

Christ came to earth to save lost souls. What is your life saying to this wicked world? Which master are you trying to please—God or man? Actions speak louder than words. Conduct yourself in such a way that others will see that you are living a life pleasing to the Heavenly Father.

—*Catherine Moore.*

World Missions

When we think of a call to missions, often the picture that comes to mind is a person in their early twenties, just getting started, and God summoning him or her to a life of service for Him.

However, a call to serve can come at any time in a person's life. Ashley, who goes to Haiti every year, said she wanted to be a missionary from a very young age—before she even knew what a missionary was! Sam spent several years teaching at a school in Bangladesh after retirement.

God is not deterred by a person's age or circumstances. Joni Eareckson Tada has reached millions from her wheelchair, and if that is not amazing enough, Nick Vujicic has done the same without any arms or legs at all!

A young person who recognizes God's call to missions does not have to wait until he is older to serve. He can organize a Bible club in his neighborhood, or he can start whatever ministry God has placed on his heart.

If old enough, a young person could consider an apprenticeship at a mission board, or he can gain college credits through a program such as Extreme Assignment with Source of Light Ministries International. For one year, Extreme Assignment students take Bible Institute classes, learn from missionaries, and go on a missions trip, while earning up to four semesters of credit at certain Bible colleges (find out more at sourcelight. org).

And what about senior citizens? God has places all over the world for them too! Many are finding great fulfillment by giving their retirement years to the Lord's work, building deep and meaningful relationships and doing something that matters for eternity.

Jack and Dottie moved to Kenya when Jack was sixty-five. They distributed millions of Bible study lessons, not retiring from ministry until he was eighty-six! They left behind fifty thousand students enrolled in Bible studies and a print shop that makes over one million Bible lessons a year. What a heritage!

Not all of us have the health and stamina to follow in the footsteps of Jack and Dottie, but there are other ways to support the kingdom, such as planned giving. Many mission boards have options concerning life insurance policies or wills as a way to give beyond what is possible on a fixed senior income.

Those who are limited physically can invest in the vital ministry of prayer (note the example of Anna in Luke 2:36-37), or reach out to the lost through internet ministries, or support outreaches to people with their same illnesses or disabilities with organization such as Joni and Friends.

Young or old, disabled or healthy, God's call is a joyous summons to give our lives to something bigger than ourselves. Those who have the courage to obey find the adventure of choosing God's work is not one they regret.

As Nate Saint said just two weeks before he was martyred for Christ, "If God would grant us the vision, the word 'sacrifice' would disappear from our lips and thoughts; we would hate the things that seem now so dear to us; our lives would suddenly be too short, we would despise time-robbing distractions and charge the enemy with all our energies in the name of Christ."

—*Kimberly Rae.*

The Jewish Aspect

Paul the apostle, also known as Saul of Tarsus, who brought the gospel of Jesus Christ to much of the first century world, is one of the most important people in the history of the faith. His assertion that he did not receive the gospel from man, but by a direct revelation from Jesus Christ (Gal. 1:12), is supported in the book of Acts, which recounts Paul's vision of the resurrected Jesus Christ on the road to Damascus. Paul had been traveling from Jerusalem to Damascus on a mission to persecute the church of God, when he was blinded by a heavenly light and experienced a vision of the resurrected Jesus Christ (Acts 9:1-5).

"Paul was born into a devout Jewish family in the city of Tarsus, capital of the small Roman district of Cilicia in Asia Minor. His father, a member of the tribe of Benjamin, named him Saul, after Israel's first king.' . . . For Paul, as an Orthodox Pharisee, his education would have started in the synagogue very young at the age of five. This is because of traditional Jewish belief that the instilling of the law must start early in life," (Wallace, "The Early Life and Background of Paul the Apostle," wwwbiblicaltheology.com).

Paul told the Galatians that he had been called from his mother's womb (Gal. 1:15), which was also true of the Prophet Jeremiah. The comparison helped the new believers understand that Paul, like Jeremiah, had been separated, or set apart, for special use by God. The Jews would have understood this based on their unique calling as a holy people set apart and chosen by God for Himself (Deut. 14:2). Paul referred to Himself as the least of all saints (Eph. 3:8) and the least of the apostles (I Cor. 15:8); however, he also made clear that he was commissioned as an apostle and was God's appointed representative.

Following his dramatic encounter with Jesus on the road to Damascus (Acts 9:1-6), Paul spent the next three years in Arabia in the wilderness following in the Old Testament tradition of Moses and Elijah. Jonah was in the belly of the whale for three days and three nights, which was symbolic of Christ in the earth for three days and three nights (Matt. 12:40). Abraham and Isaac journeyed for three days to Mount Moriah where God asked Abraham to sacrifice Isaac to Him (Gen. 22:4).

It was during Paul's time in the wilderness that he sought to understand his calling. His message was that faith in Christ alone was necessary for salvation for Jews and Gentiles. "That the Gentiles should be fellowheirs, and of the same body, and partakers of his promise in Christ by the gospel" (Eph. 3:6) was the mystery (vs. 9) to which Paul referred. He taught that as fellow heirs of the same body, believing Jews and believing Gentiles were joined together into one body in Christ, no longer separated before God. "In English a 'mystery' is something dark, obscure, secret, puzzling. What is mysterious is inexplicable, even incomprehensible. The Greek word *mysterion* is different, however. Although still a 'secret', it is no longer closely guarded but open. . . . More simply, *mysterion* is a truth hitherto hidden from human knowledge or understanding but now disclosed by the revelation of God," (Stott, *The Message of Ephesians*, InterVarsity). The mystery that Paul taught propelled the infant church to fulfill the Great Commission to go into all nations to preach the gospel (Matt. 28:19).

—Deborah Markowitz Solan.

Guiding the Superintendent

The message of the gospel is very clear and very simple: "If thou shalt confess with thy mouth the Lord Jesus, and shalt believe in thine heart that God hath raised him from the dead, thou shalt be saved" (Rom. 10:9).

Paul was deeply concerned for the churches he had established in Galatia. False teachers were coming to the area and corrupting the gospel of grace. They were teaching that there was more to the gospel than grace through faith. In essence, these folks were being taught another gospel. Lesson Eight emphasized that there is only one true gospel. Paul now continued to teach the Galatians that not only is there only one gospel, but also that it came directly from God. He did this by telling them exactly how the gospel message had come to him directly from Jesus Christ Himself.

DEVOTIONAL OUTLINE

1. Not received from human sources (Gal. 1:10-12). Paul insisted his gospel did not have its origins in merely human teaching. Rather, he had received the gospel directly from the risen Christ.

2. Received directly from God (Gal. 1:13-17). From a human viewpoint, it would be impossible for Paul to make up the gospel. He reminded the Galatians of his previous religious zeal as a persecutor of the church and a stalwart for the traditions of Judaism.

There can be only one explanation for this radical change—God had miraculously transformed Paul's life and called him to preach the gospel. It was on the road to Damascus that Christ revealed Himself to Paul. Paul had had no contact with the Jerusalem church or the other apostles at this point, and he immediately went alone into the Arabian desert.

3. Recognized by the Judean churches (Gal. 1:18-24). After three years in the desert around Damascus, Paul briefly visited the church at Jerusalem. But he maintained a low profile while there, meeting only with Peter and the Lord's brother James. He then journeyed to Syria and his homeland, Cilicia. At that time the churches of Judea knew him only as their former persecutor who now preached Jesus Christ.

All this was a clear indication that Paul's message of the gospel originated from God and not from mere humans. Therefore it must be believed.

CHILDREN'S CORNER

text: **Acts 4:1-3, 7-20**
title: **Serving in Jesus' Power**

Following the ascension of the risen Jesus back to heaven, the religious leaders in Jerusalem had a major problem on their hands. The disciples had been emboldened by Jesus' resurrection and the power of the Holy Spirit. Using this power, they had healed a crippled beggar in the temple.

The miracle was so obvious that it could not be denied. So the leaders arrested Peter and John. The next day the leaders asked them about what they had done.

The disciples confessed that the miracle was all done through the power of Jesus and His Holy Spirit. The courage of these men and the fact of the healed man could not be denied.

In an attempt to stop further miracles, Peter and John were ordered by the religious leadership to stop preaching or teaching in Jesus' name, to which the men replied, "We cannot but speak the things which we have seen and heard" (vs. 20).

—*Martin R. Dahlquist.*

Scripture Lesson Text

GAL. 3:1 O foolish Galatians, who hath bewitched you, that ye should not obey the truth, before whose eyes Jesus Christ hath been evidently set forth, crucified among you?

2 This only would I learn of you, Received ye the Spirit by the works of the law, or by the hearing of faith?

3 Are ye so foolish? having begun in the Spirit, are ye now made perfect by the flesh?

4 Have ye suffered so many things in vain? if it be yet in vain.

5 He therefore that ministereth to you the Spirit, and worketh miracles among you, doeth he it by the works of the law, or by the hearing of faith?

6 Even as Abraham believed God, and it was accounted to him for righteousness.

7 Know ye therefore that they which are of faith, the same are the children of Abraham.

8 And the scripture, foreseeing that God would justify the heathen through faith, preached before the gospel unto Abraham, saying, In thee shall all nations be blessed.

9 So then they which be of faith are blessed with faithful Abraham.

10 For as many as are of the works of the law are under the curse: for it is written, Cursed is every one that continueth not in all things which are written in the book of the law to do them.

11 But that no man is justified by the law in the sight of God, it is evident: for, The just shall live by faith.

12 And the law is not of faith: but, The man that doeth them shall live in them.

13 Christ hath redeemed us from the curse of the law, being made a curse for us: for it is written, Cursed is every one that hangeth on a tree:

14 That the blessing of Abraham might come on the Gentiles through Jesus Christ; that we might receive the promise of the Spirit through faith.

NOTES

The Gospel of Faith Foretold

Lesson Text: Galatians 3:1-14

Related Scriptures: Romans 4:1-12, 17-22; Acts 15:13-18;
Romans 15:7-12; I Peter 1:9-13

TIME: possibly A.D. 48   PLACE: from Syrian Antioch

GOLDEN TEXT—"The scripture, foreseeing that God would justify the heathen through faith, preached before the gospel unto Abraham, saying, In thee shall all nations be blessed" (Galatians 3:8).

Introduction

It seems to happen with some frequency. The phone rings, and I answer. Immediately a recorded voice that has become familiar informs me that I have won a two-day, two-night trip to some exclusive getaway. Just as immediately I hang up the phone. Why? Because I know that the "free" trip comes with a cost. There are requirements. The idyllic vacation will be interrupted by seemingly endless, high-pressure sales presentations. Some people may consider this "cost" an acceptable trade-off for the benefits received. But it is not my idea of a relaxing vacation.

There is nothing necessarily wrong with offering free gifts in order to promote one's product or business, but sometimes the "free" gift is not really free at all. In fact, many people assume this is the case, and even when offered something that is genuinely free, they immediately start wondering what the catch is. This is true in the case of the gospel.

LESSON OUTLINE

I. **THE ARGUMENT FROM THE GALATIANS' EXPERIENCE—Gal. 3:1-5**

II. **THE ARGUMENT FROM ABRAHAM—Gal. 3:6-9**

III. **THE ARGUMENT FROM THE LAW—Gal. 3:10-12**

IV. **THE ARGUMENT FROM CHRIST'S REDEMPTION—Gal. 3:13-14**

Exposition: Verse by Verse

THE ARGUMENT FROM THE GALATIANS' EXPERIENCE

GAL. 3:1 O foolish Galatians, who hath bewitched you, that ye should not obey the truth, before whose eyes Jesus Christ hath been evidently set forth, crucified among you?

2 This only would I learn of you, Received ye the Spirit by the works of the law, or by the hearing of faith?

3 Are ye so foolish? having begun in the Spirit, are ye now made perfect by the flesh?

4 Have ye suffered so many things in vain? if it be yet in vain.

5 He therefore that ministereth to you the Spirit, and worketh miracles among you, doeth he it by the works of the law, or by the hearing of faith?

Message of faith (Gal. 3:1). Paul's primary reason for writing to the Christians in the province of Galatia was to address the problem of legalism. The Galatians, who were primarily Gentiles, had been saved through faith in Christ, but certain Jewish teachers had infiltrated the churches and were teaching that faith was not enough. These teachers, whom we call Judaizers, were insisting that the Gentile believers must also observe the Jewish law, even declaring this was necessary for salvation (cf. Acts 15:1).

Paul had no tolerance for such legalism. He called this teaching "another gospel" (Gal. 1:6) and the proponents of it "false brethren" (2:4). He wrote, "If righteousness come by the law, then Christ is dead in vain" (vs. 21). He understood that salvation comes only by receiving by faith the grace of God in Christ. If it comes by the law, then Christ's death was meaningless.

In the case of the Galatians, the crucified Christ had been clearly set before them, and they had believed in Him. They had been saved and accepted by God through faith, apart from obedience to the Law of Moses. The apostle labeled it utterly foolish to now turn away from the truth that salvation is by grace through faith (3:1). Their own experience told them the teaching of the Judaizers was wrong, but many of them were acting as if they were bewitched, or under some kind of spell.

Regeneration by faith (Gal. 3:2). Paul now begins to ask his readers some searching questions to remind them of crucial truths they had already affirmed and experienced. He notes, first, that they had received the Holy Spirit through faith, not through "works of the law." This refers to their reception of the Holy Spirit when they were saved. This was clearly a work of God's grace, which they received by faith. Works had nothing to do with their regeneration, or spiritual new birth.

Sanctification by faith (Gal. 3:3-5). The Gentile believers in Galatia knew that their salvation had come through faith in Christ, wholly apart from the law. Why, then, would any of them think that they must complete their spiritual journey through their own efforts at keeping the law—that is, "by the flesh"? Why would any believer abandon the Spirit with whom the journey started? The law was not a part of salvation, so why introduce it as a requirement for one who is born again and now led by the Spirit of God?

Sanctification is the progressive growth toward Christlikeness that is empowered by the indwelling Holy Spirit. It is being "made perfect," or mature, in the faith (vs. 3). This cannot be effected by human efforts to obey the Law of Moses. How foolish it was to "suppose that a system [the law] which never could bring regeneration to sinners could still somehow bring about their ultimate transformation into the likeness of Christ" (Kent, *The Freedom of God's Sons,* BMH).

In fact, if sanctification were a matter of following the law, then all that the Galatian believers had suffered for their *faith* would be meaningless (vs. 4). These followers of Christ had been persecuted for their belief long before the Judaizers had attempted to bring them under the law (cf. Acts 14:5-6, 19, 22).

Was their suffering for the gospel of grace that they had embraced at Paul's preaching all for nothing? It would be if they now turned to law "in order to satisfy God's righteousness, [for] they would be repudiating their former position which claimed that they looked to Christ alone" (Kent). Paul's concluding words in Galatians 3:4 suggest that the believers were still clinging to faith in Christ in spite of the teaching and pressure of the Judaizers.

Paul further notes that the Holy Spirit who worked in and among them did not make His mighty works contingent upon their obedience to the law. Indeed, the works of the Spirit were evident among them even when Paul and Barnabas were preaching to them the gospel of grace. "There was nothing more of the Spirit that the Galatians could get through the Judaizers. In fact, the false teachers had contributed nothing that was spiritual or miraculous" (Gromacki, *Stand Fast in Liberty*, Kress). Paul's point is that sanctification, like salvation itself, comes through faith, not works of the law.

THE ARGUMENT FROM ABRAHAM

6 Even as Abraham believed God, and it was accounted to him for righteousness.

7 Know ye therefore that they which are of faith, the same are the children of Abraham.

8 And the scripture, foreseeing that God would justify the heathen through faith, preached before the gospel unto Abraham, saying, In thee shall all nations be blessed.

9 So then they which be of faith are blessed with faithful Abraham.

The faith of Abraham (Gal. 3:6). After setting forth the issue in relation to the Galatians' own Christian experience, the Apostle Paul now develops a scriptural argument for the gospel of grace as opposed to the Judaizers' false gospel of the works of the law. He points to Abraham, whose faith was accounted to him for righteousness (Gen. 15:6). The Bible declares Abraham righteous on the basis of his faith alone. The law, which came many years later, had nothing to do with his acceptance by God.

The children of Abraham (Gal. 3:7-9). It seems the Judaizers emphasized the necessity of being connected to Abraham, especially through circumcision, the identifying sign of God's chosen people. Thus, they taught that Gentile believers became children of Abraham and therefore heirs of the promises to Abraham through circumcision and obedience to the law that came through Abraham's descendants.

Paul declares that those who "are of faith" (vs. 7)—that is, those who (like Abraham) simply trust the Lord—are the true children of Abraham. Faith, not race or the law, is the requirement for salvation. Just as Abraham was saved by faith, so were the Galatian believers, and so are we today. If works were required, no one could be saved, for imperfect people cannot perfectly meet God's righteous requirements.

Scripture is our authority in all matters because it comes from God Himself. Paul cites Scripture to show that God's plan was always to "justify the heathen through faith" (vs. 8). "Heathen" denotes Gentiles. This is the gospel—that sinners, whether Jews or Gentiles, are justified, or declared righteous, through faith, not through works.

The promises to Abraham from the very beginning foresaw that God's blessing would come on those who were true heirs of Abraham by faith. While it is true that Abraham's physical descendants would be specially blessed by God, His blessings were not limited to them. The initial promises to Abraham, which are at the core of what we call the Abrahamic covenant (cf. Gen. 12:23), included the assurance that in Abraham "shall all nations be blessed" (Gal. 3:8). The word for "nations" here is the same word translated "heathen" earlier in the verse. The blessing is justification, or spiritual salvation, which is free to all who trust in Christ, faithful Abraham's greatest descendant.

THE ARGUMENT FROM THE LAW

10 For as many as are of the works of the law are under the curse: for it is written, Cursed is every one that continueth not in all things which are written in the book of the law to do them.

11 But that no man is justified by the law in the sight of God, it is evident: for, The just shall live by faith.

12 And the law is not of faith: but, The man that doeth them shall live in them.

The curse of the law (Gal. 3:10-11). The Judaizers insisted that keeping the law was necessary for salvation as well as sanctification. Paul showed from the Galatians' own experience based on Paul's preaching that this was not the case. Then he argued from the life and experience of Abraham that it is by faith, not by keeping the law, that one receives God's gracious salvation. Now he turns to the nature of the law itself to show that it was never intended to save or to sanctify.

Those who "are of the works of the law" (vs. 10) stand in contrast to those who are "of faith" (vs. 9). As Paul had just said, it is those who are of faith who are blessed, for salvation comes through faith alone. Those who seek the blessing of salvation through keeping the Old Testament law are cursed rather than blessed.

Paul quotes Deuteronomy 27:26 to show that the law condemned anyone who did not keep it in its entirety, and keeping the law perfectly is not possible. It is clear, then, that acceptance with God is impossible through human effort. This is the curse of the law. It ultimately condemns those who seek to obey it. It cannot save.

The apostle again asserts, "No man is justified by the law in the sight of God" (Gal. 3:11). As proof, he cites Habakkuk 2:4: "The just shall live by faith." Here "the just" refers to those who have been justified by faith, and they thus live by faith. They do not live by the law. Thus, the Old Testament itself declares that "one stands in a right relationship to God and lives before him by faith" (Barker and Kohlenberger, eds., *The Expositor's Bible Commentary*, Abridged Edition, Zondervan).

The opposite of faith (Gal. 3:12). The Judaizers argued that while faith is, in fact, necessary, it must be accompanied by law keeping. Paul states that the two principles are opposites and cannot be mixed. Gromacki summarizes the thought by saying, "Faith does not express itself in legalism. Faith and the law are not two sides of the same coin. Faith says that man must live before he can do, but law says that man must do before he can live. Faith charges 'Believe and live,' whereas the law commands 'Do and live.'"

Those who want to live by the law are bound to keep it all, and this is something they cannot do. This is why faith—and faith alone—is the only way to receive God's gracious gift.

THE ARGUMENT FROM CHRIST'S REDEMPTION

13 Christ hath redeemed us from the curse of the law, being made a curse for us: for it is written, Cursed is every one that hangeth on a tree:

14 That the blessing of Abraham might come on the Gentiles through Jesus Christ; that we might receive the promise of the Spirit through faith.

The redemptive work of Christ also argues for the gospel of grace that Paul and the apostles consistently preached and taught the Galatians. The law condemns us by pointing out our sins. It cannot save, no matter how earnestly we seek to obey it. Because we cannot fully and perfectly obey the law, we stand under its curse of condemnation.

Christ redeemed us from the curse of the law by becoming a curse for us (vs. 13). Under the law, the hanging or impalement of criminals gave public testimony to the curse the law pronounced upon them for their deeds. Deuteronomy 21:23 affirms that anyone who is hanged on a tree is cursed before God. By dying as our Substitute on the cross, Jesus Christ paid for our sins and thus delivered us from the curse the law pronounced on us. He redeemed, or ransomed, us from our just condemnation. Our salvation, therefore, is His work, not ours. We do not attain it, maintain it, or add to it by any works we do.

Galatians 3:14 tells us the purpose of Christ's redemption. He died so that the blessing of Abraham might come to Gentiles, as well as Jews, through faith in Jesus Christ. The blessing of Abraham is justification—being declared righteous by God (cf. vss. 8-9). Apart from Christ's death, which paid the debt of sin, no one could be declared righteous.

Christ's redemption also secured "the promise of the Spirit through faith" (vs. 14). As Paul already indicated in verse 2, the Holy Spirit is received and comes to dwell in a person when that person exercises faith in Jesus Christ. Once again, this blessing is not the result of law keeping but the result of personal faith in Christ.

The Apostle Paul was confronting a very real threat to the churches in Galatia and beyond. The legalism the false teachers were promoting appealed to human pride in being able to accomplish by one's own efforts acceptance with God. Such teaching, however, would lead only to frustration and spiritual bondage.

Paul countered the Judaizers with a series of arguments that assured his Galatian readers that the gospel of salvation by grace through faith—which they had heard from him and believed—was, in fact, the truth of God. We must not get lost in the details of Paul's arguments. The basic truth Paul argues for and we must grasp is this: we are saved through faith, and we are to live by faith.

Legalism is the attitude that we must do things in order to be accepted by God. Scripture tells us we do good works because we are already accepted through faith. When we walk by faith, we find joy and freedom, and we present to the world a faith that is real and attractive, not a burden.

—Jarl K. Waggoner.

QUESTIONS

1. What was Paul's primary reason for writing Galatians?
2. What in the Galatians' past experience with the Spirit should have shown them the error of the false teachers?
3. What is sanctification, and what did the Judaizers teach regarding it?
4. What did the experience of Abraham teach about faith?
5. Who does Paul say are the "children of Abraham" (Gal. 3:7)?
6. How did God's promise to Abraham foresee that Gentiles would be justified by faith?
7. What is the curse of the law?
8. How does faith stand in contrast to the law?
9. How has Christ redeemed us from the curse of the law?
10. What two purposes of Christ's redemption does Paul list?

—Jarl K. Waggoner.

Preparing to Teach the Lesson

In our lesson this week, we learn that God had planned the gospel of faith long before we came on the scene. It was always in the heart of God to redeem man, and He foretold this good news a very long time ago, even during the time of Abraham.

TODAY'S AIM

Facts: to show that God had foretold the good news of faith in Jesus even during Abraham's time.

Principle: to remember that the gospel of faith was not an afterthought with God. He planned it deliberately to redeem us. It has never changed.

Application: to realize when we put our trust in what God has planned for us, we will find redemption.

INTRODUCING THE LESSON

Planning takes deliberate attention to detail. Think of the last time you had guests who let you know that they were coming to visit. You hopefully did not wait till the last minute to prepare for their coming. You got your home clean, you changed the sheets, and you did all that your guests needed for their stay. This is what God did for us in planning our redemption from sin. He took deliberate steps to let us know that a Redeemer was coming. This ancient good news is still the same today.

DEVELOPING THE LESSON

1. The spirit is received by faith (Gal. 3:1-5). This gospel truth was foretold long ago. Yet the Galatian believers had left this truth and were already following after other doctrines. Paul reminded them that the truth about Jesus being crucified for them had already been explained to them clearly. But they had been deceived and were in danger of turning from this saving truth to follow a false gospel.

It is easy to go astray from the truth. Salvation does not come through the Law, it comes through God's saving grace through faith.

Paul chastises them for thinking that having begun their Christian walk in the Spirit, they could make themselves perfect by fleshly works. In so doing they were making their suffering worthless. It is the Spirit alone who leads us to perfection. God had shown them His miracles by those who brought them the Holy Spirit, not by those who preached keeping the law.

We cannot live by faith and simultaneously follow the law as a way to salvation. If our new life is born of the Spirit, we must continue to live by that same Spirit. Our suffering will then have meaning. Notice that more than once in this section (vss. 1, 3) Paul says that the Galatians are foolish, trying to live in two worlds at once. Ask your students to identify ways in which we neglect God and rely on the flesh, even as the Galatians did.

2. Abraham made righteous by faith (Gal. 3:6-9). Scientific facts change around us as new discoveries are made. But the gospel is the same, even from the time of Abraham. He believed God, and that was accounted to him as righteousness because of this faith. We are all children of Abraham if we believe and trust in God as he did. The Jews boasted that they were saved by being physical descendants of Abraham. Paul asserted that the true children of Abraham are those who have Abraham's faith.

Paul pointed out that the Scriptures foretold a time when the Gentiles would become righteous before God by faith and not by works of the law. Just as God counted Abraham righteous through faith, the Gentiles would also become the heirs to God's kingdom through faith alone. This is still true today. If we believe the gospel through faith, we will also be blessed like Abraham, who saw Christ's cross in the future through faith.

Remind your students that God's way of salvation has never changed through thousands of years. He still calls us to trust Him in simple faith.

3. The righteous will live by faith (Gal. 3:10-14). The Law was designed to open the door to the true gospel of Christ (cf. Gal. 3:24), not to be the ultimate truth. The Law only brings a curse on those who fail to keep it, and no one can keep the Law perfectly. It is designed to show us our failure. The Jews broke the law down into 613 little laws so they would be sure to keep all of them. Every law has to be kept faithfully—an impossible task.

Where the Law failed us, the gospel of faith stepped in to give us victory. Paul makes it clear that only faith can justify a person. Jesus came to break the curse of the Law because He fulfilled the demands of the Law and died for our sins. The Law stated that anyone who hangs on a cross is cursed. Jesus fulfilled that for us and opened the way to make us right before the holy God.

The gospel of faith has not changed throughout the ages. Abraham of old and we today have the same way to enter into the presence of God. Abraham saw this through the eyes of faith. We are likewise made right with God through faith in what Christ has already done for us. We experience the same blessing in the same way— through faith.

Emphasize to the class that saving ourselves through good works is futile. Jesus came to give us life, and He has already paid the costly price for us. This is not something to be taken lightly but to be received by simple faith in the gospel that was foretold so long ago.

ILLUSTRATING THE LESSON

Abraham looked forward to the cross through faith. We look back at the cross through faith.

CONCLUDING THE LESSON

We cannot impress God with our good works, nor can we work our way into heaven. The gospel is very clear and simple. Jesus has already paid the price for our sins. This truth has been the same for thousands of years. Even during the time of Abraham, salvation was by faith in God. The gospel demands a response of faith. It makes us able to enter the kingdom of God, where we will forever enjoy God's blessings along with Abraham. The gospel of faith has not changed.

ANTICIPATING THE NEXT LESSON

Next week, we will reaffirm that the gospel means putting our faith in the Lord Jesus Christ. There can be nothing more wonderful than this.

—A. Koshy Muthalaly.

PRACTICAL POINTS

1. There is nothing we do can to earn our salvation (Gal. 3:1-4).
2. Our righteousness is determined by our faith, not our works (vss. 5-6).
3. All nations are blessed because of Abraham (vss. 7-9).
4. It is impossible to uphold everything that is written in the law (vs. 10).
5. The law points out our failures; faith brings a right standing with God (vss. 11-12).
6. Christ's work on the Cross fulfilled God's law and secured our redemption (vss. 13-14).
—Charity G. Carter.

RESEARCH AND DISCUSSION

1. Many people believe that hard work or good deeds assure them of salvation. Why is it easier to believe that we need more than faith to be saved (Gal. 3:2)?
2. Explain how some people who were saved by faith resort to proving themselves through works (vs. 3).
3. Abraham simply believed God and was considered righteous (vs. 6). What does that tell us about God's view of faith?
4. Who are "the heathen" and how are they justified by faith (vs. 8)?
5. Discuss how the just (the righteous) live by faith (vs. 11).
6. How should Christ's redemptive work on the Cross impact the way we interact with others (vs. 13)?
7. Describe the ways in which you and your family have benefitted from the "blessing of Abraham" (vs. 14).
—Charity G. Carter.

ILLUSTRATED HIGH POINTS

Set forth, crucified among you?

Soon, nearly everyone may be exploring virtual reality via personal goggles. The experiences are becoming more and more realistic and the price is going down. Although we may dodge and duck invisible projectiles and utter "oohs" and "ahhs" as we marvel at virtual wonders, the truth is that nothing is really happening.

However, this is not the case when it comes to the preaching of the gospel. For the Galatians, as for us, when meaningful content (the gospel) is presented by a delivery system (a godly preacher), and illuminated by a powerful agent (the Holy Spirit), a true and transforming experience may occur.

Works of the law, or . . . faith

In 1985, when asked why he attended the same conservative convention for seventeen years, Ronald Reagan famously answered, "You dance with the one who brung ya." This saying, now a favorite axiom in political circles, advocates loyalty to one's original benefactors.

Before Reagan, it was an oft-repeated adage of a certain down-homey University of Texas football coach, Darrell Royal. He first used it during a 1965 Longhorn losing streak. After being asked why he had not bothered to change his game strategy, like Reagan he famously answered, "You dance with the one who brung ya."

Recorded as a song in 1927 with the title "I'm gonna dance with de guy wot brung me," several artists have performed songs with similar titles. Remember, do not switch partners after you get to the party. It was "Mr. Grace" who brought you to salvation; why would you leave him just to dance with a real stinker like "Mr. Works"?
—Therese Greenberg.

Golden Text Illuminated

"The scripture, foreseeing that God would justify the heathen through faith, preached before the gospel unto Abraham, saying, In thee shall all nations be blessed" (Galatians 3:8).

The Bible is full of prophetic messages; many of these messages foretold truths about events that would unfold at some point in the future. They were given primarily by prophets, God's chosen spokesmen.

Those wise enough to listen to God's messages would find comfort and hope in times of trial, warnings about judgment to come for disobedience, and insight into God's special promises to His people.

Much of the New Testament is the recorded fulfillment of Old Testament prophecies. Although all the prophecies were fit together to bring about God's perfect plans, no prophecies were more precious than those of the coming Saviour and the gospel of faith.

Although God's free gift of grace is for all people, many of the Jews did not believe Gentiles could be true children of God. False teachers taught that Gentiles must first become Jews through circumcision and obedience to the Law of Moses before God would accept them.

Paul's letter to the Galatian church was written in part to help the church understand the sufficiency of Christ's work on the cross. Christ had completed all the work needed to provide and secure salvation (John 17:4). The Galatians did not need to add to that finished work (nor could they).

Evidently frustrated by their confusion regarding the tension between grace and the law, Paul tried to reason with the Galatian believers. He asked them a rhetorical question: "This only would I learn of you, Received ye the Spirit by the works of the law, or by the hearing of faith? Are ye so foolish? having begun in the Spirit, are ye now made perfect by the flesh?" (Gal. 3:2-3).

Paul then presented another compelling argument for the gospel of faith. This is seen in the golden text, wherein God promised to "justify the heathen through faith." This message was given to Abraham.

Wanting descendants yet having none, Abraham was promised many children by the Lord (Gen. 15:5). This was not a promise of an immediate large family, for Abraham had only two sons, Ishmael and Isaac, that the Bible devotes space to. This prophecy looked to the distant future and was, at bottom, spiritual in nature (cf. Gen. 17:6-7; Gal. 3:16).

Abraham was a man of faith, and as such, God blessed him and considered him righteous (Gen. 15:6). The spiritual children of Abraham are those who, like him, simply trust or believe God. Just as with Abraham, their faith is "counted . . . for righteousness."

It is important to note when this promise was given to Abraham. It was not after he was circumcised, as if given in response to any work on his part, but rather it was before his obedience (Rom. 4:9-12). This point refutes the teachings of those promoting a works gospel.

God's promise, given so long ago, is to justify or declare, sinners (which, according to Romans 3:23, includes all people) not guilty. He acquits the guilty when they place their trust in His Son and His saving work. The true gospel is the gospel of faith. Like Abraham, have you believed? If so, you are blessed!

—*Christine M. Morrison.*

Heart of the Lesson

A street near me is known to be a speed trap. The police ticket anyone going over the speed limit. Motorists complain that they were not violating the law since they were only one or two miles per hour above the limit. In reality, they did break the law because they were traveling faster than the law allows. Going just a few miles above the speed limit may seem insignificant compared to going fifty miles over, but it is still a violation of the law.

Paul emphasized that the Jewish people were under a curse because they were incapable of obeying the law. Breaking one law rendered them guilty and ineligible for heaven. God, however, has made salvation available for all who put their trust in Jesus Christ.

1. The Galatians' efforts (Gal. 3:1-5). The Galatian believers had strayed from the truth. They had begun to elevate the Jewish law, thinking that adhering to it strictly would somehow solidify or ensure their salvation. This disappointed Paul, so he asked them several questions about their conversion. He wanted them to understand that keeping the law did not secure their redemption. Faith was the only thing necessary.

Every humanly-derived religion today teaches that salvation comes by doing good deeds or by performing specific tasks. People think they must perform certain rituals to reach heaven. Sadly, these people are mistaken. They do not realize that obtaining salvation is simple. Acts 16:31 states, "Believe on the Lord Jesus Christ, and thou shalt be saved." Christ is the only route to salvation. He guarantees eternal life in heaven for all who put their faith in Him.

2. Abraham's faith (Gal 3:6-9). The book of Genesis repeatedly tells of Abraham's trust in God. The law had not yet been given; it was his faith that established his standing. This made him a good model for the Galatians. Because of Abraham's faithfulness, God rewarded him with many descendants and counted him as righteous. Paul points out that God had planned to bless all nations with salvation through Christ long before Abraham's time.

Abraham is still a good example for Christians everywhere. He simply had to believe, which is all that is required of us today. God did not bless Abraham alone; He also blessed the Jews. And just as God planned, He made salvation available to the Gentiles through faith. He has blessed people of every nation by offering the gift of salvation, and He will continue to bless us in this way until the end of time.

3. Christians' trust (Gal. 3:10-14). Paul begins by saying that if the Jews broke one law, no matter how small, they were guilty of breaking the whole law. While the law teaches holy principles, it does not justify us before God but condemns us. Paul quotes Habakkuk 2:4 when he says, "The just shall live by his faith" (Rom. 1:17). Christ went to the cross to save us from the curse of the law. The Jewish law said that anyone hanged on a tree was cursed. That meant Christ was condemned. Because Christ was punished for man's sin on the cross, the blessings of Abraham and the Jews are now available to the Gentiles.

Anyone who places his trust in Christ will receive blessings. Thankfully, we are no longer under the law, and Christians do not have to follow those restrictive laws to be saved. Believing in Christ is all that is necessary. God still changes lives. Has He changed yours?
—*Catherine Moore.*

World Missions

A Muslim has a dream about a man in white who says He is Jesus. He wakes up and looks for a Christian to tell him more.

A young girl leaves her family worshipping their ancestors and goes outside, looks up at the stars, and wonders who made them.

A tribal village has a prophecy that one day a stranger will come with a book that will tell them the way to heaven.

All over the world, God has put eternity into the hearts of men. Revelation teaches that there will be in heaven redeemed people from every tribe, tongue, and nation (Rev. 5:9; 7:9). Yet according to Wycliffe Bible Translators, "There are an estimated 160 million people without access to *any* Scripture in their heart language . . . At least 1.5 billion people are without the *full* Bible in their first language."

How are people to be saved from every tongue if they do not have a Bible? Despite the huge number above, Wycliffe president Bob Creson is optimistic. "The Bible is being translated into more languages and at a faster rate than ever before. . . . 'Every year now there are 130 to 160 new translations that are started.'" Creson believes the remaining nearly 1,900 languages in need of a Bible will have something in process within the next ten years. He says right now "'there is an opportunity to invite people to be a part of something that is pretty historic'" (christianpost.com). (To be part of helping the translation projects, go to www.wycliffe.org).

How can people of every tribe and nation be saved if no one goes to tell them the good news? We have a message of genuine hope to give, unlike any other religion.

Buddha went searching for the great enlightenment, and in the end he decided that all life is suffering. Hindus ring bells to get the gods' attention. Tribal worshippers have fetishes to show their fear and submission to unknown spirits. Religion is a long history of man trying to connect with God.

But how many find Him? How many find peace in all their effort and striving? Religion in and of itself cannot save.

Yet out of this swirling, engulfing darkness comes light: God reached down for us. Christianity is the one and only faith in which God connects with man. It was God who so loved a wicked, lost, searching world that He sent His own Son to earth. God the Son Himself came to be with man. No false gods can make this claim. No false god abandoned the free exercise of his power due to His love. There is no god like the true God.

We must not be like other people, these who strive to reach God by their own efforts. We must be very careful that, though we seek to live lives of holiness and adherence to God's commands, we are not presenting a gospel of works. No, we must reflect the glory and beauty of the truth that we have been reached and given salvation through grace alone!

All nations are to be blessed by the gospel. Christians present the good news of the glorious prospect of a relationship with God Himself. To all those around us let us spread the good news. Let us be part of the reason that one day in heaven there will be believers from every tribe, tongue, and nation!

—*Kimberly Rae.*

The Jewish Aspect

In the Hebrew Bible, Abram is considered the first Jew and the father of the Jewish people. He was instructed by God to leave his country and go to a land that God would show him (Gen. 12:1). In an act of faith, Abram obeyed God and left behind everything he knew to begin a new civilization in an unknown land. God established his everlasting covenant with Abram (Gen. 17:2-9) and changed his name from Abram—"exalted father"—to Abraham—"father of many." When Abram was 99 years old, and his wife Sarai was 89, God promised that he would make Abram a great nation and that all the families of the earth would be blessed through him (Gen. 17:1-8; cf. 12:2-3).

God said that Abram's descendants would outnumber the stars. "And he believed in the Lord; and he counted it to him for righteousness" (Gen. 15:6). The word "believed" in Hebrew is *aman*—to be firm or sure, steadfast. It meant more than just knowing something to be true. It meant that Abraham was firm in his devotion and obedience to God. "The use of aman in this passage indicates that Abram did not just give mental assent to God's promises (Ge. 15:5), but he relied on that promise and made a personal commitment" ("Hebrew Definitions," www.preceptaustin.org).

"In a number of verses the Hebrew Old Testament uses the word 'hashab' to refer to God making just or righteous judgements in His Role as Supreme Ruler and Judge. In Genesis 15:6, 2 Samuel 19:20 and Psalm 32:2, the word 'hashab' means 'to impute'" ("Hebrew and Greek Words About Justification," www.internetbiblecollege.net.)

Paul taught that when Abram put his trust in God, the Lord credited this to him as righteousness. Ancient Judaism, however, extolled him not for his faith but for following God's commands and for the *brit milah*—the covenant of circumcision (Gen. 17:10). "Abraham is central to Judaism because he is widely regarded as the father of the Jewish nation. In addition, he is seen as the exemplar of the servant who is faithful to God in all things, and who follows his commands. Additionally, Abraham is not only the founder of the Jewish nation, but the receiver of the covenant [circumcision] to which all practicing Jews are bound," (Why is Abraham Important to Jews?" www.reference.com).

Paul taught the Galatians that the most important link to Abraham was the link of faith and not genetics or circumcision. He stated that even in Abraham's day it was clear that the blessing of righteousness, by faith, was intended for every nation because of God's promise that through Abraham all nations would be blessed. Paul said that the just had to live by faith and that no man was justified by the law in the sight of God (Gal. 3:11). The Hebrew prophet, Habakkuk, also taught that the just shall live by his faith (2:4). Paul affirmed this when he said that Abraham's righteousness came because he believed God and not as a result of following the law.

Paul emphasized that no one could keep the entirety of the law (Gal. 3:10). Jews knew that the Hebrew Bible stated that all the words of the law must be kept (Deut. 27:26). God had instructed the Israelites, "Ye shall therefore keep my statutes, and my judgments: which if a man do, he shall live in them: I am the Lord" (Lev. 18:5). Throughout Jewish history, however, they continuously disobeyed God and His commandments. David, the psalmist, said, "They kept not the covenant of God, and refused to walk in his law" (Ps. 78:10).

—*Deborah Markowitz Solan.*

Guiding the Superintendent

Despite what others were telling the churches in Galatia, Paul's gospel had always been that one's relationship to God depended on faith in Christ and not faith in Christ plus obeying Jewish laws and traditions.

Paul's gospel had always been simple and yet profound. There just is no place in one's Christian experience for salvation by works "made perfect by the flesh" (Gal. 3:3).

To prove his point about the gospel, Paul first examined the initial salvation experience of his readers and then brought forth evidence from history about how Abraham was saved.

DEVOTIONAL OUTLINE

1. The immediate past (Gal. 3:1-5). Paul wastes no time in getting to his point. "Are ye so foolish? having begun in the Spirit, are ye now made perfect by the flesh?" In other words, You began by God's grace, but now you think you must perfect yourselves by your own efforts.

They were acting irrationally. This was inexcusable! Even the best of human effort will not increase one's standing before God!

Their new behavior was contrary to what they believed in when they were saved. Paul reviewed all the work of the Holy Spirit that they all had experienced at salvation—the indwelling of the Spirit, their filling by the Spirit, and their gifts from the Spirit.

2. The distant past (Gal. 3:6-14). Paul next reviewed what happened to Abraham and what the Old Testament in general had to say about salvation by faith.

Because Abraham was a faith hero to Jews, it would be only natural for Paul to use him as an example. What was true about Abraham would be very important. "Abraham believed God, and it was accounted to him for righteousness" (Gal. 3:6). Those who believe are the children of Abraham. Faith was not just for Abraham. God intended that all who believed, including Gentiles, would be justified as Abraham had been—through faith.

To further strengthen his point, Paul cited several Old Testament passages to show that it was never God's intention to bring about righteousness by the law. The Law was a curse, not a cure. The Law was temporary. The Law was all about doing, not believing. And, finally, Christ has removed the Law's curse.

CHILDREN'S CORNER

text: **I Samuel 3:1-10, 19-21**
title: **Samuel: Ready to Serve**

Being a servant of God is not just reserved for adults. Samuel started serving the High Priest of Israel as a mere lad.

One night, Samuel heard a voice calling him. He assumed it was the aged high priest. No, Eli assured him that he had not called. Two more times Samuel heard the voice calling him and ran to Eli. Finally, the priest realized that it was the Lord who was calling. He told the boy to return to sleep, and if the voice called again to answer, "Speak, Lord; for thy servant heareth" (I Sam. 3:9).

Again the boy heard the voice, but this time he told the Lord he was listening. This began a lifelong relationship and ministry for Samuel. All Israel would soon recognize that Samuel was indeed God's prophet.

—Martin R. Dahlquist.

Scripture Lesson Text

GAL. 3:15 Brethren, I speak after the manner of men; Though it be but a man's covenant, yet if it be confirmed, no man disannulleth, or addeth thereto.

16 Now to Abraham and his seed were the promises made. He saith not, And to seeds, as of many; but as of one, And to thy seed, which is Christ.

17 And this I say, that the covenant, that was confirmed before of God in Christ, the law, which was four hundred and thirty years after, cannot disannul, that it should make the promise of none effect.

18 For if the inheritance be of the law, it is no more of promise: but God gave it to Abraham by promise.

19 Wherefore then serveth the law? It was added because of transgressions, till the seed should come to whom the promise was made; and it was ordained by angels in the hand of a mediator.

20 Now a mediator is not a mediator of one, but God is one.

21 Is the law then against the promises of God? God forbid: for if there had been a law given which could have given life, verily righteousness should have been by the law.

22 But the scripture hath concluded all under sin, that the promise by faith of Jesus Christ might be given to them that believe.

23 But before faith came, we were kept under the law, shut up unto the faith which should afterwards be revealed.

24 Wherefore the law was our schoolmaster to bring us unto Christ, that we might be justified by faith.

25 But after that faith is come, we are no longer under a schoolmaster.

NOTES

The Gospel: Faith in Christ

Lesson Text: Galatians 3:15-25

Related Scriptures: Romans 4:13-16; Romans 3:19-28;
Romans 10:1-13; Hebrews 11:1-10

TIME: possibly A.D. 48   PLACE: from Syrian Antioch

GOLDEN TEXT—"The scripture hath concluded all under sin, that the promise by faith of Jesus Christ might be given to them that believe" (Galatians 3:22).

Introduction

Billy possessed an amazing skill. If you told him how old you were and the month and day of your birth, he could instantly tell you what day of the week you were born on. His ability bordered on genius. Yet Billy was not a genius. In fact, he was mentally handicapped. He had little ability to carry on a conversation, would get lost if he left his house, and could not live on his own.

Billy had "savant syndrome," a condition in which a person who is developmentally handicapped displays brilliance in a limited area. Billy could instantly calculate the day of a person's birth with absolute accuracy. However, he could not do simple math, make change, or balance a checkbook. While he could do amazing calculations in his head, he could not relate this ability to life.

Few people are savants in this sense. However, it is not at all uncommon for even Christians who are very knowledgeable of the Bible to find it hard to relate those facts to the whole of Scripture and to life. Nowhere has this been more the case than in understanding the Law of Moses. A careful study of Paul's teaching, especially in the book of Galatians, provides the answers we all need.

LESSON OUTLINE

I. **THE LAW AND THE COVENANT—Gal. 3:15-22**

II. **THE LAW AND THE CHRISTIAN—Gal. 3:23-25**

Exposition: Verse by Verse

THE LAW AND THE COVENANT

GAL. 3:15 Brethren, I speak after the manner of men; Though it be but a man's covenant, yet if it be confirmed, no man disannulleth, or addeth thereto.

16 Now to Abraham and his seed were the promises made. He saith not, And to seeds, as of many; but as of one, And to thy seed, which is Christ.

17 And this I say, that the covenant, that was confirmed before of God in Christ, the law, which was four hundred and thirty years after, cannot disannul, that it should make the promise of none effect.

18 For if the inheritance be of the law, it is no more of promise: but God gave it to Abraham by promise.

19 Wherefore then serveth the law? It was added because of transgressions, till the seed should come to whom the promise was made; and it was ordained by angels in the hand of a mediator.

20 Now a mediator is not a mediator of one, but God is one.

21 Is the law then against the promises of God? God forbid: for if there had been a law given which could have given life, verily righteousness should have been by the law.

22 But the scripture hath concluded all under sin, that the promise by faith of Jesus Christ might be given to them that believe.

Paul had clearly taught the Galatians that salvation is a gracious gift of God that is received through faith in Christ. The experience of Abraham supported this (vs. 6). Since the true sons of Abraham are those who share his faith in God, they are the heirs of the spiritual promise of blessing given to Abraham (vss. 7-9). The false teachers, however, wanted to require even Gentiles to follow the Law of Moses. Paul therefore begins to explain the relationship of the law to the covenant God made with Abraham.

Human promises (Gal. 3:15). The Judaizers insisted that faith is not enough; the Law of Moses must be added to faith. This completely misrepresented both the covenant with Abraham and the law, which came many years later. The false teachers knew the law very well, but their teaching confused people with regard to

how the law related to the promise to Abraham or to faith in Christ.

In speaking "after the manner of men," Paul is using a common custom of the time in relation to agreements to illustrate his point. The apostle points out that even human covenants are binding. They cannot be annulled, and nothing can be added to them once they are ratified.

Divine promises (Gal. 3:16-18). What is true of human covenants is even more certainly the case with God's covenant promises. They cannot be annulled or added to. This is the Apostle Paul's point as he now turns to a divine covenant, specifically the Abrahamic covenant. The Abrahamic covenant is introduced in Genesis 12:1-3. The various elements of it are elaborated in Genesis 13, 15, 17, and 22, and it is repeated to Abraham's son Isaac (26:2-5) and to Isaac's son Jacob (28:13-15). Particularly in view here is the spiritual aspect of the blessing God promised to Abraham and his descendants, namely, "being justified by faith and having all the blessings of salvation" (Wiersbe, *Be Free,* Cook).

Paul writes that God's promises were made to Abraham and his "seed" (Gal. 3:16). Here he is speaking of Christ. While Abraham's physical descendants (seed) are the exclusive heirs of some of the provisions of the covenant, and all believers—those "of faith" (vs. 7)—share in the spiritual blessings of the covenant (vs. 29). Christ is uniquely the Seed through whom those blessings come.

It was in Christ that the sin problem was dealt with. And by faith in Him, the blessing of the covenant is extended to all believers.

Paul writes that the law came 430 years after the Abrahamic covenant. This number has been questioned since it would have been more than

600 years from the time the promise was given to Abraham until the Law was given to Moses. Paul is probably referring to the "time from the *ratification* of the covenant to Jacob just before he went to Egypt (Gen. 46:1-4) until the giving of the law at Sinai a few months after the exodus" (Kent, *The Freedom of God's Sons,* BMH). This agrees with the figure given in Exodus 12:40.

Paul's point is that the Law of Moses, which came many years after Abraham, could not annul God's promises to Abraham. Neither could it add to the covenant promises (Gal. 3:17).

If the law could add anything to faith, God's covenant would not be a promise at all but would be dependent on human effort (vs. 18). However, the covenant with Abraham was not just an agreement between humans. As Wiersbe points out, "Abraham did not make a covenant with God; *God made a covenant with Abraham.*" It was a one-sided covenant made while Abraham slept (Gen. 15). Thus it was a divine promise that ruled out human effort.

All this warns us against the subtle temptation to add something to faith. Nothing could ever be greater than the salvation we have through faith in Christ, because that salvation is solely dependent on the God who created us. It is by God's grace received by faith alone. It is not earned by keeping the Mosaic Law or doing good works.

Divine purpose (Gal. 3:19-22). If the Mosaic Law could add nothing to the promise of salvation through faith, what was its purpose? The answer is that it was "added because of transgressions." This statement suggests that the law was given in order to restrain sin. That certainly was one purpose of the law, for it defined what was and was not acceptable and assigned punishment for violating it.

However, Paul's language here can also be understood as saying that the law was given for the sake of revealing sin and its true character as the transgression of God's standards of righteousness. In other words, the law was given to condemn sinners, not save them (vs. 22).

Furthermore, the law given to Moses was temporary. It was to be in force just until "the seed should come to whom the promise was made" (vs. 19).

The Seed, again, is Christ. When He came, the purpose of the law was fulfilled. "The law was designed to prepare Israel to receive the covenant promise by putting its faith in the promised seed, namely Christ . . . For the individual the purpose of the law is terminated when he puts his faith in the seed of Abraham (Christ) and thus receives the promise of justification by faith alone" (Gromacki, *Stand Fast in Liberty,* Kress). The promise of justification by faith is forever; the Mosaic Law was temporary.

Paul notes as well that the law was "ordained by angels in the hand of a mediator." The law was given through angels and delivered to the people by a mediator, Moses. The involvement of angels in giving the law is also stated in Acts 7:53 and Hebrews 2:2. This angelic activity is absent from the Old Testament account, leaving it somewhat of a mystery, though Paul and his readers acknowledged the truth of it. There is, however, a distinct purpose in citing the involvement of angels and Moses. It sets the Law of Moses apart from the Abrahamic covenant and demonstrates its inherent inferiority.

This is seen in Galatians 3:20, where the apostle notes that in contrast to the law, the covenant with Abraham was given directly by God. A mediator represents two parties to an agreement, not just one. As mediator, Moses stood between God and the Israelite nation. There was no mediator of the covenant with Abraham. It was given directly by God to Abraham with no human mediator and no angels involved.

Paul is not dismissing the law. It too had come from God, and He had important purposes for it. But the Judaizers were elevating the law to a place of supreme importance and giving it purposes God never intended by making it the means of attaining righteousness and salvation. Paul is simply pointing out that the Abrahamic promises were greater than the law in that they were permanent and had no mediator.

Paul next anticipates a question that would naturally arise from his teaching: "Is the law then against the promises of God?" (vs. 21). That is, does the law contradict the teaching of salvation by grace? The apostle's answer: "God forbid," or more literally, "May it never be." Law and grace are not conflicting concepts but complementary ones. It was not Paul who was introducing the idea that law and grace are in conflict but the Judaizers, who were teaching that the law could give life. If that were true, there would be a clear conflict with the biblical doctrine of grace. Indeed, there would be no need for grace, for righteousness would come by the law.

In verse 22, the apostle explained how the law and God's grace complement each other rather than conflict with each other. In doing so, he returned to the true purpose of the law. He writes, "But the scripture hath concluded all under sin." Here "scripture" refers to the law. The Greek word translated "hath concluded" means "to shut up together on all sides" (Vine, Unger, and White, *Vine's Complete Expository Dictionary of Old and New Testament Words,* Nelson). The law reveals that all, without exception, have sinned.

Only when people recognize that they stand condemned before God because they fall infinitely short of His righteous standards are they pre-

pared to receive the promise of God's grace through faith in Jesus Christ. The purpose of the law was to reveal sin so that sinners would see their desperate need and ultimately believe in Christ for salvation. "Seen from this angle, even the law flowed from God's grace, because it prepared people to receive the Lord Jesus Christ when he came" (Barker and Kohlenberger, eds., *The Expositor's Bible Commentary, Abridged Edition,* Zondervan).

THE LAW AND THE CHRISTIAN

23 But before faith came, we were kept under the law, shut up unto the faith which should afterwards be revealed.

24 Wherefore the law was our schoolmaster to bring us unto Christ, that we might be justified by faith.

25 But after that faith is come, we are no longer under a schoolmaster.

Before faith (Gal. 3:23-24). The law was temporary, and its primary purpose was to reveal people's sin and thus their need for the Saviour. But how does the law relate to those who have come to faith in Christ? Are they still obligated to keep it, as the Judaizers taught? Indeed, are we Christians today to seek to keep the Mosaic Law? The Apostle Paul begins to address this issue in verse 23.

First, he looks backward, saying, "Before faith came, we were kept under the law." "Faith" here is literally "the faith." In view is the "faith of Jesus Christ" (vs. 22), not simply faith in general, which has always existed. Before this faith in Christ appeared with Christ's coming into the world, "we were kept under the law" (vs. 23). The reference is to Jewish people, of whom Paul was one.

The Jews were "kept," or guarded, under the Law of Moses and "shut up" by it. Here "shut up" translates the same word used in verse 22 for "hath concluded." The picture is of the law holding people in custody even while pointing out their sin. This seemingly hopeless condition was temporary, however. It continued only until the faith was fully revealed in Christ.

While on the one hand the law acted as a jailer, shutting people up in sin, on the other hand it also acted as a "schoolmaster" (vs. 24). We should not think of a schoolteacher here, for the term *paidagogos* refers to a guardian or guide. In Roman and Greek society, this guardian was typically a slave entrusted with the protection, management, and discipline of a child.

By depicting the law as a guardian, Paul is showing that it did not give life, as the false teachers claimed, but rather regulated life. Furthermore, just as the guardian prepared the child for maturity, "the law was a preparation for the nation of Israel until the coming of the promised Seed, Jesus Christ" (Wiersbe). It pointed them to Christ so that they might be justified by faith. (Gal. 3:24).

After faith (Gal. 3:25). When Christ came, the law, which pointed to Him, was no longer needed. For the Jewish people, this meant that when they placed their faith in Jesus Christ, they were no longer under the guardianship of the law. The law had served its purpose.

Again, Paul is teaching that the law, though it served a good purpose, was temporary and is no longer needed by the Christian. But what about Gentiles, who were never under the law? The same held true for them. Once they had realized their need for Christ and come to faith in Him, it would be a disaster for them to place themselves under a guardian, as the Judaizers wished them to do. This would be giving up freedom in Christ for the bondage of keeping a law they could never fully obey, a law that would only condemn them.

The law is good. It had an important role for the nation of Israel, and it can teach us much even today about God and humanity. But in Christ we are free from the law. It is by faith we are justified before God—and by faith we are to live for God by the power of God the Holy Spirit. Yes, in Christ there are commands to obey, but we obey out of gratitude and by the Spirit's power—not to make ourselves acceptable to God but to offer acceptable praise to Him.

—*Jarl K. Waggoner.*

QUESTIONS

1. What point does Paul make in referring to human covenants?

2. Who is the "seed" to whom God made promises (Gal. 3:16)?

3. Why is it important to note that the law was given long after the promise to Abraham?

4. How was the Abrahamic covenant different from human agreements?

5. What is meant by the law being "added because of transgressions" (vs. 19)?

6. What demonstrates the superiority of the Abrahamic promise over the Mosaic Law?

7. Does the law conflict with faith? Explain.

8. What was the role of the law for Israel?

9. How did a "schoolmaster" picture the work of the law (vs. 24)?

10. Why are Christians not under the law?

—*Jarl K. Waggoner.*

Preparing to Teach the Lesson

As this lesson is being written, news about catastrophic multiple shootings fill the air waves. It is a clear indication that we live in a world full of sin. This week we explore the only answer to this dilemma in the true gospel of Jesus Christ.

TODAY'S AIM

Facts: to show how we can receive God's promises when we receive what Jesus has done for us.

Principle: to receive the gospel of Jesus and inherit the promises that God has made to us.

Application: to remember that when we received Jesus by faith, we receive the remedy for our sin.

INTRODUCING THE LESSON

Have you ever had a promise made to you but you expected that the promise would never materialize? Then, one day, the person who made that promise to you shows up and makes good on his promise. What an exciting day that becomes! In the Old Testament we find that God made several promises that pointed to the coming Messiah. When Jesus came into our world, all those promises by God became a reality.

DEVELOPING THE LESSON

1. God gave a promise to Abraham (Gal. 3:15-18). As human beings, we make promises to one another. Normally we expect promises to be kept. Our trust that a promise will be kept is based on the trustworthiness of the one who made it. In the same manner, we find that God made a promise to Abraham and his son Isaac (cf. Gen. 12:3,7; 17:7). Their descendants were set apart to be the heirs of God's blessings as a nation.

Paul points out that the promises made by God were made to Abraham and his seed (Gal. 3:16). The word "seed" here is a direct reference to Jesus, the Messiah. Paul also reminds us that the Law was not given until 430 years after Abraham. Paul affirms the fact that God cannot and will never break His promises.

Did God change His mind about sending the Messiah when the Law came on the scene through Moses? Paul is an expert in theological reasoning. He challenges us to think. The blessing could not be received by law-keeping. The Law was just a forerunner to the ultimate promise from God in Christ. God is always faithful to His promises. God's answer to the world came in the form of a promise. At that time, this promise was yet unfulfilled because the Law could never provide the salvation we need.

2. The Law was temporary till the promise came (Gal. 3:19-20). Paul asks a very relevant question as he continues his argument for the gospel. Why was the Law given? It was given only for the time till Christ came. It was needed as a temporary measure to convict people of their sin problem. God gave His Law to Moses, through angels on Mount Sinai.

Normally mediations require two parties to agree on something. In contrast to the Law of Moses, God did not use a mediator for the Abrahamic covenant. God was His own mediator. This shows the superiority of this earlier covenant, which climaxes in the gracious work of Christ.

It is important for us to understand that while there is a legitimate use for the Law, by itself it is not a plan of salvation. The better promise came through Jesus Christ and the saving power of His gospel. He fulfilled the requirements of the Law through His sinless life and vicarious death so that we who believe will not be punished for our sins. Christ set us free to enjoy the benefits of the gospel through faith in what He has provided for us.

3. God's promise is received through faith in Jesus (Gal. 3:21-25). Paul reminds us that God's law does not contradict the promise of God. However, it does not go far enough to provide a solution for our sin dilemma. If the Law could give us righteousness, then we could have also been saved by the Law. But that cannot happen because the Law falls short of that. Eventually we will break the Law, no matter how much we try to keep it. The gospel makes us righteous through Jesus' perfect righteousness.

Here is what the gospel does. We were under sin's power. Through the gospel, we believe in Jesus and receive His righteousness through faith. This is the only way to appropriate the perfect righteousness that God requires. The Law shows us our need of the gospel because it makes us see our sinfulness. But now that Jesus has come, He has opened the way for us through faith in Him. Help the class to see that while the Law brought failure, the gospel opens all the promises of God to us.

The Law was like a temporary teacher or tutor who taught us about sin and righteousness until the true gospel came. But now that the true gospel has come, we do not need the tutor any more. Trusting Jesus in faith has opened the way to become right with God. The Law trained us, like a schoolmaster who guided us for a time. Jesus brought the true gospel to us. We are now free from bondage under the law of sin because Jesus is all that we need to save us from sin.

Get your students to think seriously about what it means to be absolutely free from the Law and to embrace the freedom that comes through knowing our Lord Jesus. How does this impact our everyday lives?

ILLUSTRATING THE LESSON

The Law led the way to Jesus and His true gospel.

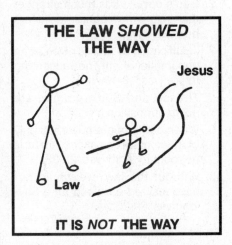

THE LAW *SHOWED* THE WAY

Jesus

Law

IT IS *NOT* THE WAY

CONCLUDING THE LESSON

It is interesting that Paul spent so much time teaching the Galatian believers that the Law was now outdated because the true gospel is here and can be received by faith. Many of us, even in church, carry unnecessary burdens because we feel that we have to do something to earn our salvation. The problem that the Galatian church faced is the same problem that we sometimes deal with today. Usually this manifests itself as legalism within the church.

The gospel has offered us freedom from having to do things to get right with God. God gave us the gospel to be received through faith in Christ. Sin has already been paid for. And who does not want to be free?

ANTICIPATING THE NEXT LESSON

Next week we will gain insights about how we have been adopted as sons.

—A. Koshy Muthalaly.

PRACTICAL POINTS

1. Once a person has made a covenant, that covenant stands on its own (Gal. 3:15).
2. God's covenant is much stronger than man's covenant and cannot be voided (vss. 16-17).
3. Justification by faith is given as an unconditional gift, not according to law (vss. 18-19).
4. The law and God's promise are not in opposition (vs. 20-21).
5. When our lives are governed only by rules and regulations, there is no room for faith (vss. 22-23).
6. Without the law, we would not have realized our need for a Saviour (vss. 24-25).

—*Charity G. Carter.*

RESEARCH AND DISCUSSION

1. What is the significance of Abraham's promise being made to his "seed" rather than his "seeds" (Gal. 3:16)?
2. The promise God issued to Abraham had nothing to do with the law. So why is the law frequently discussed when people talk about that promise (vss. 18-19)?
3. What is the main difference between the law and God's promise (vss. 20-21)?
4. How do we receive the promise of faith (vs. 22)?
5. Describe life prior to trusting Jesus and what life is like now (vs. 23).
6. Why does the law no longer serve as our guardian (vs. 25)?

—*Charity G. Carter.*

ILLUSTRATED HIGH POINTS

Confirmed, no man disannulleth

Anna was an eighteen-year-old slave girl whose owner lived near a Christian family, the VanCamps.

Eventually, Mr. VanCamp found Anna behind a building, beaten and sick with fever. With love, he went to the slave dealer and bought her. Thereafter, he and his wife loved and cared for her as their own. To ensure her care after their death, they bestowed upon her both their properties and her freedom. Sadly, upon their passing it was discovered that, though Mr. VanCamp had the best intentions, the freedom papers had not been signed!

In man's world, a contract is confirmed by pen and ink. In God's kingdom, His promises are confirmed with a cross and our Saviour's blood.

Saith not . . . to seeds, . . . but as of one

British born stock broker Nicholas Winton cancelled his ski vacation to visit Czechoslovakia, where he met the (mostly) Jewish refugees. Perceiving that the Czechs would soon be invaded by the Nazis, he took it upon himself to save the children. He took the names of children from parents who wanted their dear ones taken to England for safekeeping.

Just days before the Nazi invasion, Winton organized the first transport by plane out of Prague. He then continued to organize more transports by plane, railroad, and boat—eight in all. Between March and August of 1939, he managed to rescue 669 endangered children.

Often, God blesses just one individual to bless many others. God chose to save the world with a single blessed man willing to give His own life to rescue all who are willing to sign onto His plan.

—*Therese Greenberg.*

Golden Text Illuminated

"The scripture hath concluded all under sin, that the promise by faith of Jesus Christ might be given to them that believe" (Galatians 3:22).

In his letter to the Galatian church, Paul tried to make clear the purpose of the Law of Moses and the promise God gave to Abraham hundreds of years before.

Galatians is an especially helpful book for believers who have grown up in a church that put heavy emphasis on rule keeping and little emphasis on the grace and freedom Christ gives.

Aware of the ongoing tension of the relationship between law and grace, Paul decided to appeal to the Galatians' logic. He pointed out the validity of promises made among regular people (Gal. 3:15). How much more trustworthy, then, is the very Word of God, who cannot lie (Num. 23:19)?

God made a promise of a coming Messiah to Abraham and his seed (Gal. 3:16). This was a permanent covenant invoked by God that could not be changed or revoked (vs. 17).

The Judaizers, however, were influencing the Galatian church with their distorted teaching. These corrupted doctrines were especially alluring because they contained partial truths.

The Law, for example, was very important, but not for the reasons the Judaizers promoted. The Law serves as a tool to show sinners their need to depend on Christ (Gal. 3:24), since nobody can keep the Law perfectly (cf. Matt. 5:19-20; Rom. 3:10).

Paul knew that the believers' attempts to win God's favor by following rules and traditions were due to faulty thinking. By these fruitless attempts, it was as if the Galatians were rejecting the true gospel.

Paul wanted his readers to consider the chronological order of the promise of salvation through faith in Christ and the establishment of the Law of Moses. The promise came first—in fact, 430 years before anyone was even given the Law.

There was no reason for the Galatians to question the faith they had expressed in Christ; it did not somehow lack sufficiency for salvation.

The Word of God reveals that the entire human race is under sin's control (Rom. 6:17) and will, left in this unregenerate state, suffer sin's punishment (vs. 23). The glorious way out of such a desperate condition and fate is for those who are still lost to put their faith in the true gospel of Jesus Christ.

Some may ask, "What is faith?" Hebrews 11:1 tells us, "Now faith is the substance of things hoped for, the evidence of things not seen." Much of Hebrews 11 shows how precious faith is in the eyes and heart of God (vs. 6).

Paul wanted the Galatian church to rest secure in the entirety of the true gospel. They received the promise of salvation when they believed in Jesus Christ, and they would be kept by His righteous power (I Pet. 1:5), not by keeping the law.

Do not complicate faith like so many others. Instead, keep your eyes on Jesus, "the author and finisher" of your faith (Heb. 12:2).

There is a saying, "Keep it simple, silly." Acts 16:31 says, "Believe on the Lord Jesus Christ, and thou shalt be saved." That, my friend, is simple!

—Christine M. Morrison.

Heart of the Lesson

An individual goes to the bank to borrow five thousand dollars. He or she signs a contract to pay a certain amount each month. At the end of the allotted time, the loan balance should be zero. Instead, this person decides to stop making payments before the contract ends, violating the agreement. In direct contrast to such a broken agreement, God made a covenant with Abraham years ago that still applies to Christians today. God always keeps His promises and never breaks them. Paul reminded the Galatians of God's faithfulness in his letter.

1. God's promise (Gal. 3:15-18).

Paul was attempting to persuade the Galatians to believe God's Word was true. He recounted the promise God made with Abraham. This agreement was confirmed through Jesus, a descendant of Abraham. Paul proclaims that the promise made to Abraham can never be annulled. In other words, no one can alter God's agreements. This covenant allowed the Galatians to have a relationship with God through Christ.

Every day, people sign contracts to finance a new home, a different vehicle, or a frivolous trinket. Most people keep their promises and pay the loan off on time. There are some people, however, who fail to keep their contract. The loan company has to take these people to court to obtain the money that was borrowed. God does not operate that way. God's covenant with Abraham is a gift, not a loan.

People should be thankful that God made the agreement with Abraham, which even now allows people to have an intimate relationship with Christ. As God promised, Jesus came to provide salvation for lost souls. Without this contract—this gift—no one is able to be saved. Christians should praise God each day for this promise that has been fulfilled through Christ. Furthermore, Jesus has promised to return to earth and take Christians to heaven someday. We know that He has kept all His previous promises; He will keep this one too.

2. The law's purpose (Gal. 3:19-25).

The Galatians needed to understand the purpose of the law. The Jewish law told people that they were sinners, but it could not free them from their punishment. Paul compares the law to a "schoolmaster," a tutor (usually a slave) who had charge over the heirs of a household before they came of age. The law's authority or jurisdiction ended, however, when Christ died for sinners and faith came, that is, became available to all nations, Jews and Gentiles alike. The Galatian church needed to trust that God would keep His promise to justify them through their faith.

Christ's atonement ended the need for Jewish law. Jesus' death provided for the freedom of every individual. God's promise to Abraham was fulfilled and still applies today. Sometimes people allow their faith to falter and forget that God has faithfully kept His promises. That is why it is crucial to keep studying God's Word and coming into His presence in prayer. These things will remind you of His faithfulness. Placing trust in God is the only way to achieve peace and freedom.

Have you received God's freedom? Have you liberated yourself from the tedious requirements the world has placed on salvation? All you need to do is place your trust in the Almighty God and receive the greatest gift given to man. Then, have faith that God will keep you safely in His loving arms and take you to live with Him in heaven.

—*Catherine Moore.*

World Missions

"I lived in fear without hope," said Beni from Togo. "I wore an amulet against evil spirits. It was a life of darkness—without forgiveness or love."

In New Mexico, prisoner Mario said, "I want to be a new person. I'm tired of this life. Can you send me those study booklets that the other prisoners are reading?"

At a camp for handicapped teens in Michigan, after the sermon a blind boy stood up and said loudly, "I would get saved now if I knew which way to go!"

These words represent millions who need the gospel we enjoy. Christians in America are blessed with overwhelming spiritual abundance. We have access to as many Bibles as we want, plus resources in books and on the internet that we can freely peruse and study without fear of persecution.

What are we doing to get this great gospel to the world? When was the last time we truly sacrificed so others could know Christ?

In northern India, Mamta went blind due to a wrong medication put into her eyes. She travels with Usha, a girl with polio, and the two have played a major part in starting four churches.

Samar Pradhan and his family have served with Source of Light Ministries International since 1980. All of his work could be supported with 200 dollars per month. At present, he receives nothing. He would like to host a series of camps to train Christians in his area on how to reach Muslims. He could do this with 700 dollars, but the money is just not there.

Villages beg for missionaries to come teach them the truth. People groups long for Bibles in their own language. Right now there is a world in need of salvation, a plenteous harvest waiting for the truth.

What is our part in all this? As God calls us to give to the work being done around the world, many mission boards are just waiting for funds to be able to get the gospel to more people.

One of these missions agencies is Source of Light Ministries International, based out of Madison, Georgia. They print and distribute a great abundance of Bible lessons and other materials around the globe. In the Philippines, in just one month over 10,000 Bible lessons were distributed in a prison ministry, and 105 people came to faith in Christ. In West Bengal, a new believer shared his booklet from Source of Light with 30 of his friends. Twenty of them professed faith in Christ.

Funds are greatly needed. National missionaries can be supported with accountability through this ministry. With an 800 dollar donation, 18,000 Bible lessons could be printed on a huge roll of paper, or there are multiple other opportunities to give. (www. sourcelight.org).

Remember Beni from Togo? He received Christ and now says, "From that moment on, my life was changed and is now filled with so much hope. I no longer live in doubt. I live with the expectation of my Saviour from heaven."

Living for ourselves is so far short of the life God intends for us; it dishonors the value of the gospel we carry. As a statement attributed to Ben Franklin sets forth, "A man wrapped up in himself makes a very small bundle." We are not meant to hoard the truth.

The harvest truly is plenteous. The laborers are few. Today will you pray, give, or go so more lost souls like Beni can be saved? —*Kimberly Rae.*

The Jewish Aspect

When Paul told the Galatians that all were under sin (Gal. 3:22), this was in agreement with the Hebrew Bible's statement that man's heart is evil from youth (Gen. 8:21). The Psalmist David spoke fervently of his sin. "For I acknowledge my transgressions: and my sin is ever before me" (51:3). God also sent the prophets to guide and warn His people of their sin. "The literal meanings of the Heb. And Gr. Words variously rendered 'sin,' 'sinner,' etc. disclose the true nature of sin in its manifold manifestations. Sin is transgression, an overstepping of the law, the divine boundary between good and evil (Psa. 51.1; Lk. 15.29); iniquity, an act inherently wrong, whether expressly forbidden or not; error, a departure from right (Psa. 51.9; Rom. 3.23); missing the mark, a failure to meet the divine standard; trespass, the intrusion of self-will into the sphere of divine authority (Eph. 2.1); lawlessness, or spiritual anarchy (1 Tim. 1.9); unbelief, or an insult to the divine veracity (John 16.9)" (*The Scofield Reference Bible*).

Ancient Jews knew that it was impossible to keep the entirety of the law (Deut. 27:26), and atonement for sin was required. Animal (blood) sacrifices were the primary ritual for forgiveness of sins in ancient Judaism (Lev. 17:11). Paul explained that since man could not keep the law, the righteousness of God comes by faith in Jesus Christ and His blood sacrifice (Rom. 3:20-25). This righteousness without the law, he said, was witnessed by the law and the prophets (Rom. 3:21). David sang of God's righteousness (Ps. 51:14). The prophet Isaiah spoke of the righteousness of God, as did the prophet Jeremiah. "Behold, the days come, saith the Lord, that I will raise unto David a righteous Branch, and a King shall reign and prosper, and shall execute judgment and justice in the earth. In his days Judah will be saved, and Israel shall dwell safely: and this is his name whereby he shall be called, THE LORD OUR RIGHTEOUSNESS" (Jer. 23:5-6).

When Paul spoke of the redemption that is in Jesus (Rom. 3:24), the Jewish believers in Rome would have understood the meaning of redemption from the Hebrew Bible. "Finding its context in the social, legal and religious customs of the ancient world, the metaphor of redemption includes the ideas of loosing from a bond, setting free from captivity or slavery, buying back something lost or sold, exchanging something in one's possession for something possessed by another, and ransoming. . . . As one who delivers his people, Yahweh is called Israel's 'Redeemer,' especially in Isaiah where 'redemption' is a key metaphor (41:14; 43:1; 44:6; 47:4)," (Elwell, ed., *Baker's Evangelical Dictionary of Biblical Theology*, Baker).

Paul explained to the Romans that it was the confession of their faith that brought salvation (Rom. 10:9-13). When he said, "But what saith it? The word is nigh thee, even in thy mouth and in thy heart: that is, the word of faith, which we preach" (vs. 8), he was quoting Deuteronomy 30:14. When he said, "For whosoever shall call upon the name of the Lord shall be saved" (Rom. 10:13), he was quoting the prophet Joel, "And it shall come to pass, that whosoever shall call on the name of the Lord shall be delivered" (2:32). Many ancient Jews obtained a good report based on their faith (Heb. 11).

—Deborah Markowitz Solan.

Guiding the Superintendent

If the gospel is as simple as Paul has been claiming, a very basic question arises. If salvation does not involve the Law, then why was the Law given in the first place:/ Second only to that question: Why would God allow it to rule for over fifteen hundred years?

The text of Galatians now addresses these questions.

DEVOTIONAL OUTLINE

1. The promise not changed (Gal. 3:15-18). The idea of promise is used in the text to refer to the initial pledge given to Abraham: "He believed in the Lord; and he counted it to him for righteousness" (Gen. 15:6).

A very simple illustration is used by the apostle to explain his point. When two parties make an agreement it is called a covenant. A third party cannot years later change it. For merely one of the two parties to add or subtract from the details of the covenant would be a betrayal.

God's promise made to Abraham was essentially made with Christ. So the Law given 430 years later could not change the original promise.

The promise coming years before the Law had no bearing on the Law. It was all of God's grace.

2. Show people their guilt (Gal. 3:19-20). If the purpose of the law was not to change the promise, what was its divine purpose? It was "added because of transgressions" until Christ would come. The law, then, was never intended to save anyone. Rather, it was added to the promise to convict people of their sin and their need for salvation. When Christ came, it would no longer be needed.

3. Drive the Sinner to Christ (Gal. 3:21-25). All along, the law's purpose was to point people to Christ. Therefore, the law and promise could never be in conflict. The Law was an expression of God's justice that pointed ultimately to the fulfillment of the promise to Abraham.

The Law also imprisoned the sinner until Christ came. The Law constrained and pushed people toward faith.

The Law was like a schoolmaster who trained and prepared us for faith in Christ. Now that Christ has come, the teacher is no longer needed.

CHILDREN'S CORNER

text: **Daniel 3:13-18, 21-26**
title: **The Three Hebrews: Ready to Die**

The king could not be angrier. He had commanded that all those under his rule were to bow before his idol of gold! He demanded to see the three men who had refused his order.

Shadrach, Meshach, and Abednego were ushered into the king's presence. Yes, it was true, they said, They did not bow when told. Despite his anger, the king offered them a second chance.

The three men told the king they were servants of God. They would trust God even if they ended up in the fire.

The angry king ordered the furnace heated up seven times hotter and had the men thrown in.

To the surprise of everyone, including the king, suddenly there were four, not three, men in the fire. In the king's own words "the fourth [man] is like the Son of God" (Dan. 3:25).

The old chorus could not be truer: "They wouldn't bow, they wouldn't bend, they wouldn't burn" (Smith, "The Fourth Man").

—*Martin R. Dahlquist.*

Scripture Lesson Text

GAL. 3:26 For ye are all the children of God by faith in Christ Jesus.

27 For as many of you as have been baptized into Christ have put on Christ.

28 There is neither Jew nor Greek, there is neither bond nor free, there is neither male nor female: for ye are all one in Christ Jesus.

29 And if ye be Christ's, then are ye Abraham's seed, and heirs according to the promise.

4:1 Now I say, That the heir, as long as he is a child, differeth nothing from a servant, though he be lord of all;

2 But is under tutors and governors until the time appointed of the father.

3 Even so we, when we were children, were in bondage under the elements of the world:

4 But when the fulness of the time was come, God sent forth his Son, made of a woman, made under the law,

5 To redeem them that were under the law, that we might receive the adoption of sons.

6 And because ye are sons, God hath sent forth the Spirit of his Son into your hearts, crying, Abba, Father.

7 Wherefore thou art no more a servant, but a son; and if a son, then an heir of God through Christ.

NOTES

Heirs Because of the Gospel

Lesson Text: Galatians 3:26—4:7

Related Scriptures: John 1:11-13; Romans 9:6-16;
Romans 8:14-17; Titus 3:3-7

TIME: possibly A.D. 48   PLACE: from Syrian Antioch

GOLDEN TEXT—"If ye be Christ's, then are ye Abraham's seed, and heirs according to the promise" (Galatians 3:29).

Introduction

While spending some time in the western United States years ago, I found myself amused by the responses of people when I told them I was from West Virgina. Quite often, the response was something like this: "Oh, I have a friend who lives in Richmond." I quickly realized that many people did not know West Virginia was a state. They thought I was from the western part of Virginia!

Impromptu street interviews are easy to find on the Internet. Many of them demonstrate in a humorous—and often appalling—way the widespread ignorance and confusion of people when it comes to geography, history, and current events. But I wonder what kinds of responses people on the street would have to questions about Christianity. I think we would be greatly disappointed to see the level of ignorance that reigns in the Western world with regard to our faith.

The issues Paul dealt with in Galatians are still with us. There is much confusion, even within Christian circles, about salvation, faith, works, and the relationship of the law to the Christian believer. The apostle clearly and thoroughly addresses such matters in the passage before us in this lesson.

LESSON OUTLINE

I. THE REWARDS OF FAITH—
   Gal. 3:26-29

II. A NEW POSITION—Gal. 4:1-7

Exposition: Verse by Verse

THE REWARDS OF FAITH

GAL. 3:26 For ye are all the children of God by faith in Christ Jesus.
27 For as many of you as have been baptized into Christ have put on Christ.

28 There is neither Jew nor Greek, there is neither bond nor free, there is neither male nor female: for ye are all one in Christ Jesus.
29 And if ye be Christ's, then are

ye Abraham's seed, and heirs according to the promise.

Starting in Galatians 2:15, Paul goes to great lengths to present the biblical doctrine of justification by faith alone—that a person is declared righteous before God solely through faith in Christ. The Law of Moses could not and cannot justify anyone (3:16); it can only make a person aware of his sin and condemnation before God (vss. 10-11). This is the true importance of the law. It shows us how sinful and hopeless we are so that in faith we turn to Christ alone.

Paul writes, "The law was our schoolmaster to bring us unto Christ, that we might be justified by faith" (vs. 24). Once we have come to faith in Christ, "we are no longer under a schoolmaster" (vs. 25). In the verses that follow, the apostle elaborates on what this truth means for believers.

Sons of God (Gal. 3:26). Through faith in Jesus Christ, all believers have become children of God. This new relationship to the Lord could never be attained through flawed obedience to the Law of Moses. Indeed, those who are under the dominion of the law are like young children under the authority of a schoolmaster, or tutor. Faith in Christ brings one into the family of God as His son. "Children of God" is literally "sons of God." The expression speaks of mature sons in contrast with children, who are still under a tutor. Those who have placed their faith in Christ are no longer held under bondage to the demands of the law. They are now mature sons and daughters of God.

Unity in Christ (Gal. 3:27-28). All believers are children of God, and this new relationship comes about through faith, not by carefully observing the Jewish law. This is the truth stated in verse 26, and it is essentially repeated in verse 27 from a slightly different perspective: "As many of you as have been baptized into Christ have put on Christ."

Baptism here does not refer to water baptism but to the baptism of the Spirit. The moment a person trusts in Christ for salvation, the Holy Spirit enters that person's life. The Spirit identifies that person with Christ and spiritually places him or her into the body of Christ (I Cor. 12:13; cf. Rom. 8:9). The apostle describes this as putting on Christ (Gal. 3:27). The believer is united so closely with Christ that he or she can be said to be clothed in Him. Faith not only brings one into the family of God but also initiates the spiritual baptism that brings one into union with Christ.

Water baptism symbolizes this union with Christ. However, like keeping the law or doing any other work, it can do nothing to actually bring this union about.

In his dealings with the Galatians, Paul found it necessary to combat false teaching by emphasizing that Gentiles did not have to become Jews and follow the law in order to be saved. Justification is by faith alone for both Jews and Gentiles; therefore, all are "one in Christ Jesus" (vs. 28). All believers, regardless of earthly distinctions of race, gender, or position, share "in a vital union with [Christ], whereby they share His life, His perfect righteousness, and the prospect of participating in the promises He will receive as the Messianic Heir" (Kent, *The Freedom of God's Sons,* BMH).

Some social distinctions must necessarily be made in this life, but they have no bearing on one's relationship to Christ. All who come to Christ in faith are united as one in Him.

Every Christian is unique and distinct, but all believers have come to Christ in the same way—by faith. All are united in Him as one body

(I Cor. 12:13), and all are essential to the proper working of that one body, which we call the church. There is no place in Christ's church for pride or self-centeredness. We who are saved by grace are to be gracious to one another.

Heirs of the promises (Gal. 3:29). All who belong to Christ by faith and are therefore in Him are also "Abraham's seed, and heirs according to the promise." Since Christ is uniquely Abraham's "seed," or Descendant (vs. 16), all those who are in Christ are likewise Abraham's seed and heirs of the promises made to him.

Abraham was given some promises that were for him personally and others that were for his descendants through Isaac and Jacob, the nation of Israel (cf. Gen. 12:1-2). The promises that all believers inherit are those blessings promised to all "families of the earth" (vs. 3). Through Christ, Abraham's Descendant, believers of all nations receive the blessing of justification and all the spiritual blessings that flow from that divine work.

Paul's point is clear: "The Mosaic Law . . . could not make men sons of God, Abraham's seed, nor heirs. [These blessings] are due solely to God's promise which is received by faith" (Kent).

A NEW POSITION

4:1 Now I say, That the heir, as long as he is a child, differeth nothing from a servant, though he be lord of all;

2 But is under tutors and governors until the time appointed of the father.

3 Even so we, when we were children, were in bondage under the elements of the world:

4 But when the fulness of the time was come, God sent forth his Son, made of a woman, made under the law,

5 To redeem them that were under the law, that we might receive the adoption of sons.

6 And because ye are sons, God hath sent forth the Spirit of his Son into your hearts, crying, Abba, Father.

7 Wherefore thou art no more a servant, but a son; and if a son, then an heir of God through Christ.

From children in bondage (Gal. 4:1-3). Believers have a new position in Christ as sons and heirs, as Paul states. These benefits come through faith in Christ, not through keeping the Mosaic Law, as some in Galatia were teaching. But the law was given by God and is thus good. How, then, does it relate to the new status all believers in Christ enjoy? Paul presented an illustration to show how believers in Christ are related to the law.

Paul had spoken of believers as heirs of the promises given to Abraham. Now he goes back to picture an heir who is still a child. Such a child is no different from a servant in the household. In fact, until he is recognized as an adult by his father, the heir may well be under the supervision of servants. While legally he was "lord of all" (vs. 1) and would inherit what his father owned, as long as he was still a child, he was under the guardianship of "tutors and governors (household managers)" (vs. 2). The family servants had authority over him.

Paul is apparently drawing from Roman custom with this illustration, but he applies it to himself and his fellow Jewish believers. When they were children, he writes, they "were in bondage under the elements of the world" (vs. 3). Before they came to Christ, they were "children." This term is used to picture spiritual immaturity. Before they were converted, they did not have the freedom of full-grown sons and heirs. In fact, they were enslaved to the "elements of the world."

What were these "elements"? The term could refer to demonic forces that enslaved the pagan Galatians, or it could be a general reference to religious bondage, whether Jewish or pagan. The context, however, suggests that the Law of Moses is in view. The law kept the Jewish believers in bondage, and now it threatened to enslave Gentile believers, as the false teachers sought to impose it on them.

How could the good law of God be a slavemaster? Before Christ came, the Jewish people stood condemned by the law God had given them. It pointed out their sin but offered no permanent solution for it. As such, the law kept people in the bondage of sin. However, as Paul notes, the law not only revealed people's sin; in revealing sin it also acted as a schoolmaster to show people the hopelessness of human works and the need to turn to Christ that they might be justified, or declared righteous, through faith (3:19-25).

The law was a tutor instructing people regarding God's requirements and their own sin so that when Christ came, they would trust Him to save them. The Judaism of Paul's day, however, saw the law as the means of salvation and thus left people in bondage to their sin.

Through redemption (Gal. 4:4-5). The transition from children in bondage to freedom and sonship was accomplished through Christ's coming into the world and purchasing redemption for all who believe. His coming occurred in "the fulness of the time." That is, it was exactly in accordance with God's timeline. Prophetically, the time was established in Daniel 9:24-27. Historically, it was a time when the world was perfectly prepared for His arrival.

At the perfect time in God's eternal plan, He "sent forth his Son, made of a woman, made under the law" (Gal. 4:4). The wording here stresses both Jesus' deity and His humanity. He is fully God and also fully man. The apostle also emphasizes that as a Jew, Jesus was born and lived under the Mosaic Law and thus was obligated to keep it. Unlike His fellow Jews, however, Jesus kept the law perfectly (cf. Heb. 4:15), and this qualified Him to redeem His people (Gal. 4:5).

"Redemption" refers to setting someone free by paying a price. "It emphasizes that through His death, Christ set the believer free from enslavement to sin" (Enns, *The Moody Handbook of Theology,* Moody). The price paid for our salvation was His death on the cross. In relation to Jewish believers, Christ's death redeemed those who were "under the law" (vs. 4) and its bondage.

Before Christ's coming, those like Abraham who had faith in the Lord were counted as righteous before God (cf. Gen. 15:6). But they could be counted as righteous only on the basis of Christ's death, which actually paid for their sin. In God's perfect timing, Christ came and died in their place to redeem them.

In the context of the apostle's argument, the implication is clear: "since Christ redeemed and set free those who were under the Law, why should Gentile converts now wish to be placed under it?" (Walvoord and Zuck, eds., *The Bible Knowledge Commentary,* Cook). Indeed, why would anybody want to trade such freedom for spiritual bondage?

Those who are redeemed by Christ also receive adoption as sons. The concept of adoption here is not concerned with being moved from one family into another, as we think of adoption today. Rather, it is conferring on one the full rights of sonship. Those who have been born into the family of God by faith are like heirs who have reached adulthood and are no longer under guardians. In no way would God require those He has redeemed and made His sons through faith to put themselves under the bondage of the law, whether they are Jews or Gentiles.

To sons and heirs (Gal. 4:6-7). Through the redemption of Christ, believers have been lifted to a new spiritual status. They are mature sons of God. The Holy Spirit resides within them and gives them assurance of their relationship with God (cf. Rom. 8:14-16) so that they are able to cry out, "Abba, Father" (Gal. 4:6).

"Abba" is the Aramaic form of the word "Father." It conveys a sense of intimacy. We who have been redeemed through Christ's death can, as sons of God, address our Father personally and with the greatest affection as One we know and love.

The Apostle Paul summarizes his whole argument in this section in verse 7. Interestingly, he switches from the plural "ye" to the singular "thou." In so doing, he is addressing believers individually. Each of the believers in Galatia had been redeemed by Christ. Each one was no longer a slave in bondage to the law but free. More than that, every one of them had the privileged position of God's son.

Kent points out, "This answers the question of why the law is not binding on Christians as it had been on Old Testament saints. The period of the law's guardianship ended with Christ's coming. Full sonship is the present believer's experience."

Because he is a son, the believer in Christ is also "an heir of God through Christ." He inherits the promises to Abraham and his seed (cf. Rom. 8:17).

And his inheritance is based solely on faith in Christ, not on keeping the law.

The Galatians were confused by false teachers who were seeking to lead them back to a righteousness based on the law. Yet because of their faith in Christ, Paul could still call them sons and heirs. That he had to carefully and forcefully correct them, however, reminds us that even Christians can be taken in by deceptive and destructive teaching. We must strive to be biblically knowledgeable, diligent in defending the truth of God's Word, and consistent in applying that Word to our lives as we walk by faith.

—*Jarl K. Waggoner.*

QUESTIONS

1. To what does "children of God" in Galatians 3:26 refer?

2. What does it mean to be "baptized into Christ" (vs. 27)? How does this relate to water baptism?

3. What earthly distinctions do not exist in Christ?

4. What promises to Abraham do all believers in Christ inherit?

5. What picture does Paul use to illustrate the believer's relationship to the law?

6. What was the bondage under which Jewish believers had been held?

7. In what sense is the law a slave-master?

8. To what does the "fulness of the time" refer (4:4)?

9. What is redemption, and how is our redemption accomplished?

10. What is the picture presented by "adoption of sons" (vs. 5)?

—*Jarl K. Waggoner.*

Preparing to Teach the Lesson

Being an heir is a blessing. It carries the idea of inherited wealth left by someone who loved us enough to remember us in their will. This week we learn that we are heirs of God through the saving power of the gospel.

TODAY'S AIM

Facts: to show how the gospel makes us heirs of God as His children.

Principle: to remember that the gospel transforms us from slaves to the law to become children of God and heirs to His promises.

Application: to realize that when we leave the Law behind and receive the gospel, we inherit all that God has for us.

INTRODUCING THE LESSON

Imagine that you are poor and have struggled financially. One day you get a letter in the mail that tells you that a rich relative has left you a fortune! It would change your life, and you would jump for joy! That is the contrast between the burden of being under the Law versus the joy of inheriting the promises of the gospel when we trust Jesus as our Lord and Saviour. This week we learn how Jesus, through His gospel, purchased our freedom and gave us an inheritance.

DEVELOPING THE LESSON

1. Heirs according to promise (Gal. 3: 26-29). Paul asserts that when we put our faith in Christ, we become children of God. Just as children inherit the traits of their parents, we put on the traits of our Lord Jesus when we are baptized into Him and become His children. This is an analogy that all of us can understand. As we grow in faith, we become more and more like Jesus.

Get the class to think about what it means to put on Christ (Gal. 3:27) and to become more like Jesus as we mature in our faith.

When we become children of God, we begin to see others in God's family as brothers and sisters. We no longer consider worldly distinctions such as Jew or Gentile, slave or free, male or female as important. Paul is not saying that these identities do not exist, but that we now are members of the same family with the same Saviour and Lord. We are now to behave like Jesus. We are one new family, and our Lord Jesus binds us together.

Our old identities do not really matter anymore because we are now children of God, brothers and sisters in Christ, with the same Heavenly Father. We are one in Him. There is no reason for any segregation.

Paul concludes this section by asserting that if we belong to Jesus, then we are the seed of Abraham. As we belong to Christ, we are the genuine children of Abraham, so we also inherit all the promises given to him.

2. Subject until the right time (Gal. 4:1-2). What does it really mean to be an heir? Paul uses an example that we can easily understand.

Underage children are not ready to become heirs, even though their names are on the official documents of inheritance. Even though they are wealthy, they must submit to authority just like servants with no inheritance because they must remain under the care of temporary guardians who manage their affairs for them. The underage heir takes on his wealth and authority only at a time of maturity appointed by the official will.

Help your students understand what Paul means by this analogy about heirs and their inheritance. Paul's words are divinely inspired. He is able to explain heavenly concepts in language that is trustworthy.

3. Receiving full rights (Gal. 4:3-7). Challenge the class to think about the fact that we are in for an inheritance in Christ. Paul explains that before Christ came we were in bondage to the evil forces of sin in the world. But now that Jesus has come, we have been adopted into God's family through faith in Christ. God planned this with us in mind even before the beginning of the world.

When the time was just right (vs. 4 "fulness of the time") God sent us His Son Jesus, who was born of a woman, Mary. Jesus was under the authority of the Law. Through Christ, the glorious gospel was unveiled to the world. He did this so that we might be redeemed from under the Law and made God's very own sons and daughters.

God is now our Father. He adopted us into His family (cf. John 1:12). He gave us the right to receive His inheritance because we are now His children. Notice that Paul says the Spirit is given only to those who are God's children (Gal. 4:6), and He dwells within us. The power of the Spirit is part of our inheritance. God dwells within us now and works in and through us. We can now call Him Father.

We are no longer slaves, but children of God. Slaves do not inherit anything, but children do. We are God's children and therefore we inherit all the promises of God through faith in our Lord Jesus.

ILLUSTRATING THE LESSON

We are not slaves but children of our Heavenly Father, and so we inherit all His promises.

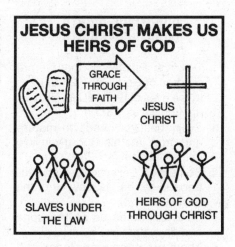

JESUS CHRIST MAKES US HEIRS OF GOD

GRACE THROUGH FAITH

JESUS CHRIST

SLAVES UNDER THE LAW

HEIRS OF GOD THROUGH CHRIST

CONCLUDING THE LESSON

Leave the class with the wonderful truth that we are not slaves any longer. We are free from religious bondage. When we put our faith in Christ, we have received the right to inherit the promises of our Heavenly Father because we are now children of the Almighty. His Spirit now resides in us and empowers us. And all this has taken place because of the gospel of Jesus Christ. When we appropriate the good news, we receive our inheritance.

Paul wrote, "In [Christ] also we have obtained an inheritance, being predestinated according to the purpose of him who worketh all things after the counsel of his own will: That we should be to the praise of his glory, who first trusted in Christ. In whom ye also . . . believed, ye were sealed with that holy Spirit of promise, which is the earnest of our inheritance until the redemption of the purchased possession, unto the praise of his glory" (Eph. 1:11-14).

ANTICIPATING THE NEXT LESSON

Next week, we explore the gospel in action. We seek to understand what Christians should do after receiving the gospel.

—A. Koshy Muthalaly.

PRACTICAL POINTS

1. Our faith assures us that we are children of God (Gal. 3:26-27).
2. In the eyes of God, all His children are equal (vss. 28-29).
3. Every believer needs to mature and grow into his God-given role in the kingdom (4:1-2).
4. Some new believers are still entrapped by the distractions of the world (vss. 3-5).
5. God welcomes us as His sons and daughters (vs. 6).
6. There are certain privileges and responsibilities afforded to children that are not available to mere servants (vs. 7).

—Charity G. Carter.

RESEARCH AND DISCUSSION

1. What is the way to become a child of God (Gal. 3:26-27)? Explain what we have to do as well as what God does.
2. Since we know that God views all His children the same, how should that knowledge impact the way we view other Christians and how we respond to one another (vs. 28)?
3. How are young heirs the same as servants? Why must they await their father's appointed time to assume familial status (4:1-2)?
4. What does it mean to be adopted as a child of God (vs. 5)? Describe the benefits that are reserved for family members and restricted from unbelievers.
5. At what point are the children of God no longer like servants but are full heirs (vs. 7)?

—Charity G. Carter.

ILLUSTRATED HIGH POINTS

Redeem them that were under the law

Fourteen-year-old Braxton Moral is set to graduate from Harvard one week before he also graduates from high school. A gifted child, by third grade he felt unchallenged, confused, and depressed. His worried parents tried to get him into the nearby community college, but he was turned away because of his young age. Braxton decided he would rather be a Harvard grad anyway and enrolled as a distance learner. He is thinking, naturally, of running for president in 2040. Education was a great help for young Braxton—answering life's questions and giving him direction. Yet even as he loves and embraces school, he will get what he needs and speedily graduate to a greater calling.

The law of God is a good thing. It educates us as to God's holiness as well as our own wretchedness. However, once we get this education, let us not tarry there. It is time to repent and graduate to a walk of faith in Christ!

Have put on Christ

It is exciting to know that part of the Christian's salvation experience is a wardrobe change (of sorts). We have put on Christ, both legally and experientially. Daily, we are being transformed into His likeness, but we just might bring that reality into greater focus as we follow some of these tips.

1) Understand Christ's point of view. Do we see situations from our perspective or through His eyes? What is His manner, speech, and temperament?

2) Have we studied Him throughout His Word?

3) Do we practice following Him daily?

—Therese Greenberg.

Golden Text Illuminated

"If ye be Christ's, then are ye Abraham's seed, and heirs according to the promise" (Galatians 3:29).

In order to legally be considered an heir, one must be named as such by whoever is leaving an inheritance.

The giving and receiving of inheritances, the passing down of valuable possessions, almost always occurs within families. After all, what father, especially if he has prospered to any degree, does not desire to leave his children or grandchildren things he holds dear or knows will better his heir's lives in some way (cf. Prov. 13:22)?

Amazingly, sometimes a person's life can be radically changed as a result of simply being named heir to the family inheritance, even though they were born into that family through no effort of their own.

Most often it is financial gain of some sort that comes to mind as we think of inheritances. Scripture, however, tells us that there are heirs to whom God Himself has promised an inheritance—an inheritance far more valuable that any earthly one (cf. I Cor. 2:9).

To be an heir of the King of kings and Lord of lords is an incredible gift. But how does one rise to such a royal position? Even if a person does grasp how to become a child of God, how does he remain assured throughout his life that God is his Father?

This is one of the questions that the Galatians evidently struggled to fully resolve. The Apostle Paul, therefore, wrote them a letter in hopes of helping them understand the matter.

Paul feared that the Galatians were being led away from their simple and pure devotion to Christ (cf. II Cor. 11:3). They were complicating the gospel and its message of grace, which had freely been given to them as believers.

False teachers were troubling the church (Gal. 1:7), demanding that they become Jews and keep the Law of Moses in order to be accepted by God. Paul strongly disputed this argument because he knew from his own experience the futility of such thinking and efforts.

It is out of God's great love and mercy that He freely offers grace through His Son Jesus Christ (Eph. 2:4-6). No one can earn this gift. Like a good father, the Lord wants to bless His children with it (Luke 11:13).

The golden text gives us further understanding of how each of us is made an heir or child of God. It starts with belonging to Christ, which is a matter of believing, trusting in him as Lord and Saviour. This act of faith brings us into the family of God (John 1:12), positioning us as an heir of God.

Just as Abraham's belief in God's promise made him righteous (Gen. 15:6), so it is with every person. Paul had reminded the Galatians earlier in chapter 3 that the true children, or seed, of Abraham were those who, like Abraham, believed God (vss. 6-7).

The Galatian believers, having already believed in Christ for salvation, were heirs of God. How sad that they seemed to forget and began to act like orphans and fearful slaves (cf. Rom. 8:15).

Do you belong to Christ? If you do, then you are one of Abraham's descendants—an heir—because of the gospel!

—*Christine M. Morrison.*

Heart of the Lesson

I recently encountered a young girl whose parents had both passed away in a short period of time. Because she was a minor, she needed someone to take charge and become a protector of her estate. Fortunately, a relative agreed to become her guardian. When she becomes an adult, this young lady will inherit all of her parents' estate. Until then, her relative will protect her and her inheritance. Paul illustrates how Christians are heirs to all the benefits of Christ.

1. One in Christ (Gal. 3:26-29). Paul states that all saved individuals are children of God. Everyone comes to salvation the same way—by trusting in the Saviour. There are no nationalities, social categories, or genders that determine God's favor. All those who have received salvation belong to Abraham's family.

Society places celebrities in high esteem. People highly value the queen of England, the president of the United States, entertainers, and outstanding athletes. In God's eyes, these individuals are no more important than a lowly servant. While they may have more social obligations than a common citizen, they need to receive salvation the same way as everyone else. When prestigious persons stand before God, their social status vanishes. God does not look at people the way society does. He looks at the heart—not the outward appearance (I Sam. 16:7).

2. A child as a slave (Gal. 4:1-3). Young children are unable to care for themselves. If they inherit great wealth from their parents, they must rely on a protector to meet their needs and take care of their inheritance until they become adults. Basically, they have the same status as servants, who have no rights. Paul teaches that before coming to faith in Christ, we are like young children under the authority of others and are treated like servants rather than as heirs.

In Jewish society, a child becomes a man or woman at twelve years old. In today's society a child becomes an adult at eighteen. A child inheriting an estate must wait until adulthood to access the inheritance. He is not yet equipped to manage the property.

People prior to salvation are like young children. They do not yet understand the truth about salvation. They do not realize that redemption is theirs through simple faith in Jesus Christ.

3. One of God's sons (Gal. 4:4-7). Before Christ came, the Galatians were also like small children. They lived in bondage to law and rituals and knew nothing of the glorious inheritance to which God had chosen them. But then God sent His Son to earth. Jesus came, not only to free the Jews from the limitations of the law, but also to free the Gentiles from the control of various religions. When individuals become children of God, they become members of His family. As such, they are entitled to all the rights and privileges of an heir.

As soon as a person trusts in the Heavenly Father, he or she immediately becomes a member of the family of God. This person is no longer a slave to sin and can refer to God as Father. He or she is able to inherit everything that the Heavenly Father owns. Christ's death bought sinners' freedom and made them heirs to the throne. What a wonderful transformation to go from a slave to a child of God with just a simple request for forgiveness! This should result in all Christians shouting for joy.

—*Catherine Moore.*

World Missions

Should believers from the West support national missionaries in the East?

As heirs together of the grace of God, some would say we who have such wealth and prosperity should share it with our brothers and sisters in Christ ministering in countries with much fewer resources. Others argue it creates problems. Examples can be found for both perspectives.

An Indonesian missionary received $100,000 from a partner church in America and used every dollar for his Bible college and national missionaries. He would not take offered money for a vacation for him and his wife, asking to use the money for God's work instead.

In India, however, a Hindu man admitted he acted as a Christian missionary just to get a salary.

In Bangladesh, a national minister who had connections to Western missionaries was assumed to be rich, and the resultant social and financial expectations made for a huge burden to him and a drain on his work.

There are pros and cons on both sides of this discussion.

Potential benefits of supporting national missionaries include:

1. National missionaries already know the language and culture. They can be more effective more quickly than Western missionaries.
2. They need much less support.
3. It follows the command to do good to the household of faith (cf. Gal. 6:10).
4. It meets a need in the body of Christ. A laborer is worthy of his hire, but if there is no money for them to go, how can they serve if we do not help?

Potential problems with supporting national missionaries include:

1. It can create dependence on Western funds instead of on God.
2. It can create expectations and even jealousy among other nationals.
3. Sometimes believers or even non-believers join a ministry for the money they might get.
4. At times there arises a lack of accountability or misuse of funds.

In light of these back and forth considerations, what are we to do?

For starters, we should be careful not to give for wrong reasons, such as guilt to gain approval or status with God or other believers. We must keep a close watch over our hearts, which can so easily be lured into acting out of wrong motivations.

By reflecting back to lesson 8, we see that true reasons to give or not to give are the same as to serve or not. We should be motivated by the desire to be obedient to God out of our love for Christ.

As with many things in the kingdom, the issue is not about finding a standard that applies to all situations, but rather taking each individual situation to the Lord for guidance and wisdom.

This is not to say that if we give, we throw off the need for accountability or trustworthy transactions. One way to deal with this matter is by having partners in ministry or by giving to ministries that have accountability measures in place.

The decision about supporting national missionaries should be a vertical one (meaning something we take to God for an answer) rather than simply a horizontal one (based on people, results, or other earthly factors). If we freely offer our earthly treasure to God, we can be sure He will direct the use of it in the best way for His kingdom.

—Kimberly Rae.

The Jewish Aspect

Immediately after Adam and Eve disobeyed God in the Garden of Eden, God said that there would be hostility between the serpent's seed and the seed of the woman (Gen. 3:15) and that the woman's seed would eventually bruise (destroy) the head of the serpent. God later instructed Abram (the seed of woman) to leave behind all that he knew and to follow after Him. Abram (later Abraham) and Sarai (Sarah) experienced years of struggle before their son was born (Gen. 21:1-3).The seed that was promised was threatened throughout the Hebrew Bible. One such threat came when God instructed Abraham to offer Isaac as a sacrifice. God, however, used this to test Abraham's faith in Him. When Abraham passed the test, God once again confirmed the blessing of Abraham's seed (Gen. 22:17).

God also promised that, through Abraham, all the nations of the earth would be blessed (Gen. 12:1-3). It was, however, not exclusively the physical seed to which God had referred (Gen. 26:4; 28:14). Paul taught, "And if ye be Christ's, then are ye Abraham's seed, and heirs according to the promise" (Gal. 3:29). He explained that Abraham was justified by faith (Gen. 15:6) and that the children of God were those who had faith in Christ (Gal. 3:26).

An heir, in the Hebrew Bible, is someone who inherited or possessed something. Early Jewish believers were taught that they were heirs of the promise (Heb. 6:17), heirs of salvation (1:14), and heirs of righteousness (11:7). Heirs of God meant that believers received all that God had promised to His children. It also meant that God Himself was their inheritance. "The Old Testament is rich in its usage of the inheritance metaphor. The terms for inheritance occur over two hundred times, most frequently in Numbers, Deuteronomy, Joshua and Psalms. While Jewish inheritance laws were specific and complete (Num 27:8-11), almost all of references to inheritance in the Old Testament are theological, not legal. In the theological sense, to inherit means to 'receive an irrevocable gift' with an emphasis on the special relationship between the benefactor and the recipients" (Elwell, ed., *Baker's Evangelical Dictionary of Biblical Theology,* Baker).

Paul told the new believers, "For ye have not received the spirit of bondage again to fear; but ye have received the Spirit of adoption, whereby we cry, Abba, Father" (Rom. 8:15). The spirit of bondage to fear was the spirit of slavery to the law. The Spirit of adoption (the Holy Spirit) conveyed warmth, affection, gentleness and love, which is why the believers could call God "Abba, Father." "Abba is a Hebrew or Syriac word, signifying Father; why then is the word Father added in the Greek? To signify, that God is Father both of Jews and Gentiles" (Poole, *A Commentary on the Whole Bible,* Macdonald).

"Old Testament legal adoption was not prescribed in Jewish law or practiced by the Israelites. . . . The adoption metaphor was not lost to Israel, however. God declares that He is the father of the nation Israel, whom He loves as his child (Isa 1:2; Hosea 11:1). He told Pharaoh, 'Israel is my firstborn son" (Exod 4:22). . . . Although not precisely adoption passages, the instances of declared sonship in the Old Testament provide a theological foundation for Israel's designation as the children of God" (Elwell, ed.).

—Deborah Markowitz Solan.

Guiding the Superintendent

Over four thousand years ago and hundreds of years before the Law was given, God appeared to a man by the name of Abraham. He told Abraham His intentions to bless the world using his descendants. This blessing or promise was for a son from Abraham. At the time Abraham was childless and well past the child-producing age. But he believed God's promise "and he [God] counted it to him for righteousness" (Gen 15:6). Eventually this promised seed would find its fulfillment in Jesus Christ (Gal. 3:16). Those who, like Abraham, believe in God's Seed (that is, Jesus Christ) will inherit the promises made to Abraham (Gal. 3:18).

DEVOTIONAL OUTLINE

1. Heir of God's promise (Gal. 3:26-29). Those who put their faith in Jesus Christ become heirs of the great promises to Abraham; all that was promised to Abraham is now given to them.

The apostle likens faith to putting on Christ, as one who puts on clothes, thus making the believer clothed with Christ. All those who believe in Christ are made one with each other regardless of race, origin, or gender.

Since the believer belongs to Christ, he or she is Abraham's seed and, thus, inheritors of the promises.

2. Heir of God Himself (Gal. 4:1-7). Not only is the believer an heir of the great promises to Abraham, he or she is also "an heir of God through Christ."

The apostle used the illustration of how a child was raised when he or she was a minor to describe mankind's state while under the law.

Education in those days was handled mostly through hired "tutors and governors" (vs. 2). When a child reached adulthood, as determined by the father, the child would be fully adopted into the family as an heir. Before this time, even if the child was an heir, he or she was still treated as a servant.

Life under the Law is likened to life as a slave (Gal. 3:23-24). So why would anyone want to go back to this stage of life? It is much like a person who enjoys grade school but once out has no desire to go back. There should be no real desire to go back.

Now that Christ has come the believer is no longer a slave but has received "the adoption of sons" (4:5). As a result the believer is a son and an heir with total benefits.

CHILDREN'S CORNER

text: **Acts 8:26-40**
title: **Philip: Ready to Give the Gospel**

Philip, one of the first church deacons (Acts 6:5), was suddenly approached by an angel with an important task. He was to go south of Jerusalem toward Gaza.

He was led to meet an important royal official from Ethiopia (East Africa) who was returning from worship in Jerusalem. The man was reading in Isaiah (ch. 53) about Jesus the sacrificed lamb. The Ethiopian had no idea who or what Isaiah was saying.

This was a perfect teaching moment for Philip. He clearly explained about Jesus Christ and the gospel. The man trusted in Christ there on the spot and wanted Philip to baptize him. No sooner was this done than the Lord took Philip away for another task.

—*Martin R. Dahlquist.*

Scripture Lesson Text

GAL. 6:1 Brethren, if a man be overtaken in a fault, ye which are spiritual, restore such an one in the spirit of meekness; considering thyself, lest thou also be tempted.

2 Bear ye one another's burdens, and so fulfil the law of Christ.

3 For if a man think himself to be something, when he is nothing, he deceiveth himself.

4 But let every man prove his own work, and then shall he have rejoicing in himself alone, and not in another.

5 For every man shall bear his own burden.

6 Let him that is taught in the word communicate unto him that teacheth in all good things.

7 Be not deceived; God is not mocked: for whatsoever a man soweth, that shall he also reap.

8 For he that soweth to his flesh shall of the flesh reap corruption; but he that soweth to the Spirit shall of the Spirit reap life everlasting.

9 And let us not be weary in well doing: for in due season we shall reap, if we faint not.

10 As we have therefore opportunity, let us do good unto all men, especially unto them who are of the household of faith.

NOTES

The Gospel in Action

Lesson Text: Galatians 6:1-10

Related Scriptures: Romans 15:1-4; II Timothy 2:24-26;
II Corinthians 9:6-15; I John 3:14-19

TIME: possibly A.D. 48   PLACE: from Syrian Antioch

GOLDEN TEXT—"As we have therefore opportunity, let us do good unto all men, especially unto them who are of the household of faith" (Galatians 6:10).

Introduction

Years ago, a popular singer recorded a song that proclaimed the joys of marriage. It spoke of commitment to the wedding vows and standing by each other forever. It is understandable why it soon became a popular choice for wedding songs. Ironically, the singer himself was in his fourth marriage. While the words of the song were fine and the singer was no doubt sincere, it seems clear that he was unable or unwilling to put his words into practice.

Our lives are always tested by our commitment to our words. Are they merely meant to impress others, or are they put into practice in our daily lives? Do we spout the truths of Scripture without really living those truths?

In his letter to the churches of Galatia, the Apostle Paul went to great lengths to counter the false teaching of those who wished to impose the Old Testament law upon believers in Christ. He clearly and forcefully set forth the biblical case for justification by faith and the need to continue in faith. But while Paul was a very scholarly man, he knew that following Christ is more than assenting to a system of belief. One cannot be Christ's follower without following Him day by day in our attitudes and actions.

LESSON OUTLINE

I. **CHRISTIAN COMPASSION—**
   Gal. 6:1-5

II. **CHRISTIAN WORKS—**
    Gal. 6:6-10

Exposition: Verse by Verse

CHRISTIAN COMPASSION

GAL. 6:1 Brethren, if a man be overtaken in a fault, ye which are spiritual, restore such an one in the spirit of meekness; considering thyself, lest thou also be tempted.

2 Bear ye one another's burdens, and so fulfil the law of Christ.

3 For if a man think himself to be something, when he is nothing, he deceiveth himself.

4 But let every man prove his

own work, and then shall he have rejoicing in himself alone, and not in another.

5 For every man shall bear his own burden.

Compassion for the fallen (Gal. 6:1). After presenting important theological truths in the first four chapters of Galatians, Paul begins in chapter 5 to apply those truths to the Christian life. He explains how Christians should live in light of the freedom they have in Christ.

Galatians 5:26 tells us that if we walk in harmony with the Spirit who dwells within us (vs. 25), we will not be focused on ourselves, seeking our own glory and enrichment. Instead, we will be looking for ways to express Christlike compassion. Such compassion especially should be shown toward one who is "overtaken in a fault" (6:1).

This can mean either that the one overtaken was surprised by the fault itself and did not mean to fall into sin, or it can mean the person was surprised when someone discovered his sin. In either case, the person has fallen into sin. It is clear too that the offender is a Christian whom his fellow Christians are to restore.

Why does Paul introduce this hypothetical case in his letter to the Galatians? Warren Wiersbe offers an interesting answer in light of Paul's lengthy refutation of the legalistic Judaizers: "Because nothing reveals the wickedness of legalism better than the way legalists treat those who have sinned. Call to mind the Pharisees who dragged a woman taken in adultery before Jesus (John 8)" (*Be Free,* Cook). In contrast to the legalists, those who are spiritual should act compassionately and seek to restore the fallen Christian.

The Greek word translated "restore" in Galatians 6:1 is used elsewhere of mending nets so that they are useful for fishing (cf. Matt. 4:21; Mark 1:19). What is envisioned here are more mature, or spiritual, believers restoring a sinning brother or sister to usefulness in the church. This affirms that Christians do in fact fall into sin at times. It also tells us that although all believers should exhibit the fruit of the Spirit, there are various levels of fruitfulness among Christians simply because the Christian life is a continuing process of growth and development of Christlike character.

Those who are more mature in the faith are to look out for those who are struggling with sin, and they are to restore them by urging repentance, offering forgiveness, and encouraging them in the right way. They are to do so in a "spirit of meekness" (Gal. 6:1), or gentleness. This is the same word used in 5:23 and emphasizes that those who do the restoring must be exhibiting the fruit of the Spirit. They must also take heed to themselves, that is, be aware of their own potential for falling into sin.

Compassion for the burdened (Gal. 6:2-5). While the command to bear one another's burdens may have many applications, in this context it refers particularly to restoring a sinning brother or sister. Through prayer, confrontation, forgiveness, and acceptance, we can relieve that individual of the heavy burden he or she bears.

When we do this, we also fulfill the "law of Christ" (vs. 2). This phrase is used only here and in I Corinthians 9:21. To what does it refer? Some have argued that it refers to all the commands of Christ. However, it seems better to "identify the law of Christ with the admonition to love one another (Gal. 5:14), for there is a clear link between Galatians 5:14 and 6:2 . . . If we carry the burdens of other believers, we show our love for them" (Schreiner, *40 Questions About Christians and Biblical Law,* Kregel).

The Old Testament injunction to love one's neighbor is quoted several times in the New Testament (cf. Matt. 22:39; Rom. 13:9; Jas. 2:8), including Galatians 5:14. More specifically, the law of Christ is to love one another *as Christ has loved us* (John 13:34-35). Wiersbe gives a succinct summary: "'The law of Christ' is: 'Love one another' (John 13:34; 15:12). Paul has already discussed the 'law of love' (Gal. 5:13-15), and now [in 6:2] he is applying it."

Galatians 6:3 is a stern warning against pride. Pride, or conceit, can hinder Christians from acting in a compassionate way to bear one another's burdens. When they think so highly of themselves that they look down on others as inferior and refuse to help those who are entrapped in sin, they are deceiving themselves, for their sinful pride makes them no better than their sinning brother or sister. In fact, "measured by God's standards, no one amounts to anything" (Barker and Kohlenberger, eds., *The Expositor's Bible Commentary, Abridged Edition,* Zondervan).

Instead of proudly standing in judgment over those who have fallen into sin, we need to examine our own works. We are exhorted, "Let every man prove his own work" (vs. 4); this warns against comparing ourselves to others. We are to "prove," or test, the quality of our work by God's standards, not man's. Only when we measure up to the standard of God's will for us can we legitimately be satisfied. But though we can take satisfaction in the work we have done for God, we are still "nothing" (vs. 3) and must not rejoice that we have done more than someone else.

The words "every man shall bear his own burden" (vs. 5) might at first seem to contradict the call in verse 2 to bear one another's burdens. However, an entirely different situation is in view here. "For" ties verse 5 to what immediately precedes it so that the burden he speaks of here is not sin but the work of verse 4, that is, the "normal duty which falls upon every man" (Ridderbos, *The Epistle of Paul to the Churches of Galatia,* Eerdmans).

In Galatians 6:5, Paul is simply saying that each person is responsible for his own work before God. Another person's failure does not excuse anyone. Furthermore, two different words for "burden" are used in verses 2 and 5, further distinguishing the two different ideas.

As followers of Christ, we are responsible to act compassionately toward our fellow believers who are burdened. This is a true expression of Christlike love. Our actions, however, must always be accompanied by a humble attitude.

CHRISTIAN WORKS

6 Let him that is taught in the word communicate unto him that teacheth in all good things.

7 Be not deceived; God is not mocked: for whatsoever a man soweth, that shall he also reap.

8 For he that soweth to his flesh shall of the flesh reap corruption; but he that soweth to the Spirit shall of the Spirit reap life everlasting.

9 And let us not be weary in well doing: for in due season we shall reap, if we faint not.

10 As we have therefore opportunity, let us do good unto all men, especially unto them who are of the household of faith.

Sharing with leaders (Gal. 6:6-9). With verse 6, the Apostle Paul shifts emphasis slightly, from our obligation to show compassion to the fallen and burdened to our duty to engage more widely in other good works.

As Christians, we are to share with those who faithfully teach us the Word of God. "Communicate" is an old English word for "share," which is what the Greek word here (*koinoneo*) means. It can refer to sharing in fellowship with others or to sharing material things. The latter is the clear meaning here. Those who benefit from faithful teaching are to share "all good things," including money, with their instructors.

Believers are to provide financial support for those who labor in the church in teaching the Word. Such teachers, usually designated as elders or pastors, are worthy of support, as the New Testament consistently teaches (cf. I Cor. 9:14; Phil. 4:15-18; I Tim. 5:17-18).

The direction to support godly teachers is followed by the important principle set forth in Galatians 6:7. The principle is universal, but here it seems to be connected specifically to the context of Galatians. "Be not deceived; God is not mocked" probably refers to the Galatians' honoring of false teachers who were actually deceiving them while failing to support faithful teachers of the Word. This was equivalent to treating God with contempt.

Paul reminds the Galatians that one reaps what he sows. This is a scriptural principle (cf. I Cor. 9:10-11; II Cor. 9:6). If the Galatians did not support honest, selfless, faithful teachers of Scripture, they would reap dire spiritual consequences in their lives.

The illustration of sowing and reaping pictures at least three spiritual truths, as noted by Robert Gromacki (*Stand Fast in Liberty,* Kress). "*First,* like begets like. Righteousness is not produced by the sowing of sin. *Second,* the more one sows, the more one reaps . . . *Third,* one reaps more than one sows." These are truths we need to keep in mind as we examine our lives before God.

Galatians 6:8 elaborates on the principle of sowing and reaping and in so doing gives the principle a wider, ultimate application. Sowing to the flesh reaps "corruption," Paul writes, and sowing to the Spirit reaps "life everlasting." One who consistently pursues a life geared toward pleasing fleshly, human desires will reap corruption, or moral decay. A self-centered life proves that a person is not a Christian but one who seeks to "fulfil the lust of the flesh" (5:16).

The person who sows to the Spirit is the one who walks in the Spirit. As a follower of Christ, such a person values eternal riches above temporal ones. He directs his life toward the things of God and thus proves by the life he lives that he is a follower of Christ, who will reap eternal life.

We must not become confused here. Paul is not saying that an effort to do the right thing will bring the reward of eternal life. This would contradict what he teaches throughout the book of Galatians. He is simply saying that one who consistently pursues the things of God does so because he believes in Christ, and he will reap eternal life. A Christian can sin, as we all know, but he cannot persist in such a lifestyle if he is truly born again. The Christian must continually choose to sow to the Spirit so that his life is a true reflection of who he is in Jesus Christ.

While the ultimate result of sowing to the Spirit is eternal life, the principle of sowing and reaping applies temporally as well. Just as the Galatians would reap blessings from supporting godly teachers, so we can expect to reap blessings even in this life by sowing to the Spirit.

The blessings for godly living, however, are not always immediately evident in this life. In fact, pursuing that which is pleasing to God often results in persecution. Indeed, persecution at some point in our lives is assured (cf. II Tim. 3:12)! As a result, we can easily become discouraged and grow "weary in well doing" (Gal. 6:9), even to the point of losing heart and giving up.

Paul's words urge us to continue doing that which is good and praiseworthy. The principle of sowing and reaping is firm and unchanging. The harvest of divine blessing will come, but it will come in God's time. That blessing might come soon, or it might come later. But since it is spiritual in nature, it can even come in the midst of persecution (cf. Matt. 5:10-12). We must maintain this perspective, trusting Him and doing what honors Him regardless of our present circumstances.

Doing good to all (Gal. 6:10). Our good works are not to be limited to supporting those who instruct us in the faith. In fact, they are to be unlimited in scope, reaching "all men." This means we are to do good to believers and unbelievers alike of both genders and of every race, nationality, social status, or religion. Such action mirrors the Lord Jesus, whose concern is for all people. Our opportunities might be limited to some extent, but we can all express the love of Christ to others. Let us not fail to do so while those opportunities exist.

Though we have an obligation to all people, our first priority is to our own spiritual family, the "household of faith." This recognizes the special bond we have in Christ to support and encourage one another; indeed, this is where most opportunities to do good are likely to be found.

When we fully grasp the great theo-logical truth Paul teaches in Galatians—that salvation is God's gracious gift received by faith alone apart from any human effort—our lives will be transformed. And as we continue to grow in our understanding of the depth of Christ's love, we will seek to share that love with others through compassionate, humble, selfless service that demonstrates our gratitude to God. In doing this, we will also reap God's blessing both in this life and in the life to come.

The reason the gospel makes a difference is that "It is the power of God unto salvation to every one that believeth; to the Jew first, and also to the Greek" (Rom 1:16).

—Jarl K. Waggoner.

QUESTIONS

1. What is our responsibility to one "overtaken in a fault" (Gal. 6:1)?
2. With what attitude should our efforts be undertaken?
3. What is the law of Christ, and how do we fulfill it?
4. What warning did Paul give in verse 4?
5. What is the burden we all bear?
6. What obligation do we have to those who faithfully instruct us in the Word?
7. How does the principle in verse 7 relate to verse 6?
8. How does the principle of sowing and reaping relate to our daily lives?
9. Why is it easy to grow "weary in well doing" (vs. 9)?
10. In doing good for others, what is our responsibility, and what is our priority?

—Jarl K. Waggoner.

Preparing to Teach the Lesson

In our final lesson for this quarter we will explore the gospel in action. The gospel is meaningless if it is not lived out. Let us take a closer look at how this works.

TODAY'S AIM

Facts: to show how love can be practiced in our everyday world.

Principle: to show genuine love, it has to be shown in action.

Application: to demonstrate that when we say that we love others, we must show it in action.

INTRODUCING THE LESSON

Many unbelievers are offended by Christians because we often do not practice what we preach. Sometimes we are also called hypocrites because of this. In order for our faith to be seen as genuine and worthy of a listening ear, we need to be a whole lot more practical in our faith. People need to see us doing something about what we believe. Many do not doubt that we have a powerful message, but they are turned off when we do not practice our faith.

Our lesson this week calls our attention to the practical dimension of our faith that reaches outward to others in the church and in the community.

DEVELOPING THE LESSON

1. Help fellow Christians (Gal. 6:1-3). Love looks on the other person with compassion, knowing that we need the same grace ourselves when we make mistakes. If we bear the name of Christ, we must be able to show grace to others, especially within our local churches. Our faith must be marked by meekness, not self-righteous arrogance. Meekness suggests strength under control. As believers in Jesus, we must show this kind of strength. We must steer others back to the right track.

Instead of showing self-righteous arrogance, Paul encourages us to share the burdens of others.

This is practical Christianity. We need to help others in need. In doing so, we obey the law of Christ. This law is very different from the obligations of the Mosaic Law. Jesus calls us to obey Him in love out of a willing heart, helping others. When we think we are too good to stoop to service, Satan is deceiving us. Jesus calls us to serve others in humility.

Help the class to identify several practical ways in which they can show their love to the community around them. Very often this can be done without preaching!

2. Do your own work well (Gal. 6:4-6). Meekness opens the door to humility. We learn to take responsibility for our own behavior as Christians.

When we take a good look at ourselves, we will be able to assess our own actions and see if they measure up to Christ. When we do what we ought to do, we will have the joy of satisfaction. We will not have to see if we measure up to a fellow believer in church, because Jesus is our standard.

In verse 5 Paul says that "every man shall bear his own burden." This seems to be in contradiction to what he said in verse 2 about bearing one another's burdens. What Paul is saying in verse 5, is that we need to take responsibility for our own behavior and not make excuses for our faults. It speaks of personal accountability for our actions. As Christians, we are called to be a responsible people.

Some of this responsibility is to be seen when we share what we have with those who teach the Word. Love takes care of those who teach the Word. In what ways can we honor those who teach us? List some practical ways in which this can be done.

3. Do what is good (Gal. 6:7-10). Paul concludes this teaching with some dire warnings. First he reminds us that we cannot fool God. He knows everything. What we sow is what we will reap. This means that what we put in, we will get back. If we seek only to satisfy our earthly desires, we will get back only death. If, on the other hand, we seek to please the Spirit of God, we will reap that which is eternal.

Harvests take time. So sometimes this could mean that we may have to wait patiently for the harvest, but it will be worth waiting for what God will give us. Help the class to see that only what they sow will determine what they reap. Encourage them to sow only toward everlasting life. We are not to get discouraged while doing what is right. We will reap our reward one day.

As Christians, we are to demonstrate our love through doing what is right, especially toward those fellow believers who are in our local congregations. Help the class to think of ways they can specifically help their own "household of faith" (vs. 10).

ILLUSTRATING THE LESSON

Love is practical. It must be seen in action both within the church and in the community.

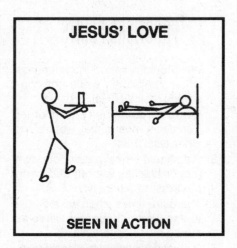

JESUS' LOVE

SEEN IN ACTION

CONCLUDING THE LESSON

Sometimes we see that our local churches are active and very busy taking care of the needs of the people in our local churches, and rightly so. This certainly should be a top priority for us as followers of our Lord Jesus. But a congregation that is isolated from the wider community is not visible in displaying the expressions of Christian love. Therefore it is limiting its opportunities to demonstrate to the world what Jesus is like. Love must become love in action where the needs are greatest.

We certainly see this demonstration of the love of Christ in His own public ministry. The book of Acts shows us how the early church reached out into the community at large and met their needs.

Paul challenges us here this week that we are to "do good unto all men, especially unto them who are of the household of faith" (Gal.6:10). This is a commandment that, as Christians, we really cannot ignore, for love by its very definition seeks to reach out to all others in need.

ANTICIPATING THE NEXT LESSON

Next quarter is about "Faith and Providence." Study Genesis 11:31—12:9 to see how Abram was called to a life of faith.

—A. Koshy Muthalaly.

PRACTICAL POINTS

1. We should respond in gentleness when people sin while not condoning their sin (Gal. 6:1).
2. Being in community with other Christians means that we are not alone (vss. 2-3).
3. We should strive to carry our own responsibilities without becoming a burden to others (vss. 4-5).
4. There are times when we are able to encourage those who serve as our spiritual leaders (vs. 6).
5. Righteous actions yield positive results; sinful actions yield negative results (vss. 7-8).
6. We should always strive to do what we know is right (vss. 9-10).

—Charity G. Carter.

RESEARCH AND DISCUSSION

1. Reflect on a time when you encountered someone who thought too highly of themselves (Gal. 6:3). How was it evident?
2. If bearing the burdens of others helps us fulfill the law of Christ (vs. 2), explain why we are also instructed to bear our own burdens (vs. 5).
3. Give several concrete examples, whether positive or negative, of people who reaped what they had sown (vss. 7-8).
4. Discuss why it is sometimes easy to become "weary in well doing" (vs. 9). What should motivate us to keep doing good things?
5. Why is it important for us to do good to everyone (vs. 10)? Explain why we are to especially do good to fellow believers.

—Charity G. Carter.

ILLUSTRATED HIGH POINTS

In the spirit of meekness

Two doors served in the same house filled with rough-and-tumble kids. All day long, they endured endless disrespectful kicking and slamming. After the children went to bed, they discussed their day. The ornate front door would say, "I can't take it anymore, these are the rudest people," and the simple bathroom door would console, "They are only children. Give it time."

Nevertheless, the living room door vowed that the next time it happened, she was determined to just break— and that is what she did. At first, she felt quite vindicated. The children were scolded by their parents. However, being broken now, the homeowners discarded and replaced her. The bathroom door continued with the family, which matured nicely.

Shall we, by impatience with others, break our own Christlikeness?

We shall reap, if we faint not

The fabled king advertised for a personal assistant. He assembled a vast array of candidates and presented them with a challenge. They were to take a pot with a hole in the bottom and attempt to fill the pot with water from the local pond.

Immediately, many walked away. Others began and soon quit.

Only one hopeful man continued the effort. Over and over he filled the pot only to have it leak out onto the shore. Hours turned to days and then to months.

The pot never filled, but the pond emptied, and there in the middle was a diamond ring, which he promptly gave to his king. The king said, "This ring is a reward for your patience and hard work. You are fit for the job."

If we obey and faint not, saved souls are both our treasure and His.

—Therese Greenberg.

Golden Text Illuminated

"As we have therefore opportunity, let us do good unto all men, especially unto them who are of the household of faith" (Galatians 6:10).

Walking in humility and loving others through encouraging words and simple acts of service demonstrates Christ's love to the world. Such a lifestyle also assures the believer about his place within the family of God (I John 3:18-19).

Believers can find many verses throughout the Bible that offer wisdom about how to treat and relate to others, both nonbelievers and fellow Christians.

Ultimately, helping and serving others accomplishes three things: it fulfills the law of Christ (Gal. 6:2), realizes the call of every believer (cf. Rom. 15:1-4), and shows the true gospel in action. The latter part of James 2:18 puts it this way: "I will show thee my faith by my works."

Nearing the end of his letter to the Galatian church, the Apostle Paul gave some fatherly instructions to the believers in how they should care for one another.

Having suffered much discouragement as a Christian, Paul knew his fellow brethren would encounter difficulties in which they would need each other's help. They would experience personal failures (cf. Gal. 6:1) and have burdens to carry (cf. vs. 2).

Paul advised them to stay humble when such situations did occur. If they became self-righteous, they would be deceived and set themselves up for possible failure in their own lives (vss. 1, 3).

Paul also invoked an agricultural principle in his letter: sowing and reaping (vs. 7). These actions and their results would have been familiar to the Galatians and would prompt them to sow good seeds into the lives of others. In sowing generously, they would reap generously (II Cor. 9:6).

As the believers trusted God, persevered in doing good, and applied this principle, God would honor their obedience and multiply their own harvest (II Cor. 9:10-11; Gal. 6:9). Serving others will never yield a bad crop!

The golden text urges all believers to do good, giving help to all people where and when it is needed. Where there is life, there is yet opportunity and time with which believers can choose to love others.

Although believers should serve all people, they should make a special effort to bless other believers. This is because Christians' acts of love and support reveal their true love for God (I John 4:21).

Giving higher priority to fellow believers is easy to understand when we look at our own families. Do they not receive priority when we can help or support them in some way? We often help family members before they even ask!

Must believers really do good to those outside of the family of God? Why would such a command be given?

Believers show the gospel in action when they reach out to serve those who are yet lost. God may use your witness to impact them and grant them the gift of repentance that leads to salvation (cf. II Tim. 2:24-26).

Make the most of what time is left, beloved. Obey God and demonstrate the true gospel by doing good unto all!

—*Christine M. Morrison.*

Heart of the Lesson

Several times I have been given too much change when making a purchase. To the amazement of store clerks, I returned the extra money. Patrons standing behind me in line have remarked, "Why don't you keep the money? The store will never miss it." I have even returned to the store to pay for items that have been mistakenly omitted. I do this because I have to live with my conscience, and I know that God sees my actions.

At the conclusion of his letter to the Galatians Paul emphasized putting the gospel into action. He wanted these people to understand that nothing is hidden from the One who sees all.

1. Helping fellow believers (Gal. 6:1-5). Paul wanted his Galatian readers to realize that Christians falter. Instead of scolding a stumbling individual, we should lovingly encourage the person, just as we would want them to do for us. Sharing another believer's burden helps lighten the load.

All people err. No one is perfect. This should make people—especially Christians—more tolerant of the imperfections in others. God is forgiving, even though people continuously make the same mistakes. Why should Christians keep condemning one another when we are all imperfect? As Paul says, "Who art thou that judgest another man's servant? to his own master he standeth or falleth. Yea, he shall be holden up: for God is able to make him stand" (Rom. 14:4).

Helping someone overcome sin not only helps the person who is troubled but encourages the comforter too. As believers in the true God, saved individuals should be willing to aid a fellow sufferer (II Cor. 1:4). Praying to God for guidance may provide direction on how to assist and what to say. Be-

lievers can then be satisfied that they have done the Lord's work. Christians should not think they are superior to anyone else (Phil. 2:3). They need to remember that they are sinners.

2. Doing good to all (Gal. 6:6-10). Paul reminded the Galatians that while people are able to fool others, they cannot deceive God. A farmer plants a field of corn. When he diligently works the field, he expects a good harvest. When the farmer gathers his crop, he expects to pick golden ears of corn—not peas or potatoes. If people sow evil, they will harvest evil. If they sow good seeds, they reap a good harvest. There is no way around this.

We must not tire of helping others, especially fellow Christians, since these are the deeds that the Lord commands and lead to blessing. This truth should have encouraged the Galatians to help all people, but especially their brothers and sisters in Christ.

People today are just like the Galatians. They need to be reminded to do good. Evil comes too easily; it is more natural for sinful men to imitate the world. Furthermore, people are often criticized for doing good and small deeds tend to go unnoticed. But God is watching—and so are others. Kindness is never shown in vain.

Doing good is similar to sowing good seeds. Both reap a good harvest. Helping others is one reason people are placed on this earth. Christians should be especially focused on helping fellow believers. Whenever there is an opportunity to assist, children of God should take advantage of the occasion. Believers should encourage fellow brothers and sisters to look forward to their heavenly rewards

—*Catherine Moore.*

World Missions

Opportunity can be defined as:

1. *A favorable juncture of circumstances.*
2. *An amount of time or a situation in which something can be done.*
3. *A good chance for advancement or progress.*

Galatians 6:10 tells us to do good as we have opportunity. Do we have opportunity, according to the definition? Let us take a closer look.

1. *A favorable juncture of circumstances.*

If we have more than one set of clothes and more than one meal's worth of food, we are among the physically better off of the world. Anything above the need of today's food and shelter is a surplus and means we have enough to share.

Yes, we have opportunity.

2. *An amount of time or a situation in which something can be done.*

God has given each of us a lifetime. He has graced us with talents and abilities specific to our role in the body of Christ. If we ask, He will show us how we can use those gifts to serve Him.

Yes, we have opportunity.

3. *A good chance for advancement or progress.*

"We are more than conquerors through Him who loved us" (Rom. 8:37), and we know God's Word will not go forth without effect (Isa. 55:11).

Yes, we have opportunity.

So then, what will we do with the great opportunity we have? God says to use it to do good to all men, but especially to our fellow believers. Who among the body of Christ is most in need? This would certainly include the persecuted, impoverished, wounded, orphaned or widowed, war-torn, weary in ministry—the list could go on and on.

In just one issue of *The Voice of the Martyrs* magazine, prayer is asked for:

- children in Nigeria, Colombia and other places where parents have been killed for their faith, that they will remain strong in the Lord.
- children in Sudan fleeing bombs every day, and for the safe distribution of medicines and Bibles.
- children in Southeast Asia forced to choose between their families and Christ.
- children disowned by parents, like Sonxi in Laos, whose parents told her she would be better off as a prostitute than a Christian.

The magazine also tells of Rachel, threatened at gunpoint at age eight in Vietnam; of Susan, imprisoned at thirteen in Uganda; and of Nankpak, whose family was killed in Nigeria when he was eight.

Through The Voice of the Martyrs website (www.persecution.com), you can sign up to receive their free monthly magazine, purchase a prayer calendar, donate to help the Families of Martyrs, write to encourage believers imprisoned for their faith, help send Bibles to restricted nations, and more. That is just one ministry, one way to help fellow believers in their suffering. There are many more—so many opportunities.

Hebrews 13:3 says, "Remember them that are in bonds, as bound with them; and them which suffer adversity, as being yourselves also in the body."

We have so much to share: our time, our finances, our prayers—our very lives. What would God have you give? What opportunities has He provided for you to do good to the household of faith?

—*Kimberly Rae.*

The Jewish Aspect

When Paul instructed the Galatians to do good to all men (Gal. 6:10), he was referring to Proverbs: "Withhold not good from them to whom it is due, when it is in the power of thine hand to do it" (Prov. 3:27). When Jesus said that the second greatest commandment is to love your neighbor as yourself (Matt. 22:39), He was quoting from the Hebrew Bible (Lev. 19:18). "Talmudic sages Hillel and Rabbi Akiva commented that this is a major element of the Jewish religion. Also, this commandment is arguably at the center of the Jewish faith. As the third book of the Torah, Leviticus is literally the central book. Historically, Jews have considered it of central importance: traditionally, children began their study of the Torah with Leviticus, and the midrashic literature on Leviticus is among the longest and most detailed of midrashic literature" ("Christianity and Judaism," www.wikipedia.org).

There are over 130 references to love in the Hebrew Bible, many of which provide specific instructions regarding how to love. "If thine enemy be hungry, give him bread to eat; and if he be thirsty, give him water to drink" (Prov. 25:21) is just one example.

John wrote, "My little children, let us not love in word, neither in tongue; but in deed and truth" (I John 3:18). Paul taught that all the things that were written in times past were for the instruction of the believers (Rom. 15:4) and that everyone should be more concerned about their neighbors than themselves (vss. 1-2).

"A large part of Jewish law is about treating people with kindness. The same body of Jewish law that commands us to eat only kosher food and not to turn on lights on Shabbat, also commands us to love both Jews and strangers, to give tzedakah (charity) to the poor and needy, and not to wrong anyone in speech or in business. In fact, acts of kindness are so much a part of Jewish law that the word 'mitzvah' (literally 'commandment'), is informally used to mean any good deed" (Rich, "Love and Brotherhood," www.jewfaq.org).

The early believers were also instructed to be gentle, patient, and meek and not to strive with others (II Tim. 2: 24-25). Meekness is lauded throughout the Hebrew Bible, specifically in the Psalms and Proverbs. Ancient Jews understood that it was the meek who would inherit the earth (Ps. 37:11). David thanked God for His great deliverance and said it was God's gentleness which had made him great (II Sam. 22:36). Moses was the meekest man on the face of the earth (Num. 12:3). The Hebrew word for meek—*anav*—conveyed an individual's devout dependence upon the Lord (Zeph. 2:3).

Paul reminded the early believers, "But this I say, He which soweth sparingly shall reap also sparingly; and he which soweth bountifully shall reap also bountifully" (II Cor. 9:6). This was taught in Proverbs: "There is that scattereth, and yet increaseth; and there is that withholdeth more than is meet, but it tendeth to poverty" (11:24). Paul used another agricultural metaphor when he said that their actions bore consequences. "Be not deceived; God is not mocked: for whatsoever a man soweth, that shall he also reap" (Gal. 6:7). Ancient Israel was an agrarian society and the concept of sowing and reaping is evident throughout the Hebrew Bible, as early as Genesis (8:22). The Jews would have understood the connection between harvest and judgment.

—*Deborah Markowitz Solan.*

Guiding the Superintendent

In the earlier chapters of Galatians Paul laid out the case for the believer no longer having to follow the Law. The Law had been added to the promise to Abraham to help people understand the true nature of sin. The Law was a school teacher to bring them to Christ (Gal. 3:24).

But being free from the Law does not mean a person becomes lawless. To trust in Christ as one's Saviour is to accept a new law—the law of Christ (Gal. 6:2). This new law is the law of love (Gal. 5:14; cf. John 13:34).

The apostle gave his readers four ways in which the believer should be always ready to live out this new law of love.

DEVOTIONAL OUTLINE

1. Restore a fallen brother (Gal. 6:1). Love must be administered with great care. Love calls the believer to restore a brother who is overtaken by sin. However, this must be done with great care to avoid being tempted.

2. Help with their burdens (Gal. 6:2-5). A true believer will lend a hand to help a fellow believer with his or her life burdens. But to do this, the believer must lay aside pride and value others above self.

The believer is also told to carry his or her own burdens. On the surface this seems to be contradictory. The *burden* of verse two refers to a heavy crushing load that is more than a person can bear, while the *burden* of verse six refers to the ordinary responsibilities that one must daily bear.

3. Support Christian leaders (Gal. 6:6-9). The text is clear. Christian love has a responsibility to financially help those who teach the Word. The law of reap and sow applies in this situation.

While this principle can have a very broad application, in context it is referring to financial support of Christian teachers.

4. Help all people (Gal. 6:10). Not only will love reach out to fellow believers when needed, it will also be ready to help anyone in need, regardless of their faith.

Whenever the opportunity arises, love will step in to help.

Scripture is clear. Christian love will reach out to help any fallen brother, any brother with a special need, or any brother who is involved in Christian teaching. If that is not enough, love should take the opportunity to reach out to those outside the church.

CHILDREN'S CORNER

text: **Acts 19:1-12**
title: **Paul: Ready to Do God's Work**

No matter where Paul might find himself, he was always ready and willing to serve God. When He arrived in Ephesus, he found a small group of followers of John the Baptist. He told them all about Jesus Christ, whom they all then received and were baptized. They also received the Holy Spirit.

Either in the synagogue or a rented lecture hall Paul daily told the people about Jesus Christ. As in most other places, Paul's message got mixed reactions. Some violently rejected him, but many willingly came to Christ. In addition to his preaching. Paul was able to work special miracles. Within two years "all they which dwelt in Asia [modern Turkey] heard the word of the Lord Jesus, both Jews and Greeks" (Acts 19:10).

—*Martin R. Dahlquist.*

by followers who agreed with and supported this system. Some of these followers were utilized as enforcers by their participation in the punishment of transgressors, such as death by stoning.

When Jesus began His ministry, He challenged the authority of the religious leaders. As the ministry of Jesus and His disciples grew, so did resentment toward them from those in power. This resentment steadily increased to the point of rage, which led to the crucifixion of Jesus, and it did not end there. Actually, it got worse as the disciples carried out the Great Commission of Christ after His death and resurrection. It is believed that all but one of the apostles was martyred for their efforts to spread the gospel of Jesus, and only God Himself knows how many others have suffered the same fate in one way or another since.

This resentment of Jesus and His disciples concerning the new message of grace has in a sense somewhat undermined even the modern church. The books of Galatians and Hebrews deal with the fact that people who had accepted the message of grace were constantly being lured back into the legalism of the Old Testament, and this continues today.

Most people equate the New Testament with the first chapter of the book of Matthew. However, the New Testament (new covenant) did not really begin until the death and resurrection of Jesus. Only then was the law satisfied. Throughout His entire life and ministry, Jesus lived in accordance with Old Testament law. Only upon His death and resurrection was our relationship with God transformed by the working of His wonderful grace. This transformation was welcomed by those oppressed by religious leaders, by those who now realized that they were incapable of satisfying the law. The early result was the new way early Christians viewed not only their friends but also their enemies. They now looked at others with humility.

Many Christians today experience the same resentment and rejection from church leaders and fellow Christians as their predecessors did. The reasons are the same. Power and traditions are threatened by the message of grace. Like trying to mix oil and water, Old Testament law does not mix well with New Testament grace. If a church insists on living legalistically, the message of grace will be distorted.

Back to Basics

WAYNE J. VASILENKO

Perhaps you have wondered at times why the modern church seems to be struggling. Why is it that most of us no longer see the dynamism like that we read about in the Bible? Why is it we sometimes feel overpowered by Satan? For many people, Christians included, it feels as though evil is taking over the world. Is Satan winning?

Although most believers think of the first disciples of Christ as pillars of faith, they were not. They were just like you and me in many ways. The only difference is that they were able to walk and talk with Jesus. You might consider that a huge advantage, but Jesus made it clear to the disciples that future believers would experience stronger faith and more power than those who were following Him during His ministry here on earth. This would continue long after His ascension back to His Heavenly Father's side until His eventual return. So the question is, Why do Christians so often feel powerless and alone?

As we study the books of Acts, Galatians, and others, we see a dramatic transformation taking place among the followers of Jesus. Previously, they had Jesus with them and drew on His faith and power, but now He was no longer there.

Remember that immediately after Jesus' death and resurrection, the disciples were in hiding, fearing for their lives. They remained in hiding until the resurrected Lord appeared to them; it was only then that they began to regain their faith and confidence.

During this time, Jesus told them that He would not be with them much longer but that they would receive power from the Holy Spirit. Jesus went on to say that both their power and the power of believers in the future would surpass what they had yet experienced. After His ascension back into heaven, this was fulfilled on what would be called the Day of Pentecost. The disciples had experienced the Holy Spirit to a degree before when Jesus sent them out on their own during His ministry, but their power seemed inadequate in some situations, such as when they failed to cast out a demon (cf. Matt. 17:14-21).

It was not because of a lack of faith, as it is translated by some, but it was because of its weakness—there is a difference! If the disciples had not had faith, they would not have even tried to cast out the demon; but their faith was very weak, as Jesus went on state. In verse 21, Jesus was referring to the unbelief, not the demon. Yes, you can have faith but fail to excercise it at times.

Since the death and resurrection of the Lord Jesus, and even before Pentecost, many changes had already taken place among the disciples. The bond between believers grew stronger as the wrath of the religious leaders, who had crucified the Lord, would now be redirected at anyone claiming to be a follower of Jesus.

This was both a fearful and an exciting time for the disciples, whose numbers were steadily growing as the reports of Jesus' resurrection spread despite opposition. The excitement came from many experiencing the risen Lord and seeing His words come to pass. As if that were not enough, now, after Pentecost, people were seeing the disciples themselves performing miracles and boldly proclaiming Jesus as the Christ, right under the noses of the religious leaders!

As bold as the disciples appeared, there was still lingering fear among believers that was caused by the threat of meeting the fate of martyrdom, which many eventually did. This lingering fear still exists today, and I believe that this has a stifling affect on the Christian faith in our time. At this time I believe the fear is more about rejection within the church itself, but with the rise of certain radical extremists the threat of actual martyrdom is once again on the rise in many parts of the world.

The only way to combat fear and uncertainty is to rely on God's Word. There are still people preaching a perverted gospel, just as there were in the early church. We are living among many false religions and false doctrines, just like the ones Paul preached against. Therefore, it is more important than ever to go back to the source itself, the Word of God.

As Christians, we possess the same resources that Jesus and the disciples had at their disposal—God's Word and the Holy Spirit. These two resources are above reproach. The Word of God is as true and unchanging as is the Holy Spirit; it is only when we deify tradition or human philosophy or opinion that we risk being misled. This is just as true for us in modern times as it was for the early church. If you are a truth seeker, there is no substitute for a personal and consistent study of the Word of God. Paul stressed this to the early believers everywhere he preached, reminding them to pay careful attention to the teachings of the early church leaders, especially to that of the apostolic witnesses.

We are the conduit through which God's Spirit flows. Remember, we have the same Holy Spirit in us today that Jesus had when He walked the earth. The Apostle Paul dedicated his ministry to the gospel message, and we must remain true to the Word of God. As in the early church, many people have perverted the truth with false teachings and legalistic beliefs. Paul taught us that the truth will be found in the Word of God forever.

TOPICS FOR NEXT QUARTER

June 2

Abram Called by God
Genesis 11:31—12:9

June 9

Dwelling in Canaan
Genesis 13:10-18

June 16

Abram Blessed by Melchizedek
Genesis 14:1-2, 11-20

June 23

Abram's Exemplary Faith
Genesis 15:1-17

June 30

Abram's First Son
Genesis 16:1-11, 15-16

July 7

An Everlasting Covenant
Genesis 17:1-8, 15-21

July 14

The Son of Promise
Genesis 21:1-10

July 21

Hagar and Ishmael Cast Out
Genesis 21:11-21

July 28

A Test of Faith
Genesis 22:1-14

August 4

God's Choice for Isaac
Genesis 24:10-20, 26-28

August 11

Isaac and Rebekah
Genesis 24:50-54, 59-67

August 18

Sons for Isaac and Rebekah
Genesis 25:19-28

August 25

Isaac's Abundant Blessings
Genesis 26:1-5, 12-14, 20-25

PARAGRAPHS ON PLACES AND PEOPLE

ACHAIA

Achaia is the name in the New Testament for the region roughly synonymous with modern-day southern Greece. "Achaia" is mentioned eleven times in the New Testament. Together with Macedonia to the north, it was one of the two Roman provinces that largely covered the land of the Greeks.

The occupants of ancient Greece were called Achaeans ("of Achaia") as far back as the time of Homer (around the eighth century B.C.). When we see Achaia mentioned in the New Testament, we can reflect upon the fact that the gospel of Christ was penetrating the citadel of western culture.

ARABIA

Arabia is a very large peninsula in southwestern Asia that stretches from the Fertile Crescent in the north to the Indian Ocean in the south and from the Persian Gulf in the east to the Red Sea in the west (thus including the Sinai Peninsula). The term is used seven times in the Bible, twice in the New Testament (both in Galatians).

There has been much discussion about just where Paul is pointing when he says he went from Damascus in Syria into Arabia (Gal. 1:17). It was there that he received teaching from God soon after his conversion. He later makes reference to Mount Sinai being in Arabia (4:25), so some believe he may have gone to the Sinai Peninsula region or the Transjordan (east of the Jordan) area with which Sinai was commonly linked. It is also possible that he meant the nearby Syrian desert, also called Arabia at times in ancient sources.

JAMES, THE LORD'S BROTHER

At least four personages named James appear in the New Testament, and this has been a source of confusion at times. The most common error is to mistake James the Lord's brother with the apostle who was the brother of John.

James the Lord's brother is mentioned a couple of times in the Gospels, which describe a time prior to his adherence to the faith (Matt. 13:55; Mark 6:3). After Christ's resurrection, this James became a leader of the church (Gal. 1:18-19); he presided over the Jerusalem Council (Acts 15) and wrote the New Testament epistle named after him.

ABRAHAM (NEW TESTAMANT REFERENCES)

Abraham is a central figure of the Old Testament. Through him and his seed all the world received and will continue to receive great blessing. His importance becomes even more clear from what the New Testament says about him. Abraham is mentioned seventy times in the New Testament. Interestingly, of the forty references that come outside the Gospels, twenty-eight come from Romans, Galatians, and Hebrews in the midst of the most detailed theological discussions of the New Testament.

Citing Abraham, the father of the faithful, the New Testament shows clearly that we are made right with God only through faith. The true children of Abraham are those who have come to trust in Christ and His saving work.

—Stephen H. Barnhart.

Daily Bible Readings for Home Study and Worship

(Readings are for the week previous to the lesson topics.)

1. March 3. A New Loyalty

M —We Used to Be Foolish. Titus 3:1-8.
T —And Such Were Some of You. I Cor. 6:9-11, 19-20.
W —Leave Fleshly Desires Behind. I Pet. 4:1-6.
T —Made Alive Together with Christ. Eph. 2:1-13.
F —Faith in the Power of God. I Cor. 2:1-5.
S —Obedience from the Heart. Rom. 6:17-23.
S —Turning to God from Idols. I Thess. 1:1-10.

2. March 10. A New Affection

M —If God So Loved Us. I John 4:7-16.
T —Love One Another. John 15:9-17.
W —Because We Love the Brethren. I John 3:14-19.
T —Love Fulfills the Law. Rom. 13:7-10.
F —Nothing Without Love. I Cor. 13:1-7.
S —May Your Love Abound. Phil. 1:3-11.
S —News of the Thessalonians' Love. I Thess. 3:1-13.

3. March 17. A New Way of Life

M —Doing What Pleases the Lord. I John 3:20-24.
T —Fulfill Your Calling. Eph. 4:1-6.
W —Grow in Christ. Eph. 4:7-16.
T —Put on the New Man. Eph. 4:17-24.
F —They Gave Themselves to the Lord. II Cor. 8:1-6.
S —Walk Worthy of the Lord. Col. 1:3-11.
S —Called to Holiness. I Thess. 4:1-12.

4. March 24. A New Understanding

M —Raised at Christ's Coming. I Cor. 15:20-28.
T —At the Last Trumpet. I Cor. 15:51-58.
W —Lord of the Dead and the Living. Rom. 14:7-12.
T —Who Can Abide the Day of the Lord? Joel 2:1-11.
F —Watch, Therefore. Mark 13:28-37.
S —Like a Thief in the Night. II Pet. 3:9-16.
S —You Are Not in Darkness. I Thess. 4:13—5:10.

5. March 31. A Growing Confidence

M —Moving on to Perfection. Heb. 5:10—6:4.
T —Confidently Drawing Near to God. Heb. 10:14-23.
W —Keep Yourselves in the Love of God. Jude 1:14-21.
T —Joy and Confidence in Trials. I Pet. 4:7-14.
F —To Be Accounted Worthy. Luke 21:29-36.
S —Confidence at Christ's Coming. I John 2:20-29.
S —Becoming Strong in Faith. II Thess. 1:1-12.

6. April 7. A Growing Awareness

M —Perilous Times Shall Come. II Tim. 3:1-9.
T —Many Antichrists Already. I John 2:12-19.
W —When Will These Things Happen? Matt. 24:3-14.
T —This Generation Shall Not Pass. Matt. 24:29-34.
F —The Lord's Coming Is Near. Jas. 5:7-11.
S —He Will Not Tarry. Heb. 10:32-37.
S —Let No Man Deceive You. II Thess. 2:1-12.

7. April 14. A Growing Resolve

M —Blessed Are Those Who Obey. Rev. 22:6-14.
T —Laboring to Enter Our Rest. Heb. 4:11-16.
W —A Steadfast Anchor of the Soul. Heb. 6:9-20.
T —Live in the Daylight. Rom. 13:11-14.
F —Faith More Precious Than Gold. I Pet. 1:1-8.
S —The One Who Overcomes. Rev. 3:7-13.
S —Wait Patiently for Christ. II Thess. 2:13—3:5.

8. April 21. Remember the True Gospel! (Easter)

M —The Gospel I Preached unto You. I Cor. 15:1-11.
T —Christ Is Risen Indeed. I Cor. 15:12-22.
W —By the Determined Counsel of God. Acts 2:22-36.
T —1Salvation in No Other. Acts 4:5-14.
F —The Glorious Gospel of Christ. II Cor. 4:1-6.
S —Reject Any Other Gospel. II Cor. 10:12—11:4.
S —Raised from the Dead. Gal. 1:6-9; Matt. 28:1-7, 18-20.

9. April 28. The Source of Paul's Gospel

M —The Gospel Committed to Paul. I Tim. 1:11-17.
T —Separated unto the Gospel. Rom. 1:1-9.
W —Made a Minister of the Gospel. Acts 26:12-20.
T —Paul's Earliest Preaching. Acts 9:13-22.
F —The Mystery Made Known to Paul. Eph. 3:1-9.
S —Obligated to Preach the Gospel. I Cor. 9:13-19.
S —Paul's Gospel Not from Man. Gal. 1:10-24.

10. May 5. The Gospel of Faith Foretold

M —A Father to Saints of Many Nations. Rom. 4:11-18.
T —Promises to the Fathers Fulfilled. Rom. 15:7-16.
W —This Agrees with the Prophecies. Acts 15:7-18.
T —On the Foundation of the Prophets. Eph. 2:11-22.
F —Salvation Also for the Gentiles. Isa. 49:1-6.
S —I Will Draw All Men unto Me. John 12:23-33.
S —Gentiles' Salvation Foreseen. Gal. 3:1-14.

11. May 12. The Gospel: Faith in Christ

M —The Necessity of Faith. Heb. 11:1-10.
T —Believe with the Heart. Rom. 10:1-13.
W —Saved by Grace Through Faith. Eph. 2:1-10.
T —Righteousness by Faith in Christ. Rom. 3:19-28.
F —No Confidence in the Flesh. Phil. 3:1-9.
S —Faith Works. Jas. 2:14-26.
S —Justified by Faith in Christ. Gal. 3:15-25.

12. May 19. Heirs Because of the Gospel

M —Overcomers Inherit All Things. Rev. 21:1-7.
T —An Inheritance Gained in Christ. Eph. 1:5-14.
W —Inheritance of the Saints. Col. 3:12-24.
T —Joint Heirs with Christ. Rom. 8:8-17.
F —All Who Receive Him Become Sons. John 1:5-13.
S —Children of the Promise. Rom. 9:6-16.
S —No Difference—All Are Heirs. Gal. 3:26—4:7.

13. May 26. The Gospel in Action

M —Be a Living Sacrifice. Rom. 12:1-10.
T —Suitable for the Master's Use. II Tim. 2:19-26.
W —Bear the Infirmities of the Weak. Rom. 15:1-7.
T —Abound in Every Good Work. II Cor. 9:6-15.
F —Live in Harmony with the Gospel. Phil. 1:21-30.
S —Doers of the Word. Jas. 1:19-27.
S —Do Good to All. Gal. 6:1-10.